A
Darker
Wilderness

A DARKER WILDERNESS

edited by Erin Sharkey

BLACK NATURE WRITING FROM SOIL TO STARS

MILKWEED EDITIONS

Published 2023 by Milkweed Editions
Printed in the United States of America
Cover design by Mary Austin Speaker
Cover photo of Bernice Wright by Jackson Davis, in Jackson Davis, Papers,
1906–1947, Accession #3072, #3072-a, Special Collections, University of
Virginia Library, Charlottesville, VA 22903
23 24 25 26 27 6 5 4 3 2
First Edition

Library of Congress Cataloging-in-Publication Data

Names: Sharkey, Erin, editor.
Title: A darker wilderness : Black nature writing from soil to stars / edited by
    Erin Sharkey.
Description: First edition. | Minneapolis, Minnesota : Milkweed Editions,
    [2023] | Includes bibliographical references. | Summary: "A vibrant collection
    of personal and lyric essays in conversation with archival objects of Black
    history and memory"-- Provided by publisher.
Identifiers: LCCN 2022030943 (print) | LCCN 2022030944 (ebook) | ISBN
    9781571313904 (trade paperback) | ISBN 9781571317346 (ebook)
Subjects: LCSH: American literature--African American authors. | American
    literature--21st century. | Ecoliterature, American. | LCGFT: Essays.
Classification: LCC PS508.B53 D37 2023 (print) | LCC PS508.B53 (ebook) |
    DDC 814/.6080896073--dc23/eng/20221003
LC record available at https://lccn.loc.gov/2022030943
LC ebook record available at https://lccn.loc.gov/2022030944

Milkweed Editions is committed to ecological stewardship. We strive to align our
book production practices with this principle, and to reduce the impact of our
operations in the environment. We are a member of the Green Press Initiative, a
nonprofit coalition of publishers, manufacturers, and authors working to protect the
world's endangered forests and conserve natural resources. *A Darker Wilderness* was
printed on acid-free 30% postconsumer-waste paper by Versa Press.

For Zoë

CONTENTS

This is how the past interrupts our lives, all of
it entering the same doorway—like the hole in
the trunk of my neighbor's tree: at once a natural
shelter, haven for small creatures, but also evidence
of injury, an entrance for decay.

NATASHA TRETHEWEY,
MONUMENT: POEMS NEW AND SELECTED

Every generation confronts the task of choosing its
past. Inheritances are chosen as much as they are
passed on. The past depends less on "what happened
then" than on the desires and discontents of the
present. Strivings and failures shape the stories we tell.

SAIDIYA HARTMAN,
*LOSE YOUR MOTHER: A JOURNEY ALONG
THE ATLANTIC SLAVE ROUTE*

Things become bearers of memory and information,
especially when enhanced by stories that expand
their capacity to carry meaning.

TIYA MILES,
*ALL THAT SHE CARRIED: THE JOURNEY OF
ASHLEY'S SACK, A BLACK FAMILY KEEPSAKE*

A
Darker
Wilderness

Foreword
MEMORY DIVINE

Carolyn Finney

"Blackness is not one or 1,000 things."
—**REGINALD DWAYNE BETTS,** *NEW YORK TIMES*

"It is dangerous to be discovered."
—**ALEXIS PAULINE GUMBS,** *UNDROWNED*

"See me, feel me, touch me, heal me."
—**THE WHO**

What sayeth the woman
who lies in green pastures
that are not
her own?

What songs
does she sing?

What sound
do her fingers make
as she tends the garden
of some other dream?

1

Does she notice
the withered skin
a reflection of a soul
that has been
forsaken?

Does she sense the heaviness
of a heart
forced to bear a load
it did not create?

What sayeth the woman
who lies in green pastures
that are not
her own?

When do we become a memory? If you do not remember us, do we cease to exist?

I recently read an article by author and critic Seph Rodney about the African American artist Jennifer Packer and her recent exhibition at the Whitney Museum, entitled "Jennifer Packer: The Eye Is Not Satisfied with Seeing." According to Rodney, we experience a "seesawing between observation and imagination" as Packer simultaneously highlights and obscures the nuances of Black life, exploring longing, loss, and wonderment while honoring the named and unnamed. Her paintings, he argues, demand that we *look*, by losing a color or a body part or even a person, by what they include and exclude, by forcing the viewer to complete the piece's visual and emotional puzzle. "What is my responsibility to see?" asks Rodney. "Who will hold us accountable when we fail in this very basic duty?"

I felt like he was talking to me. For the past nineteen years, I've been telling the story of my parents on the land in juxtaposition to a narrative of nature that has not and does not always see them, a narrative of environmental longing and belonging that has neglected to consider a darker wilderness. I've been telling the story of a Black experience with all things green, colored by an American history of extraction, exploitation, and erasure. In a country where love of land and of each other could cost you. And yet you love anyway.

There is a black-and-white photograph of my mother—it is 1958, and she is kneeling by a pond on a twelve-acre property in New York that she and my father will never own but that will become their legacy. My parents left their home in Virginia—a southern state that could not see past their Black skin in any way that mattered—and traveled to New York to find jobs and perhaps a place that might welcome them as whole beings, with dreams and potential. They left behind a past that was filled not only with the pain of limitations forced on them by others but with family, the familiar, and the memories that had stoked their dreams. My father was offered a job as a gardener and chauffeur for a wealthy family who needed full-time caretakers to live on their estate, and he accepted the position. For the next fifty years, my parents would be the only Black people to live in that affluent neighborhood and, to my knowledge, the only people there who did not own the land they called home. When I stare at the picture of my mother kneeling in the sun, in this new place for the first time—this home but not home—I wonder if she was seeking her own reflection in the pond. I wonder if she felt as though she was drowning in a life that she did not recognize, in a life that she did not know how to know. I know now that she was melancholy. As I look at the photograph, I wonder if I am, as painter Dona Nelson suggests in the exhibition catalog for Packer's show, in "the presence of a person on the threshold of absence."

> *What sayeth the woman*
> *who lies in green pastures*
> *that are not*
> *her own?*

There is another photograph I keep on my desk of my parents in 2003, standing on this very same estate, older and grayer but still upright and resolute. They are standing in the sun, in front of a weeping cherry tree that my father gave my mother to celebrate their fortieth wedding anniversary. As I look at this photo, I am reminded of Gordon Parks's *American Gothic*—a black-and-white photograph of Ella Watson, Black mother and worker, holding a broom and mop, upright and resolute, in front of the American flag. The symmetry between the two photographs is not lost on me. Their Blackness and wholeness in the face of an American history that has never embraced them on their terms. Upright and resolute. Their love and labor exploited, overlooked, and shunted to the background of a narrative that strains to ignore what it does not wish to understand.

I scrutinize the photo more closely, squinting as though blurring the edges might focus my sight. This was the last photo ever taken of my parents on the land they called home for nearly fifty years. The owners had passed away, and the new owner snapped this shot of them in front of the cherry tree they could not take back to Virginia, where a new home was being constructed, but which would be a reminder of their presence on the land. I examine the photo for signs of . . . well, for signs of what? Of impending loss? Of accomplishment? Of readiness? Of acceptance? Of wholeness? Am I looking for signs of myself?

> *What sayeth the woman*
> *who lies in green pastures*
> *that are not*
> *her own?*

For eighteen years, no one from my family went back to visit the land. We tried once, unsuccessfully, to get access, but were surprised to discover that a large, locked, wrought iron gate now blocked public entry. I felt like a kid peering through a window, seeing my past self reflected, faded, like in a dream. Staring back, waiting. I wanted to fling open those gates, not only to let us in but to let our memories out. I wanted to shout our presence to the sky—"We are HERE!" I wanted to run down the driveway I used to pretend was a river of piranhas, part of the imaginary world I constructed as a child. I wanted to see my father tending the flower beds, rich with zinnias, tulips, and snapdragons all vying for his attention. I wanted to feel my mother's eyes on my brothers and I as we played on the swing set and rolled down the hill, getting leaves in our kinky hair. I wanted to touch the rocks and grass and trees that told us who we were, despite the noise from the outside world. I wanted to remember.

What sayeth the woman
who lies in green pastures
that are not
her own?

Home has always been an overwhelmingly enticing, all-consuming, magnificent idea for me. As someone who was adopted as a baby, I struggle with the weight of the word: to me, it implies a sense of ownership, of claiming, of belonging, of recognition, of relationship, of *being* claimed, of being wanted, of being seen—of *knowing*—which I have found, in part, elusive. After I eagerly left "home" at eighteen, it was a place I returned to with feelings of both desire and trepidation. This home was where my parents, who raised me, resided and also where I found out that I was not biological kin. This home was where I looked for myself everywhere, every day, and came up wanting. This home was filled with contradictions that I'm still wading through in an effort to make sense of, well, everything. But this home was also the only place that I knew I could return to and be welcomed. I cannot say that I thought, at the time, that the land was extra special or exceptional (except that it was), but it was the only place in my life that felt like a certainty, a kind of North Star in a world that did not know how to see me (and that I did not know how to see). For better and for worse, I became myself on that land. So many firsts happened there: experiencing loss, falling in love, being denied, wrestling with anger, feeling humiliation, facing fear and losing, facing fear and winning, creating new worlds. And dreaming, so much dreaming. Daydreaming wasn't just something I did; on the land, it was a state of mind, a state of being. It was an out-of-body experience that somehow occurred within my own brown body. And that body became something more, too, as I ran, swam, biked, and climbed my way through a life I wasn't sure I had earned but was desperate to prove myself worthy of. And all the while, as I dreamed and flew, my parents toiled in the background, their own dreams fading as their children grew.

By the time my parents left our home in 2003, I had moved at least twelve times and had spent the better part of five years backpacking in Africa and Asia, ultimately finding respite in a village in Nepal for a year and a half. By 2003, I had pursued an acting career for eleven years and returned to school, where I ultimately completed three degrees. By 2003, I had married and divorced, and married and divorced again. By 2003, I had become so practiced at throwing my heart out into the world in my search for home that I almost didn't notice that I was about to lose the only home I had ever known. As my parents were getting their picture taken in front of their cherry tree, I was working on my doctorate and looking for stories about Black people and nature on the library shelves and coming up wanting. Again. As I watched the story of my parents on that land fading to black, I decided to tell a different story. It was time to hold myself accountable.

In the summer of 2021, those iron gates opened. The murder of George Floyd in the streets by a police officer and the weaponization of Christian Cooper's skin against him as he birdwatched in Central Park became the latest entries in an encyclopedia of truths, stories, and moments about Black experience in the American landscape that would be denied no longer. Memories of who we've been, which had been shoved deep into the dirt, exploded in a riot of color and ferociousness no one could ignore (though many tried). We had to say their names: past and present and in every sector of society. And it implicated everybody. Including me. In this moment of sharing stories and telling truths, I had an opportunity to return to that land I had called home, and I grabbed that moment with both hands, with desire and trepidation. And with hope.

It was one of those too-hot New York summer days; the thermometer hovered around 95 degrees Fahrenheit. I was wearing a white silk dress, in part because of the heat. But I think that I also needed to feel light, like I was floating through an experience that I might otherwise emotionally drown in. My visit was not a private affair. In this moment of remembering, organizations, institutions, and individuals with the power to forget were on their own journeys, and for some, this translated into showing up for a story they did not know how to know but that they could *feel*. Our group was a small, motley crew made up of institutional representatives, academics, documentary filmmakers, artists, friends, and a forester. And, perhaps most importantly, one of the new owners whose family now called this place home.

> *What sayeth the woman*
> *who lies in green pastures*
> *that are not*
> *her own?*

It's almost one year later, and I am still processing my visit home. I felt overwhelmed by the presence of my past reflected on the grass like sunlight on a lake. I was everywhere. My

family was everywhere. And though the place had changed—
it was no longer tended to daily; trees had been cut down,
rocks were covered with moss, and tulips and zinnias no longer greeted you from the flower beds along the driveway—we
were no less present. I kept holding my breath, afraid to exhale
lest I unleash a torrent of emotion I was not ready to share. Not
everyone deserves our truth.

But there was a moment. As part of our visit, we paid
homage to the cherry tree, which had been unceremoniously
cut down years ago. We had collectively decided to plant a new
weeping cherry tree, and we watched as the forester dug a hole
for it. He never complained, even though the heat was stifling.
And he treated the new tree with such care, patiently explaining what it needed and why we were planting it in the spot he
had chosen. When he called me over to put the new tree in the
ground, and I could feel all eyes on me, I was nearly overcome
with emotion. As I held the tree, I could feel *our* collective exhale. In that moment, I understood that this story was no longer only mine or my family's. It belonged to all of us.

I eagerly await the release of the documentary film so I can
view all this from another angle. How do *others* see our story?
I have been focused for almost two decades on the story of my
family and their love of the land that was never theirs, but I have
to ask: What of the absences? What am *I* not seeing? That land
has been home to so many others—what of my Indigenous sisters and brothers? What of the non-human species that hold
forth daily? What of the trees that reach for the skies?

As the essays in this collection show, their presence—and
our presence—is everywhere. For my family, our presence is
embedded in the absence of flower beds, of pink hydrangeas,
of apple trees; in the memories held by the land of me and my

brothers foraging in the woods, rolling in the leaves, and play-ing in the snow. The echoes of our presence can be felt in our absence, in the erasure and negligence with which we are all too familiar.

Here's what I know: we are undeniable because we are part of a larger story of place and time; because the "before" and "after" always has us in between; because we are dust to dust; because to know a thing is to love a thing, and we love deeply; and because all of our stories are in relationship—I am because you are. Upright and resolute. And the land remem-bers, even if we do not. For as the earth breathes, so do we. Because this is our home.

Introduction
MORE TO BE SHAPED BY

Erin Sharkey

S o much nature writing is about freedom and access to the vast spaces that provide crisp air and opportunities for fresh perspectives. But this collection's origins lie in a revelation that came to me while teaching nature writing in a prison setting, where participants didn't have access to such liberative experiences. I began teaching in prisons in 2016, after years of activism in response to the violences of the "injustice" system. I'd always preferred teaching in nontraditional classrooms and found that the best education happens between students across differences, whether in race, age, or socioeconomic experience. This is exactly the kind of teaching that happens in prison classrooms. And beneath this motivation, I felt an unanswered desire to understand my long-absent father, who was incarcerated for a time when I was a child.

I taught classes from memoir to lyric essay in prisons before answering a call for a new class offering and proposing a fifteen-week nature writing class for Minnesota's largest facility, a former mental hospital in the southern part of the state. I began teaching in the waning days of summer.

During the class, we marked the way nature transcended the walls of the institution. On the first day, a blaze-orange fox ran across our path to the education building. Over the length of the course, an old-growth aspen grew unbounded, peeling its curling bark, shedding its browning leaves, holding the first snowflakes on heavy branches. The writers moved through their days on a schedule imposed by a crackling voice over a loudspeaker, but they also watched birds gliding freely past the windows; industrious yellow jackets throwing their bodies against the glass; and a flock of mallards who navigated puddles in the yard, ignoring the guards watching from their towers. The course spanned the entire fall, from September, when the light stretches long into the evenings, to December, when the students craned their necks to mark the waxing moon as they made their way back to their units.

Students remembered summer trips out West, cliff jumping in Oregon, dust storms while serving in the military, working the farm as boys, and favorite winding riverside drives. Nature was a meeting place for writers with very different backgrounds: they were Black and white, Hmong and Anishinaabe. Some grew up in the city, some in the country, some on the reservation; some were from Minnesota, and some were from faraway places.

Over those weeks, the fifteen students remembered nature's power to teach us about ourselves, to help us connect with others, to mark time and its passing, to (re)gain perspective. And I learned from them that nature can shape our lives, even in unnatural conditions like those experienced by the incarcerated. Even in those confines, nature was present and worth observing.

***

I grew up in the Twin Cities, between St. Paul and Minneapolis, the city of lakes. I shook sand out of my shoes nearly every evening of the summer, evidence of days spent on the city's beaches. A golden tan bloomed on my brown skin, my nose and forehead freckled. I marked years this way. Summers were like this: kids from our southside United Methodist church crammed into a retired Bluebird bus, learning about the Bible and praising Jesus in nature under high pines and on the shores of the state's ten thousand lakes. The fall: a blaze of red and orange, tornado drills. The spring: lilacs and lilies of the valley. Floods. The winter: dozens of varieties of snow, knowledge that the coldest days are the ones with the clearest, widest skies. All of this was natural.

Each summer of my childhood, my family loaded up our maroon minivan and embarked on a road trip. The varied landscapes of North America flew by my window in a blur. For weeks at a time, we made our home in a clearing, slept in our big, gray, five-person Columbia tent, and set up our kitchen and dining room on a long picnic table and around a firepit in plain view of our new temporary neighbors. This public expression of our familial cadence, out in the open, welcomed questions about our racial makeup—two white parents, my mom and my stepdad; my towheaded little brother; the baby, adopted from Guatemala; and me, a big-boned, mixed-race, Black girl. Across the nation, I met other kids, exploring the woods and lazy streams, in national parks and wildernesses. They were white and curious. The inescapable questions—"Are you Black? Why aren't you with your real parents?"

I learned that nature is not a place where you can escape the oppressive rules of race. I learned that I had access to natural spaces because of my parents' privilege and resources, their jobs as a teacher and a bureaucrat, their time off in the summer, their own experiences with travel as children. And because of their race, which granted them comfort in the wilderness, in spaces like those campgrounds, in rural areas of this country.

In my prison nature writing class, we started with the basics.

Born in the eighteenth century, nature writing grew out of an effort to describe and categorize the attributes of birds, animals, and insects—a list that grew as more of the world was "discovered." This discovery was violent because it was a tool of colonization, with "explorers" conquering new land and, with it, nature that was unfamiliar to them. Natural history museums also flourished during this time; they often featured human specimens, particularly Indigenous peoples, as well as plants and animals. The grave-robbed remains of twenty-two Inuit endured in the archives of Chicago's Field Museum until 2011, when they were returned to the Inuit Tapiriit Kanatami in Labrador. The San Diego Museum of Man displayed human remains until 2012. The hierarchy of colonization is reproduced within natural history, in the sorting of some humans as subjects rather than scientists. The work of empire, conquering and cataloging, is the field in which nature writing emerges, making its appearance in response to conditions of the state: industrialization, capitalism, urbanization, democracy.

One of the trademarks of the genre is that it is rooted in first-person observation, so it is vital to investigate the identities of those observers. Let's consider Henry David Thoreau, one of the central figures of the field. Before Thoreau set out to live deliberately, he had ample leisure time and resources to imagine the Walden Pond project. He embarked on Independence Day of 1845 for the two-year, two-month, and two-day experiment; he had just been released from a brief stay in jail, having been arrested for failure to pay poll taxes in protest of slavery and the Mexican-American War. His debt was paid by a family member. The land his cottage was built on was owned by his friend Ralph Waldo Emerson. (Students in the nature writing class noted the similarity of Thoreau's 10' by 15' cottage to the size of the cells they occupied.)

And the genre remains dominated by white, cisgender men with access to resources. Thoreau's Walden was followed by Audubon's trees and Darwin's finches, which were then followed, over the following century, by Burroughs's trout, Leopold's gray owl, Abbey's desert, and Pollan's farm. Men who moved toward conservation. Their female counterparts considered nature and the body. Rachel Carson, Terry Tempest Williams, and Annie Dillard invited readers to consider the environmental impacts of development and the ways our spirituality can form in relationship to nature. Just as the ways we experience nature in this country are not isolated from our identities, nature writing is not neutral.

Nature writing is rooted in the American experiment (think *independence, innovation, Western expansion*), but who is left out from the canon just above? A collection addressing the presence of Black people and their contributions is itself a distinctly American project. Despite efforts to the contrary, Black Americans' relationship to nature has persisted from the Middle Passage, when our ancestors traveled the westerlies in the bellies of ships, and from our toil in the fields and the intimate domestic spaces of white families. It has persisted beyond the state's continued barriers against Black people building positive relationships to natural spaces. It has persisted beyond Jim Crow laws that legislated violence impeding free movement along the scenic highways of the South. And it has persisted beyond redlining, which relegated Black

17

communities to areas of disinvestment, near toxic, smelly uses like waste storage and industrial manufacturing, that come with a myriad of environmental and health consequences, including asthma and lupus.

These circumstances do not mean that Black people don't have a relationship to nature. On the contrary, Black folks have been instrumental in the stewardship and care of the land, and though their labor has often been carried out under poor conditions or in service to land not under their ownership, skill and innovation has been evident in their relationship with it. In her book *Black Faces, White Spaces: Reimagining the Relationship of African Americans to the Great Outdoors*, Carolyn Finney writes that though her parents cared for "someone else's land for fifty years," though they "knew more about the land than the actual owners," they would never own the land themselves. I am grateful to the earlier books, writers, and editors that have begun the work of documenting these relationships. The list of such books is fortunately getting longer all the time, but two served as inspiration for this collection. *The Colors of Nature*, an anthology of essays about nature by people of color and edited by Lauret Savoy and Alison Hawthorne Deming, illustrates that nature is a complex concept to navigate for people of many different ethnicities and cultural identities, underscoring both the ubiquity of white supremacy and the ways nature and discussions of power and land underpin the design of this nation. And *Black Nature: Four Centuries of African American Nature Poetry*, edited by Camille Dungy, is a gorgeous anthology that makes the case that Black poets push the boundaries of nature writing beyond the agrarian and the wild to the political, the historical, and the radical. This project would not be possible without such footsteps to follow.

In class, I asked students to not simply tell stories that were set in nature but to consider what those stories mean in the greater context of their lives or the larger world. This created a kind of network of meaning, connecting stories with wildly different subject matter and particulars by way of deep themes and significance.

Each essay featured here is linked to an archival object, whether by geographical connection or some relationship of subject matter. My own journey in archives started in 2016, at the tail end of my MFA journey, when I was invited for a few months to explore the Archie Givens, Sr. Collection of African American Literature at the University of Minnesota. I had never had such an opportunity before, to explore without a specific goal in mind, to let one object lead me to the next, to find my own way to meaning. The Givens Collection lives in the Andersen Library, which has an outward face—a whisper-quiet reading room with oak tables occupied by people hunched over their own investigations—and a private face—a cold cavern, at the bottom of a long elevator ride, filled with a small city of floor-to-ceiling bookshelves and a special alley devoted to Black literature, music, art, and ephemera.

My curiosity took me from garden club attendance rolls and cookbooks to maps of rural Mississippi and the narratives of people formerly enslaved there—and to a little emerald-green brochure about sharecropping, titled "Farmers without Land." Published by the Public Affairs Committee in 1937, the short volume discussed the failure of the land-use model, the environmental effects: soil depletion, boll weevils, and soil erosion, as well as poor living conditions and fewer community contracts. Right away I wanted to know what a boll weevil was. Research told me: they were beetles, hungry for the bud of the cotton plant, who laid their eggs inside and turned the cloud-white bloom into a slimy green mess, decimating crops across the South. The brochure noted that the tenant farming model was also failing because Black growers were migrating to the North.

I learned that looking at archival items requires a particular kind of curiosity because the significance is found not only in individual objects but in their assembly. The viewer has an opportunity to connect objects across time, to find connections, to follow thin strains to something the collectors perhaps did not intend. This is especially true when looking at the collections of items significant to Black history, because they have been shadowed and suppressed by the white supremacy and racism of institutions that collect and store collections. It wasn't until 2016, with the Smithsonian Institution's opening of the National Museum of African American History and Culture, that a federal institution was founded to celebrate the contributions of Black Americans. The museum had been in development since the days following the end of the Civil War. At a public presentation in April 2016, at a symposium at the African American Museum in Philadelphia titled "Shifting Narratives: Rethinking the Past to Understand the Present," the NMAAHC associate director for curatorial affairs, Dr. Rex M. Ellis, noted that a great deal of the work of assembling that collection was in working with families and church communities to acquire objects of significance that had never been on display because of distrust in institutions and concern for the respect due them.

Before I had even scratched the surface of the Givens's physical collection, I learned of a new project at the University of Minnesota: Umbra Search African American History. Named for the darkest part of the moon's shadow, Umbra aims to provide broad, searchable access to digitized materials in those collections of Black memory. The search tool aggregates over 650,000 items (a relatively small amount) from small collections, archives of all kinds, and institutions across the country. Some of the archival items featured in this anthology were located in Umbra. I stumbled upon the image featured on the cover of this collection using the search term "garden clubs." I was drawn to the photograph by Bernice Wright's gaze, direct and not seeking approval as she presents the fruits of her labor. The image description tells us only her name, that she was a member of a homemakers' club, and that she holds a dish of tomatoes grown in her garden in Caroline County, Virginia. That we have even this information is lucky. Although it is accessible because it has been digitized, the physical object is housed in a special collection at the University of Virginia and was donated in 1948 by the daughters of the photographer, Jackson Davis. According to his biography, he took over six thousand photographs documenting the conditions of rural Negro schools in the South.

Maybe searching in such an archive is about looking for oneself. An archive can serve as collective memory, though it is important to remember that the archive is not a full or neutral record. Each archive tells a story about the archivist as well as what is archived. The racist structures in place in the institutions of memory can be discerned in the archive, as can the absence of Black archivists within those institutions. One feature of an archive of Black memory is that it must, by necessity, include many items connected to unknown or unidentified makers and subjects. This project claims and reacquaints the unknown by connecting those makers and subjects to contemporary Black thinkers across time and, in turn, rewrites the record.

The essays in this anthology reflect a range of experiences with nature, some green and budding, some rusting and tired. Some pieces are positive, some negative, as varied as our various relationships with nature. The authors have reflected on the experience of living through the last half of the twentieth century and the dawning of the twenty-first while weaving those narratives with objects, some from family photo albums and some which date back many generations, to the earliest days of this nation. From a statue erected in a town square to ephemera like travel pamphlets, the items you'll find range from public and civic to private and personal.

The conversation in this book begins with a foreword from Carolyn Finney, which revisits her family's intimate relationship to a piece of land that was deeply theirs, while at the same time, not their own. In it, she ponders the presence of absence and the lasting impact of loss and asks how our relationship to land ownership and power shape us.

Themes of sovereignty and liberation visit many of the narratives that follow. In "An Aspect of Freedom," Ama Codjoe considers what freedoms live outside those doled out by a government. She asks whether freedom can bloom in protest and downpouring rain, and whether the expanse of nature is large enough to hold our sorrow and cries for liberation.

Essays by Glynn Pogue, Sean Hill, and Lauret Savoy continue exploring these themes. What is the value of vacation to the Black family, and what additional levels of comfort come from being surrounded by the familiar in the unfamiliar environs of the whiter parts of this nation? Readers will stop by a Fourth of July celebration with a family continuing a lineage of Black-owned vacation havens, visit a document from the Revolutionary War that chronicles the military service that won Austin Dabney his freedom, and, in an update to one of Savoy's essays in the seminal collection *Trace*, consider the ways race and racism are etched in place-names at the bedrock of our communities.

My contribution to these stories follows and focuses on the decade I lived and worked on an urban farm in Buffalo, New York, where I felt the natural rhythms of a neighborhood in a city defined by decay and looked up to the stars and their patterns. Next comes an essay by the brilliant writer Ronald Greer II, who is currently incarcerated, in which he reminisces on his childhood on a crumbling block in Detroit. He recalls following his curiosities through a world populated by a terrifying pack of pit bulls and figures magnetized by mystery vices, as well as the safety of his grandfather's garden.

A focus on childhood continues through the contributions of Naima Penniman and Michael Kleber-Diggs. Penniman brings us to the forest and the safe haven of her playhouse, where she and her siblings, who all shared a passion for conservation, held environmental meetings. Plants as medicine, poison, and protection. As prescription for the future. In his memory-driven essay, Kleber-Diggs evokes the sensory recollections of the days following his father's death and the ways that profound loss was held in the care and domestic movements of his grandparents' home.

The end of the journey situates us at the edges of our thinking about the natural world and our place in it. Alexis Pauline Gumbs, in a ceremony of water and stone, evokes the legacy of Audre Lorde's Black feminist poetry and tests what nature poetry can hold. Is the natural world experienced by Black people the same as the natural world experienced by white people in this country? And in the final essay of the collection, Katie Robinson invites us to linger with our fears, to make friends with the things we fear by leaning into the super- and extra-natural in our dreams and nightmares, through interspecies encounters to find nature not just beyond ourselves but inside.

It is my hope that *A Darker Wilderness* will push the limits of your definition of nature by reintroducing you to historical figures such as François Makandal, Benjamin Banneker, Audre Lorde, and Austin Dabney. By meandering the typography of this country, from Martha's Vineyard to Detroit, Alabama to Buffalo, Harlem to Antigua, and Alabama to Good Hope, Georgia. By finding meaning from the forest to the ocean, the mountains to a small fishing hole in Kansas, the soil to the stars, the Grand Canyon to the micro-movements of a wasp.

One last note. As the world was shaped by the COVID-19 pandemic and as police violence in Minneapolis led to unrest and derision and while this collection was incubating, hatching, and finding its way to assembly, I was deepening my relationship with nature. In February 2021, four friends, my wife, and I embarked on an adventure and stepped up together to steward sacred land in central Minnesota. Rootsprings is a farm and retreat center on thirty-six acres of prairie, wetlands, forest, and a small spring-fed lake. The land had been home to a spiritual retreat founded by a group of nuns from the Franciscan Sisters of Little Falls, who named the property Clare's Well. Later called Wellsprings, the acreage was eventually cared for by a couple looking toward retirement and searching for new caretakers. We took up the baton—planning, organizing, fundraising, and forming a cooperative to practice new models of ownership, beyond those prescribed by capitalism.

We moved into the red farmhouse on a frigid weekend with temps south of zero and started hosting guests right away. In the first year, we hosted more than four hundred guests in three small hermitages: one near the lake named for the civil rights activist Pauli Murray, one on the hill called Windrise, and a geodesic dome named for Octavia E. Butler. Our guests have described a feeling of being held once arriving on the land, that the instant they arrive on the property a feeling washes over them, of decompression, of release. The journey to the land might feel rife with possible threats—think Trump memorabilia, Blue Lives Matter flags, anti-Biden-Harris messages painted on the sides of barns, and signs staked into front yards along the fifty-mile drive from the Twin Cities—but the land holds them once they're here.

Minnesota is a place where people "go up north," to the houses and cabins that line the shorelines of all the lakes dotting the landscape across the state. These vacation homes are part of the privilege that is unevenly distributed among us, and I can't help but think of all the residual benefits that come from the certain opportunity they offer to be immersed in nature. Our vision is to center Black and Indigenous people and people of color (BIPOC) and lesbian, gay, bisexual, trans, and queer (LGBTQ) folks at Rootsprings and to offer a respite to hold grief and transition, renewal and cultivation, planning and visioning, recreation and celebration.

I can feel its effects on me already. Curiosity has struck me; I am fascinated by the teeming life we are in the midst of. We are feeling the ways the seasons wash over the land, the ways the activity shifts from week to week—hour to hour, even. After leaving a fern gully deep in the woods, where the light comes in golden and warm, and dancing through translucent green leaves deep in the forest, I noticed a scattering of lantern-shaped, thin-skinned little buds that resembled the hops we grew on the urban farm in Buffalo. I learned that these small yellow wind-socks were the catkins of the *Ostrya virginiana* or American ho-phornbeam or ironwood tree, as it is commonly known. In the prairie, another afternoon, the field was alive with dragonflies jetting and darting from the tiny flowers of milkweed huddled together. A few weeks later, the buds were replaced with big seedpods bouncing in the breeze, some exploding with their cotton. Deer are curious about us, pausing to watch us from across the meadow. We wake to their tracks and to those of rabbits, foxes, and wolves. One day, a couple of golden-headed mute swans landed on our little lake; the air was filled with the song of bullfrogs, the screaming of guinea fowl. And this is just the beginning of our being acquainted. There is so much more to learn and observe and be shaped by.

AN ASPECT OF FREEDOM

Ama Codjoe

Fred Hampton is still alive. July 1965. Five months after
Malcolm X's assassination. Four months after Bloody
Sunday. My mother, second-born of four girls, is a few
months away from turning thirteen. My mother, the age
Denise McNair, youngest of *the four little girls*, would have
been. Searched for in rubble and broken stained glass. Her
father glimpsed the dusty patent leather shoe poking from
under the white sheet and knew it was Denise's. My mother's Tennessee touching Denise's Alabama, where white
supremacists planted fifteen sticks of dynamite under the
back stairwell of 16th Street Baptist Church, and where,
hours after the ghastly explosion, thirteen-year-old Virgil
Ware was shot while riding the handlebars of his brother's bike. The Alabama where, on the same day five children were murdered, a sixth, Johnny Robinson, sixteen and
back turned, was killed by a police officer. Far away, in Los
Angeles, Watts is almost on fire. What is it about a traffic
stop and a city block and a sidewalk and a country road and
a Bible study and a choir room and a vestibule and a playground and a living room and a bedroom and a bed and a
driveway and a highway and a stairwell and a gas station
and a suburb and a driver's seat and a parking lot and a balcony and the door to one's own home. It's raining. It's raining in Greensboro, Alabama. Almost forty years later, Agha
Shahid Ali will write: "After we died—*That was it!*—God

left us in the dark. / And as we forgot the dark, we forgot even the rain." *Even the rain, even the rain,* the poet will repeat. The young woman, the girl, takes the shoes off her feet. She pinches the tops of them together and advances toward the camera. In May 1965, a few months before this photograph was taken, a white photographer moved with his wife and daughter from Pennsylvania to Alabama to work for the *Southern Courier.* The photograph won't run in the newspaper. The negative will be archived under the title "Young woman standing in the rain during a civil rights demonstration in Greensboro, Alabama." According to the article alongside which this photograph will not appear, a policeman, wearing a gas mask and a blue uniform, set off a smoking canister ten feet from the protestors. A policeman, wearing a gas mask and a blue uniform, gave the young demonstrators a three-minute warning. The demonstrators prayed. Before the three minutes were up, gas erupted into the air. The wind shifted the noxious smoke toward the police officers. The children and young people retreated inside the doors of St. Matthew African Methodist Episcopal (AME) Church. White men hurled gas grenades into the building. Before the demonstration, two more churches had been burned. Children and young people gathered to protest the burnings. Inside the beleaguered church, the young people decided on their strategy. They chose to return outside, to hold their ground. Rain begins to fall. In the downpour, a young woman, a girl, scarcely a teenager, takes the shoes off her feet. She is the age Denise McNair or Virgil Ware or Addie Mae Collins or Carole Robertson or Cynthia Wesley or Johnny Robinson will always be. She is eleven or fourteen or thirteen or sixteen. The girl remembers, a few years ago, when she heard the phrase *four little girls*. She remembers a photograph of Sarah Collins, *the fifth girl*, who was lying in a hospital bed, skin burned, eyes covered with white patches of cotton and gauze. The young people wanted to march to the Hale County Courthouse to protest the church burnings. The police erected a barricade. The Klan was rumored to be waiting. The girl ran into St. Matthew with the others. Rain begins to fall. She leaves the church and walks outside into the rain. She pinches the tops of her shoes together and advances toward the camera. In the background, a brick wall. Her mouth open as the rain falls. Singing and shouting and praying. She wants freedom. She shall not be moved.

We shall not
We shall not be moved
Just like a tree that's planted by the water
We shall not be moved

Picture the picture without rain, and somehow the girl in the photograph appears less free. Here I don't mean the freedom a government can grant—though she wants this too—I mean the freedom she was born with, that shaped her desire to protest two church burnings and that compelled her to walk back outside, during a rainstorm, into the face of terrorism. Electric cattle prod, billy club, tear gas, raised fist, pistol, axe handle, red brick, bullwhip, fire hose, chain, stone.

The difference between obtaining civic freedom and experiencing the psychic sensation of *feeling free* means, to start, that a person can attain one, the other, or both. Photography is a tricky medium. Who knows what the girl's expression

31

would reveal a few seconds before the photograph was taken, or slightly after she finished her next step, or if I were the one taking the photograph. But, in the particular moment the photograph depicts, the girl appears to possess a kind of freedom. Another kind—the type she petitions for with every expansion of her lungs—she has been systematically and materially denied. She is willing to die for this freedom.

Just like a tree that's planted by the water
We shall not be moved

The element of water I am, including my tears, is hemmed by skin the shape of me. Drenched by a summer downpour or softened by spring rain, I have felt an aspect of freedom.

The first time I delighted in rain, ran from it precisely because I enjoyed it, was while attending a summer program between my sophomore and junior years of high school. Because I would be cast out of the bimonthly routine of wash, press, and curls, my mother arranged for my hair to be braided for the first time. I sat patiently as the stylist orbited me, parting my hair into precise boxes and a plethora of braids. The hairstyle afforded me the luxury of being unfamiliar to myself. Wearing a woven crown, I existed, for a spell, within my own invention.

The program lasted a few brief weeks; time passed indelibly. I met new people, lived communally, fell in love at least three times, and, on a night of sober revelry, got caught in a downpour. The rain and the streetlight fell on me as I hurried across the quad. My fast friends and I ran for cover, squealing. I only pretended to care. We were carefree, even as we confided in one another about a parent's incarceration, sexual angst, or the earnest questions we believed we would answer once and no more.

To this day, my hair is mercurial. I can't predict what it will look like from one day to the next. And though I've come to adore its style, unruliness, and attitude, in an alternate version of this story, the girl I was, looking in the mirror after having her straightened hair soaked with rain, would have seen ruin. If my hair had been straightened, I would have slipped out of my damp clothes and made an excuse to stay alone in my dorm room while the others listened to music, gossiped, or made out. I would have worried and sulked, begging my hair into pink foam rollers and concealing it beneath a scarf. Even now I don't know how to advise the teenage girl I was, miles from home with no mother or hairdresser to tend to her. I have compassion for the girl who believed her hair would've needed fixing.

That night, running across the quad, rain became a test for how free I could feel. Years later, during a powerful summer shower, I turned to a lover to ask if he wanted to go outside, into the rain. Another day-turned-evening, during a steady, drizzle, I meandered uptown with my friend Angel, winding through eighty blocks of sidewalk, traffic lights, and street corners. Strolling past the windows of Manhattan high-rises, we passed thousands of people's illuminated, curtained, and emptied lives. Angel teased me for choosing, without fail, to walk in the street instead of maneuvering between mounds of garbage bags heaped onto the curb. We walked an unplanned route: up and down hills, past basketball courts, bodegas, boulders, and parks. For hours we walked and talked and laughed. All the while, a gentle rain gradually soaked us. Under its influence, we bared ourselves in some new way. In Tennessee, I've stood naked in the rain with only the moon's eye watching. I've closed a flimsy, broken umbrella and surrendered to the wind, sauntering down the dirty, glistening street that leads to my Bronx apartment. Most often, though, I listen to rain's falling tendrils without feeling the need of their caress. I appreciate the excuses rain provides: to sleep in, to beg off, to stay home.

One June, on the weekend of the summer solstice, my friend Liz and I drove upstate to a farm near Albany, New York, where we'd volunteered a few summers prior. I didn't realize until we arrived that I needed a tent. Liz offered hers to share. On the first night, rain's cooing lulled us to sleep as water leaked stealthily into the tent in tiny streams. I woke, hours before dawn, cranky, restless, and damp to the bone. We laid our sleeping bags and clothes in the driest spot we could find: across the seats of Liz's car. Irritated, I looked for a task in need of completion. We had sojourned away from New York City to work the land and to spend time in community with other artists, educators, and farmers. In silence, I weeded a small plot of land, and, as my body focused on movement, discernment, and efficiency, my displeasure dissipated. Unrushed by the ongoing rain, I quickly became consumed by the fantasy of pulling every last weed, an impossible feat. *Just one more*, I thought, as the rain poured down on my back. The next day, I pruned tomato plants while the rain drummed its fingers on the ceiling of the high tunnel. Inside the humid shelter, I trained my eyes to travel along the stem and find the parts of the plant that threatened to suck away its growth.

And what of the rage there, on the girl's face. I recognize it. I share it. It is, in part, located in how wide her mouth gapes open and how her teeth gleam. Her protest, any social protest, holds sorrow and funeral and river and deluge and song and keen and reverence and chant and defiance and anger and danger and dance and release and duress and spirit and power and togetherness and agitation and rage. My mother and the unnamed girl in the photograph were born into a system that marked them as second-class citizens. My mother, the girl, and—*write it again*—Denise McNair, Addie Mae Collins, Carole Robertson, Cynthia Wesley, Virgil Ware, and Johnny Robinson were born into Jim Crow apartheid. I am the first generation on my mother's side not born into chattel slavery or government-sanctioned segregation. When I ask my mother, today, if she is free, I can't predict what she will say. I search her face while I wait for the words to fall from her slightly open mouth. I ask my mother this question because I have no succinct answer. After contemplating, she responds in her soft voice, *As free as a Black person in America*.

One day, decades from now, the book you're holding will be out of print and no one will know the name Ahmaud Arbery, but almost every time I walk through my mother's small-town neighborhood, hugging the curbs and glancing over my shoulder, I think of Arbery, just out for a run. I notice the Southern magnolia blossoms, in various stages of bloom and decay, and feel the target on my back.

And I don't think I'm wishing this into my seeing: I believe I see, finally, when I look again, pleasure in the shape of the girl's mouth, in the way her tongue can taste fresh droplets of rain. In the way it is pleasing, even with the threat of annihilation, to move as one commands one's body to move. To sing into the mouth of the demon's lair. Electric cattle prod, billy club, tear gas, raised fist, pistol, axe handle, red brick, bullwhip, fire hose, chain, stone. Danger does not make the song more beautiful. That would be inaccurate. That would be romantic.

But by walking outside of St. Matthew AME Church and into the rain, the girl in the photograph is exercising the freedom she has. Of course, the same could be said if she chose to stay inside the church or if, after deliberating with the other children and young people, she abandoned the demonstration altogether. But with the decision to go back outside, into the rain, and hold her ground, knowing full well what awaited her, the girl in the photograph aims to use one freedom to gain another. Perhaps this is the source of the pleasure I read on her child face.

Living in the United States, one may be gripped, seized suddenly, by a double vision. Ambling along a Memphis street, the Southern red oak startles into a lynching tree. Admiring the night sky, you perceive a creased map lined with stars. You spoon sugar from a sky-blue bowl into a cup of piping hot tea. On your way to the airport or the dentist or the fairgrounds, you drive by the lush, white tufts of a cotton field. Preferring the heat, you lounge on a faded beach towel and watch a group of your friends rush into the frigid Far Rockaway waters. The sea is the Atlantic Ocean, and the sea is a cradle of bones. Your friends' laughter carries easily, as if they are splashing directly beside you and not several hundred yards away. Their breath moves like the wind stroking your face. You watch as the waves race forward and backward, forward and back. When your friends return, they rejoice at how exquisite the water felt. Relaxing, they sigh, happily spent. Later, they will shake the sand from their towels and clap their sandals together before rinsing their feet at the spigot near the beach's entrance, but for now, they stretch out their limbs on the towels beside you. They twist their hair into knots at the backs of their heads. They smile, teeth chattering from the cold.

"Petrichor" is the word coined to describe the unique scent of rain, especially after a dry spell. Maybe for the rest of her life, this particular smell reminds the girl in the photograph of the rain that drenched her young, vulnerable body. The rain, for us, she stands in still. Look at her wide, ecstatic mouth. Look at her narrow hips. Look at her left arm swinging. The girl's mouth releases a song that can't be contained. The clouds release water that can't be held in any longer. Having spent time with her, having spent time studying this photograph, I have fastened the young woman onto my vision of rain. Days from now, I will stare out the window and witness rainfall—she will appear: a fleshly apparition. Years from now, I will smell a cracked-open, mineral odor, and be reminded of the time I spent contemplating the relationship between freedom and rain.

The girl in the photograph has long forgotten this moment. The photograph did not, after all, run in the *Southern Courier*. The girl did not fold open the ten-cent newspaper on July 30, 1965 and discover a picture of herself. Thousands of marches treaded across Alabama in 1965. March, fill the jail. March, fill the jail. Children forced into paddy wagons. Singing songs of freedom. Morticians making promises to do their best: to present the mutilated beloved as "nicely" as possible. Injuries, close calls, eulogies, nightmares, and panic attacks. Shelter, strategy, self-defense, and resilience. Care and collaboration. Bridges and bombings. Five days of marching the fifty-four miles from Selma to Montgomery, often through mud and cold rain. Stinging, bruising water expelled from fire hoses. Menacing, growling, barking, biting dogs. And on and on and on and on without the chance to breathe. Perhaps, to this day, when the smell of rain invades the girl's nostrils, the girl, who is now an elder, remembers not the Greensboro demonstration but her wedding day, when her mother's friend, someone whose name she no longer recalls, comforted her by saying, *Don't worry, Darlin', a little rain is good luck.* Perhaps when, in May, a fast shower streams down the windows of her yellow house, the elderly woman thinks only of how she must rush to put the hammock in the woodshed. *The petunias,* she thinks, *I am glad they will be watered.*

If the rain is rain, if the memory of the protest has not become a scar, is the girl in the photograph—the elder in my imagination, who is now the same age as my living mother or the same age as *the fifth girl,* now a woman, Sarah Collins Rudolph, the younger sister of Addie Mae Collins; who survived, blinded in one eye, the 16th Street Church bombing; who in 2013, fifty years after the bombing, said, *Every day I think about it, just looking in the mirror and seeing . . . the scars on my face. I'm reminded of it every day*—free? If I look at the Southern red oak and see only a tree, am I free?

The first demonstration I joined was in New York City after the acquittal of the four officers who murdered the unarmed, twenty-three-year-old Amadou Diallo. Thirteen years later, I taught high school students in a Saturday art program. Sitting in a solemn circle with a dozen teens, I mentioned Diallo's name and it did not stir recognition. I felt a clenching heat in my chest when I realized they did not know Diallo, whose death had awakened me and whose name echoes mine. My feelings should not have been bruised; the young people were infants, staring into the sky of their cribs, when, mere miles away, plainclothes police officers fired forty-one shots at Diallo in the vestibule of his Bronx apartment.

Forty-one shots, I chanted as I joined the swell of people and voices. The young people did not recognize Diallo's name, but they knew the name of Trayvon Martin. I was a few years younger than Diallo when he was killed, they were a few years younger than Martin. We sat in a circle the Saturday after Martin's death. We sat in a circle a year and a half later, when Martin's murderer was acquitted. We made art to express our rage, grief, confusion, and pain. We painted signs and banners, we marched. During my life, even dying words have become a repetition. And on and on and on and on, without the chance to breathe. Two years later, we joined thousands at a protest in lower Manhattan. *I put my hands up in the air*, I chanted with the same young people who did not know Diallo's name, *Don't shoot, don't shoot, don't shoot.* I felt a sad joy when I heard my voice swell in protest with the other demonstrators'. In song, we became one mouth with many tongues, one body with many limbs. Singing and chanting in unison with others made us, for a time, larger and more powerful.

> *Ain't no power like the power of the people 'cause of the power*
> *of the people don't stop*
> *Say what?*
> *Ain't no power like the power of the people 'cause the power of*
> *the people don't stop*
> *Say what?*
> *Ain't no power like the power of the people 'cause of the power*
> *of the people don't stop*

Here, in our photograph, rain freezes into dashes and drop-lets. The right side of the photograph is occluded: damaged by light, or a ghost, or a reckoning. The top of the photograph is framed by dark leaves that release tiny rivulets of rain. The young woman, the girl, is outside because nature is large enough to hold a freedom cry. Outside the frame, others like her refuse, disobey; open their mouths in protest, terror, pleasure, or song. In a letter to me, a friend wrote, *One definition of nature is "everything that is not one's self."* In the rain, or in the ocean, or in a flood of people singing freedom songs and calling the names of our unjustly killed, I feel a part of nature, a part of nature's self, which may be anything that gives nourishment and everything that breathes.

Water is the portrait I most resemble. When I am in water, stroked by its smallest particulates or immersed in its immensity, I am aware of the weather beyond my psyche, dragged into a bodily presence I often live estranged from. I can't wade into the stars, or float on fire, or press myself, boundless, into a tulip tree's inner rings. Water lets me get close. When, under an open sky, I let water join me, I feel permeable and animal. Twice I swam in the ocean at night, in the warm gulf waters off the coast of Florida, with a group of misfit artists. After wading into the sea, I closed my eyes and fell back onto the water, letting my legs drift to the surface. On my back, I faced the full moon and the stuttering stars. I marveled at how large and buoyant I felt, how insignificant. Reluctant to leave the water, I listened to my breath's percussion lap against my eardrums. The sounds of my body, its breath and heartbeat, wet the spiraling shells of my ears. Every inch of fat on my body pinned my skeleton to the water's rim. And for those moments, I was an astronaut. The moon, which hours earlier we had watched rise, grew smaller and further from reach. Eventually, my feet righted beneath my hips in an awkward search to find the ground again. Joining the others on the shore, I wrapped myself in a borrowed towel and gazed at the black water and the black sky.

A few nights later, I went in again. Unlike the first night, the sky was overcast. A steady movement of clouds obscured the waning moon. When a friend asked if I was afraid, I replied, *It's the same ocean we swim in during the day.* But her question made me aware of the danger I couldn't see. Chest deep in water, talking to my friend, I moved my hands toward and away from my body, enjoying the water's pressure against the muscles of my arms. I noticed something peculiar but not startling, something my mind didn't fully grasp. Another artist, who had swum further out, joined us closer to the shore, and, almost in sync, the three of us noticed a cold, white light—what I had seen from the corner of my eye but hadn't been able to comprehend. Surrounding any movement our bodies made, the water glowed with oceanic fireflies, bioluminescent algae so small, thousands could fit inside a single dewdrop. I laughed out loud. Mesmerized, I waved my hand back and forth, and watched as the water shimmered.

———

I exercise one aspect of freedom—at the risk of losing another—in pursuit of yet another. The last protest I participated in was in West Tennessee with my living, breathing mother. Though we commenced the march in the early morning, it was already sweltering. I had the urge to protect her against the heat, the police, the unknown. For the first nine minutes and twenty-nine seconds we progressed in silence. My mother and I stayed physically close, but as time deepened, we separated psychically, each of us dwelling in what might be called prayer. I remembered the weeds I had pulled in silence at the farm and how I didn't want to stop until I pulled the last one. The bewilderment and anguish my students expressed, the knowledge they became initiates of, crept into my gait. I tried to fathom my mother's Southern girlhood. I recalled a family picture of my mother and her sisters, dressed in their Easter best: four little girls squinting at the sun and smiling at the camera. I heard the dying words of a dying man, which echoed the words of another. I heard a man calling for his mother. It wasn't raining. The bright sky was shockingly blue. Nervous to touch my face, I used a tissue to wipe the tears from my cheeks. Toward the end of the march, I scouted a tree with meager shade for my mother to stand under. I found water for her to drink. We chanted, call and response, along with a woman projecting her voice through a megaphone. When the woman's voice grew fatigued, another took up the lead and kept the song going.

FISHING - BOATING - BATHING - TENNIS

Taylor's Playfair

Ideally located in Oak Bluffs on the exclusive island of Martha's Vineyard.

This Guest-House offers superior accommodations to a discriminating clientele, with complete relaxation and comfort. A home, from home in informality.

We do not serve meals but there are several restaurants and dining rooms that are nearby that serve the finest of foods.

It's time to exchange the long winter months for the enchantment of America's favorite vacationland.

Come to Oak Bluffs — island of cool breezes and starlit nights . . . Swim in azure blue waters, warmed by the Gulf Stream . . . Laze on its golden beaches . . . Tour through its miles of heavenly paradise.

★ ★ ★

Make your reservations now at "Taylor's Playfair."

We anticipate the pleasure of having you as our guest.

May we hear from you soon.

BICYCLING - BOWLING - SUMMER STOCK - DANCING

A FAMILY VACATION

Glynn Pogue

Picture this: a Black family posted on the porch of a big white mansion. It's the kind of porch with columns— mad stately. They're taking up the whole space: some are seated at bistro tables, some are perched on the arms of outdoor couches, some are sitting on the steps.

It's loud.

They're cackling and carrying on. Uncle Terry is playing something old-school from a Bluetooth speaker.

They're sipping Moscow mules and mint juleps from these little mugs Aunt Wendy custom-made with each of their first names on one side and their last name on the other: the Greenwoods.

Outside, the air is balmy, but it's fresh. Every now and then they catch themselves breathing a little deeper, tryna drink in as much air as they can because they all drove here from cities full of smog, from cities on fire.

It's the Fourth of July, 2020. George Floyd was murdered two months ago. They've been trying not to watch the news since they got here. It's already been too much. They lost a great-aunt and a great-uncle to COVID-19 last week, and though they all know it's risky to be gathered together this way, they need this.

They got masks on.

But sometimes they sneak them down to see each other's smiles and, again, to breathe in all that clean air.

In the distance, they can hear the crack of fireworks. When the sun dips behind the mountains, they'll know it's time to caravan their way to a good spot to watch the show. But for now, they stay perched: listening to cicadas sing; watching deer dance across the perfectly manicured twenty-acre stretch of green grass around them; slapping each other on the shoulder when someone makes a good joke; enjoying all the glory.

———

When my mother first bought The Mansion, I resented it.

She's always talking about having a "third eye," and how that eye shows her possibilities. So that's how we ended up with a house in a little town in the Pocono Mountains called Honesdale.

My mother has been collecting things all my life: professional accomplishments, titles, antique Black memorabilia, and properties. The Honesdale mansion is the crown jewel in her collection of bed-and-breakfasts called Akwaaba Inns, a business venture she and my father started in the early '90s because they both loved meeting new people and my mother loved decor. It was about investing, too, about legacy building. Something for the generations to come to inherit.

My parents like their homes old, steeped in history and character and memories of those who came before. Their six inns along the East Coast are reflective of this passion: a Victorian mansion in Brooklyn, which was the house I grew up in; two gingerbreads on the Jersey Shore; a townhouse in Washington, DC; a Craftsman in Philly; and the

Honesdale mansion, a thirty-room former Woolworth estate. My mother branded it "The Mansion at Noble Lane," but we all call it The Mansion for short.

The Mansion hosts Black folks from around the country who come up to the mountains for an escape, for a respite, for rest. It gives the collective *us* a home away from home; we arrive as strangers and leave as family. We indulge in sensory pleasures; we get spa treatments and sip champagne by the firepit. We ride horses, hike, ski, and kayak. For some of us, these forays into the outdoors are new, but the home we'll return to afterward is deeply familiar. We wake up to the sound of soul music and a heaping plate of fish and grits served in a formal dining room. We make plans to have an afternoon picnic on the lawn with the couple we sat next to at breakfast. When we leave, we feel restored. We often say the place touched us on a soul level.

My mother always tells the story about the moment her grandmother learned about The Mansion. Grandma Lemons, who was, like, ninety at the time, said, "I couldn't even eat at the Woolworths counter, and now my baby is all up in their mansion."

The house was a point of pride for all of us. Still, I was always uncomfortable with the excess of our ownership, and when my parents bought The Mansion in Honesdale, it seemed like a step overboard. As a kid, knowing nothing about money, I thought the purchase was financially risky. It already felt like we lived in a fragile comfort, where a slow vacation season meant money would be tight during the winter.

My mother would try explaining that our money was in bricks, not necessarily the bank.

"Why have money you can't spend?" I'd ask.

Then my dad would start going on about how old white families had been doing the same thing forever: creating monopolies, buying houses, letting the value rise, passing 'em down to their kids and their kids' kids.

For my parents, owning property and working for themselves meant having power. A power that had never been reserved for us.

⁓

In the 1960s, Ouida and Geraldine Taylor co-owned a guesthouse called Taylor's Playfair in the Oak Bluffs section of Martha's Vineyard. In dark green lettering, the brochure for the inn invites visitors to enjoy the "cool breezes," "starlit nights," and "azure blue waters" of Oak Bluffs, "America's favorite vacationland." The use of "America's favorite" feels notable. As long as I've ever known about the Vineyard—as those who frequent it call it colloquially—I've known it as the favorite vacationland of the Black bourgeoisie.

In Miss Ouida's summer vacation photos, "The Taylor Family Album: Martha's Vineyard Memories," is an image of a Black family seated out on a lawn. In the shot, an elderly woman sits in a wooden chair, her hands stroking the fur of a dog at her feet. She's flanked by two young women seated on each arm of her chair, a young man sitting in a lawn chair beside her. They look chill, confident, at home. It looks like there might be a barbeque happening right out of frame and someone called them over to pose for the photo, just to capture the moment.

The image strikes me as quintessentially American: the dog, the land, the family.

The phenomenon of the summer vacation is quintessentially American, too; an aspiration right alongside the house with the white picket fence, tied up in the goal to work hard enough to gain the amount of wealth required to take time off; tied up in the need for time off because the rest of the year is spent working.

Summer vacations first emerged as an idea in America in 1869, with the publishing of William H. H. Murray's *Adventures in the Wilderness; or, Camp-Life in the Adirondacks.* America was in the midst of the second industrial revolution, and the economy was booming. In his book, Murray mused that folks were spending too much time working, and that living in a big city was unsanitary and unhealthy. He encouraged "a familiarity with Nature in her wildest and grandest aspects" as a tonic. He wrote that those, like himself, who "were 'born of hunter's breed and blood,' and who, pent up in narrow offices and narrower studies, weary of the city's din," longed for "a breath of mountain air and the free life by field and flood."

It took a few years for Murray's thinking to catch on, but soon travelers began flocking to the Adirondacks. Summer vacations to national parks across the country began to trend, and continue even to this day. But up until the Civil Rights Act of 1964, those spaces were mostly inaccessible to Black travelers—and let me and my people tell it, national parks still aren't at the top of our list, thanks to their history.

In the early 1900s, Oak Bluffs became the getaway of choice for affluent Black vacationers, in part because it was one of the first seaside escapes to allow Black folks to own land, to plant roots and have property to pass down. Taylor's Playfair and my family's inns are part of a tradition of Black-owned bed-and-breakfasts and guesthouses across the country, which offered safe places for us to lay our heads throughout history, particularly during segregation and Jim Crow. These places of refuge filled the pages of *The Negro Motorist Green Book*, a guide for Black travelers compiled by Victor Hugo Green, a mail courier from Harlem.

Known as "the bible of black travel," the guidebook was published from 1936 to 1966, listing in its pages not only guesthouses but restaurants, beauty parlors, nightclubs, gas stations, and other places that were safe for us. Green knew the journeys of Black travelers were fraught with challenges— not only the indignity of being denied service at white-only establishments but, in the worst cases, the possibility of being jailed, assaulted, or even killed in "sundown towns," which decreed non-whites leave town limits before sunset.

Later in its evolution, the *Green Book* became the go-to resource for a newly emerging class of Black leisure travelers who wanted, as the subtitle on the 1963–64 edition of the guide touts, "a vacation without aggravation." Such was the motivation for guests at Taylor's Playfair, where Miss Ouida and Ms. Geraldine said guests would find "superior accommodations" for "a discriminating clientele, with complete relaxation and comfort. A home, from home in informality."

My family and I aren't Vineyard people. I've only been there once, in the winter, but I can imagine summer scenes mirroring my family out on our porch at The Mansion: ownership, excess, indulgence, and, most importantly, leisure. Sixty years after the last publishing of the *Green Book* and after Oak Bluffs welcomed its first Black residents, I still meet guests at my parents' inns with the same desire for true relaxation without having to look over their shoulders. I still meet guests who just want a place to *be*.

In other photos in the "Taylor Family Album," I witness Black people in all varieties of ease and comfort: fly ladies strike a pose atop a giant rock on the beach; a couple on a pier smile, their bikes casually parked beside them. Looking at their photo, I wonder where they headed afterward. Maybe they rode down to the end of the pier to catch the sunset. Maybe they embraced each other in the orange glow of the sun while waves crashed around them.

My parents and I live in Brooklyn, and the rest of our family lives in the Washington, DC, area. We're all close, but proximity makes the DC relatives closer to each other. We come together for holidays and special gatherings, but there are parts of their lives I'll never understand intimately. They're tight-knit. The best type of family, a family that rides hard for one another. They show up to everyone's milestone moments, big or small—always representing us in something custom-made with our name on it, just like the mugs we sipped our Moscow mules from.

We're all up at The Mansion that Fourth of July weekend to reconnect with each other and get some peace. And to support my mom. The pandemic has been hard on the business, so my aunts and uncles booked up the house for a much-needed boost. Although it's just the family, my mom will still get up early to make everyone breakfast and fluff their pillows when they step out for the day. But this weekend is still more of a vacation for her than any other is.

After getting sufficiently tipsy out on the porch, my family heads over to the Home Depot parking lot for the fireworks show. We wind our way along the curved mountain roads, the thicket of trees surrounding us dark and shadowy against the deep blue of the night sky. We keep all the windows down so we can feel the mountain breeze rush in. I feel giddy and child-like, buckled up in the backseat, looking out at lightning bugs glowing among the trees, remembering when my father and I would catch them in mason jars.

Trump will be up for reelection in the fall and there are reminders of that shit everywhere. "Vote Trump 2020" blinks from road signs typically reserved for hazard warnings; damn near every car we pass has the same words on a bumper sticker; people's front yards are cluttered with signs with his name on them poked into the grass.

Despite the scene, my mother is in her element, in the driver's seat, shuttling me, her cousin, and her cousin's daughter down to see the show. The radio is loudly playing some Top 40 song she knows every word to. My mother loves her little town, the cute shops on Main Street, its vistas and lakes. She seems to be unbothered by the fact that this particular area of Pennsylvania is red, and that it's white as hell. If she is at all fearful of the folks up here who take pride in waving their Confederate flags, she doesn't show it. She has so much faith in people.

While Martha's Vineyard gave guests at Taylor's Playfair a Black oasis, the grounds within our large wrought iron gates are the only true safe haven here. The outside is still rife with some of the same dangers Black travelers of the past sought refuge from.

Every now and then, guests ask, "Is it safe here?" And my mother assures them they have nothing to worry about.

"The town is changing," she says.

She's not wrong; we've definitely met some allies up here. Still, I've seen the way others look at us: sometimes in disgust, other times in disbelief. On the few occasions I have gone down to the little pub in town and mentioned in casual conversation that my parents own The Mansion, the locals seemed unable to comprehend how these Black people could have so much.

Days after George Floyd's murder, my mother and I attended a March for Black Lives down on Main Street. I was low-key terrified to go. But my mother insisted we had to. "We're some of the only Black people up here. We can't be afraid of them," she said. "How can we not show up?"

I could think of several reasons. What if shit got violent? What if they used this chance to show us how they really felt about us? Pennsylvania is, after all, an open-carry state.

My mother bought poster boards and markers in red, black, and green from Walmart so we could make signs. On hers, she wrote, *Do Better. Black Lives Matter.* I wrote, *I can't breathe.*

The march was real white and kumbaya. A man was playing the guitar and singing protest songs. My head was on a swivel the whole time, as I waited for something to pop off. And ultimately it did. While we sat in a moment of silence, three pickup trucks with Confederate flags flapping from their cargo beds started to circle the park where we were gathered. Each time they circled, they revved their engines a little louder. I could feel my body getting hot.

Eventually, a few white organizers ran out into the road and told them to leave, and they did. But by then I'd seen enough. I looked at my mother and said, "We should go."

When my family pulls up at the Home Depot for the fireworks show, we see a whole lot of white folks seated in the beds of their pickup trucks. Pinwheels in red, white, and blue are spinning in the hands of small children. American flags are waving. I feel the immediate unease I always feel in the presence of so much American pride. Not only has that flag never felt like it was made for me, but in recent years displays of American symbolism have begun to feel violent.

The ceremony starts up and someone sings a piercingly high-pitched rendition of the national anthem. None of my family members' hands rise to cover our hearts. A flag is lowered and folded and given to the family of a veteran, and then the fireworks start up. A brilliant burst of purples and reds and glittering whites that fizzle away effervescently. I watch the lights illuminate the faces of my loved ones, who are all looking up at the sky, taken by the display.

As the show dies down, and people load up to leave, someone begins playing "God Bless the USA" on a loudspeaker. I listen closely to the lyrics:

> And I'd gladly stand up
> Next to you and defend her still today
> 'Cause there ain't no doubt I love this land
> God bless the USA

All I can think is *God bless this family.*

———

Three years prior to this trip, my cousin Jabari had a baby with a white girl from Kentucky. He was down there for school on a full-tuition scholarship for football. Even though he and I didn't grow up together, I loved bragging about how my cousin was going to go pro. I imagined my whole family sitting at the games, wearing his jersey with pride.

But when ol' girl got pregnant in Jabari's junior year, he moved back home. My aunt first heard the news just days before I graduated from grad school. When she cried at my celebratory party, it wasn't only because she was proud of me, it was because of her pain. I felt guilty, catching up with the latest developments through the family grapevine like gossip. People's lives were changed. Suddenly we had a baby boy to welcome into the fold of our family. And suddenly we had white family members. They all joined us on this trip: the baby, the girl, her mom, and her dad, who wears a big cowboy belt and smokes Marlboro Reds. The baby is beautiful, though, smiling all the time, so clearly loved and adored.

But with the arrival of new life came loss.

A year after the baby was born, my cousin Jordan was struck by a car and killed. He was twenty-six. He was an only child. His parents—Uncle Terry and Aunt Tonya—were destroyed, the whole family was. Jordan had been a light. Always so positive, so full of faith. Whenever we saw each other, we'd trade our latest travel stories and fantasize about the places we hoped to see next. Once, he and my cousin Jamaal made a random visit to New York and stayed the night at my apartment. I was so excited to host them. To be the cool older cousin.

I took them out for Indian food at a little spot in the East Village, and we ate with our hands, our fingertips getting stained with curry, and got drunk on cheap beer. We cracked jokes and lovingly talked shit about each other's parents. In the Uber home, they were enamored by the pace of the city, by its beautiful chaos. Back at my apartment that night, I gave them extra blankets and a set of towels, then set them up in the guest bedroom. I remember thinking they were being so dramatic for sleeping foot to head.

"We're family, y'all! Grow up," I said.

"Nah, you know Jordan likes to cuddle," Jamaal joked.

I slept soundly that night, knowing they were in the bedroom next door. I think we all felt the comfort and safety of each other's company. I made them breakfast the next morning and sent them off back to DC. When we hugged, we told each other, "Be safe," because that's how we always say goodbye to friends and family. It's so automatic it just slips out of my mouth. Sometimes I don't even consider all the dangers we need safety from as I'm saying it, and the power in those words as a send-off: "Be safe."

Jordan was gone not long after.

At his funeral, I sat in the pews weeping. I wished I knew him better, I wished we had had more times like that brief sleepover in the city. I wept seeing my family so broken.

When Uncle Terry decided to come up to The Mansion for the Fourth, my aunt Kim charged my father with keeping him company. My father packed cigars for them to smoke. After the fireworks show, we all head back to the house to sit around the firepit and drink more Moscow mules. I watch my father and Uncle Terry dip back off to the porch to talk. I can see the bright orange glow of their cigars in the darkness.

The next morning, we all wake up to a heavy fog hanging over the lawn. We eat a big breakfast with all the fixings: French toast, grits, eggs, turkey bacon, fresh fruit, and mimosas for good measure. Everyone is splitting up to do activities. Some are taking the baby to a petting zoo, a group of my aunts are going on a boat ride around the lake, and others just want to chill around the house and post up on the porch again or maybe sway in one of the hammocks.

My father suggests some of us go for a hike, and I'm game. I'm not usually a hike type of girl, but it seems like a nice way to get in some fitness. Uncle Terry decides to come, and my cousins Jabari and Armani too.

I ride over to the trailhead with Uncle Terry, in his two-seater convertible. He drops the top and we go zipping around the mountain, my braids flying in the wind.

To enter the mouth of the forest we have to cut through a field of waist-high grass. It's just green, green, green, all around us. The sun is bright and high. We're laughing and yelling out our names to hear our voices echo across the land. Once we descend into the forest, a noticeable hush falls over our group. Under a dense covering of tangled trees and vines, the air is cool and still, save for the occasional bird chirp and the distant sound of a stream. We take careful steps down the muddy trail, clinging to low branches for support. When we find our groove, Uncle Terry pulls out his speaker and starts playing some '80s rap I don't recognize.

"Aye! This is the joint!" my dad exclaims when he hears the beat spill out of the speaker.

There are wildflowers everywhere along the path. I take pictures of each variety as we trudge on; my dad plucks some to take home to plant. When it's time to make our way up and out to the other side of the forest, though, things start getting real. The incline is steep and rugged, and every now and then we take breaks to bend over, put our hands on our knees, and breathe.

My cousin Armani and I are the first to finish the hike. We emerge and immediately collapse into a bed of tall wildflowers. I'm loopy with endorphins. It smells like sun. Like a hot day. There's so much sky.

The rest of the group joins us a few minutes later. We are all sweaty, with the lightness you feel in your body after you've been active. Like all the deep breaths and exhales you took— panting, heaving—drew every bit of old stale air and energy from your lungs and filled it with something fresh. Like you can feel the blood coursing through your veins. In that moment, I realize vacations in nature can also bring healing, especially when alongside those you love. This day in the forest, those moments on the porch, have brought us peace and closeness. After such a year, after so many years.

That night, as I scroll through the photos I took earlier, I find one of Jabari twirling dandelions between his fingertips, holding his arms out, his face turned up to the sun. He looks so tender, so joyous, so at ease.

On our final morning we begin the chaotic dance of getting ready to leave. My aunties are rushing around, packing to-go plates for snacking on during the long drive ahead. I'm checking underneath beds to make sure nothing has been left behind.

Outside, as all the men in the family pack up the cars, there's a cacophony of:

"Where's my charger?"

"I think someone packed my backpack by accident, can y'all check your trunks?"

"Has anyone seen the baby's elephant toy? You know he'll never fall asleep on the drive without it!"

"Don't forget the cooler! I think it's in the kitchen!"

"Tell your mom to hurry up, I'm not tryna hit all that traffic on the turnpike."

And then a blur of gratitude for this time together and for one another:

"Let's do this again, y'all!"

"Maybe we can make it an annual thing!"

"As long as Peanie is still mixing up them Moscow Mules!"

"I'm coming hiking next time!"

"I'll be back for the s'mores!"

"I love you."

"Be safe."

"I love you."

"Make sure y'all call when y'all get home."

"I love you."

And then the hugs—deeper, tighter, and longer than usual. Emphatic slaps on the back, wet kisses on the cheek that leave lipstick stains.

Trunks and car doors slam, ignitions rev.

My parents and I walk up to the porch and watch as our family members pull out of the driveway, gravel crunching underneath their tires. We wave and wave until they're out of sight.

STATE OF GEORGIA.

To the Honourable the _Geo. Gray_ and the Members of
Council, now fitting in Augufta for the Purpofe of granting
Lands in the two new Counties of Franklin and Wafhington

The PETITION of _Nathan Barton_

as a refugee in the State aforefaid,

SHEWETH,

THAT your Petitioner is entitled to _two hundred and_
fifty Acres of Land, as a Bounty for his
Services, purfuant to the Certificate hereunto annexed: That your
Petitioner is defirous of taking up the faid Lands in the County of
Washington ————————

May it therefore pleafe your Honourable Board to grant your
Petitioner _two hundred and fifty_
Acres of Land in the County of _Washington_
on the Right aforefaid, and on his complying with the
Terms mentioned in the late Land Act; and your Petiti-
oner will pray.

THIS LAND IS MY LAND

Sean Hill

Sometime around 1765, a man named Austin Dabney was born in the British colony known as the Province of North Carolina—a decade or so before that colony and its twelve siblings, which would become our union of states, declared their independence and entered the violent birth throes of this nation—before later moving to what would become Wilkes County, Georgia. During the war, those British colonists (both Tories/Loyalists and Whigs/Patriots) fought to determine their fate in this land: the story of this country. And under the command of Colonel Elijah Clark, Dabney, barely into his teen years, joined them, fighting valiantly for the colonies' independence, for the recognition of their sovereignty. Austin Dabney fought in one of the war's important battles—the Battle of Kettle Creek—a major victory for the Patriots. On August 14, 1786, Georgia granted Dabney 250 acres, as was due all Revolutionary War veterans in recognition of their military service. I know Dabney's story because of kept records, archives; the document granting Dabney land is preserved by the Georgia Archives, which is maintained by the University System of Georgia.

Austin Dabney was sent to face musket and artillery fire as the substitute for the man who laid claim to him as property, one of those colonists with a new idea of themselves. Austin Dabney, this man who was held as property, fought with courage and received a crippling injury in the Battle of Kettle Creek. When the state granted Dabney land, the legislature also appropriated seventy pounds to pay for his freedom. There is a document—a petition of manumission—recording that transaction as well.

———

This essay is a kind of accounting or assertion, while it is also, like all essays, an attempt at understanding and articulating. I'm looking at and reflecting on the intersection of Black military service, land ownership, and migration in these United States, which comes back around to our engagement with nature and the land—our fight for and claim to a home—and Austin Dabney and his story are my lens. Nineteenth-century slave narratives included the statement "Written by himself" to assert authenticity and claim authorship, and this essay is the same kind of project, seeking to claim an authentically authored identity. I'm trying to get at the ways Black folks engage with nature, in order to elucidate our humanity for those who are still in the dark. I need to say there are various ways to be a part of this world. I'm making a case for reframing what we think of as engagement with nature.

———

The document, the language, that granted Austin Dabney his freedom was penned in flowing cursive script. This document fascinates me. It is full of definitions and self-definitions. It identifies itself as an act—"An Act / To emancipate and set free Austin a mulatto"—before embarking on a 129-word sentence, in the fashion of legal documents and eighteenth-century explanations, that begins with "Whereas Austin a mulatto man at present the property of the Estate of Richard Aycock, esquire." (According to the Oxford English Dictionary, "mulatto" comes from the Spanish and Portuguese word for "young mule," the hybrid of a horse and a donkey. Mulattoes are folks of mixed Black and white ancestry, especially those having one white parent and one Black parent.) Austin, who could have been the son of Aycock or some other white man, is thus defined twice ("mulatto" and "property") in relation to the man who claimed to own him.

The lengthy sentence goes on to describe Dabney's military conduct: "During the late revolution instead of advantaging himself of the times to withdraw himself from the American lines and enter with the majority of his colour and fellow slaves in the service of his Brittainick Majesty and his officers and his vassals, did voluntarily enroll himself in some one of the corps under the command of Col. Elijah Clark." (Many Black men served in the Continental Army and fought on the side of the Patriots, but with the British promising freedom, many more fought with them.) It continues by attesting that Dabney "in several actions and engagements behaved against the common Enemy with a bravery and fortitude which would have honored a freeman," and carries on by saying that the result of his valor was that "in one of which engagements he was severely wounded, and rendered incapable of hard servitude," and rightly concludes that "policy as well as gratitude demand a return for such services and behavior from the Commonwealth." This stitching together of clauses speaks to the fabric of ideas, if not ideals, of the nascent nation. Dabney's actions merited reward, but in the

matrix of economics, chattel slavery, and imposed racial definitions in service of white supremacy issuance of that reward
wasn't exactly straightforward.

And this is the state's outlining and enacting its obliga-
tion: "Be it Enacted that the said Austin be, and he is hereby
emancipated and made free, and he is and shall be hereby entitled to all the liberties, privileges, and immunities of a free
Citizen of this State so far as free negroes and mulattos are
allowed, and is, and shall be, entitled to annuity allowed by
this State to wounded and disabled soldiers." The restrictive
language here, "so far as . . . allowed," clearly erects borders
and parameters for "free negroes and mulattos," a group to
which Austin Dabney will legally enter, but a group that at
this time would never be the same sort of free Citizen as anyone considered white.

What was land to a person in the late eighteenth and early
nineteenth centuries? What did it mean for Dabney to own
land? What grew on that land? Cash crops and sustenance?
What was cultivated there? A sense of security?

In 1821, Austin Dabney was again awarded land by grant
for his service in the Continental Army, but this was a couple
of years after other veterans, white veterans, had received their
own allotments. Because of his race and racism, Dabney had
been banned from the 1819 land lottery.

Dabney attached himself to a white soldier, Giles Harris,
whom he fought beside and in whose home he convalesced.
That family, the Harrises, perhaps proved useful to him in
several ways, not least in negotiating the wilderness of the

slavery-era South as a man of color. Dabney helped fund the education of William Harris, Giles's son, at Franklin College, which would become the University of Georgia, whose archives would hold Dabney's documents. And when Dabney died in 1830, he bequeathed what land he'd accumulated to William. A few years later, William would honor Dabney by naming his son Austin Dabney Harris.

In the early 1970s, around two centuries after the fight for independence, I was born in Milledgeville, Georgia, where I was also raised. My parents and I first lived in a white clapboard house with blue trim that sat on a raised brick and cinder block foundation, next to my maternal grandmother's home on the south side of town. Kinfolk lived all around. That house had been in our family for a long time and would later be passed on to other families just starting out. Before I can remember but after I learned to walk, my parents bought a trailer and placed it next to my paternal grandmother's house on the north side of town—in a community her generation called New Town. My father was delivered into this world by a midwife on that property, and save for four years in college and the year spent beside my mother's mother, it's where he's lived for nearly three-quarters of a century.

A big mulberry tree stood next to our trailer, and a fine fig bush and pitifully puny peach tree nestled next to my grandmother's house. I remember playing in the front yard under the shady pecan tree and in the backyard under the apple tree and scuppernong arbor.

When we'd go to visit my mom's mom, "out cross the creek" as my dad would say, there was an apple tree behind her house, too, and pecan trees and crepe myrtles, and a pomegranate tree next to the house we'd lived in. This is some of the flora I have early memories of. For fauna, there were turtles and terrapins, frogs and toads, birds—so many birds—and squirrels and an occasional rabbit or opossum or raccoon. And with the "Go outside and play" of whichever adult was watching me at the time, I was free to explore.

At some point, my dad purchased five acres of land out in the country, heading north out of town. We called it The Land. He would take me there to walk it sometimes. There was a dirt road that ran along the north side and a creek that ran along the south side and a powerline easement that ran along the east side. There were a couple of houses at the far end of the dirt road. We would find homemade wooden live traps on the land and check them. Once we found an opossum in one. Some of my formative experiences with nature and my father happened on the untended and overgrown five acres just off the road. A few years ago, my father was approached by the landowner on the other side of the creek about selling his property. He asked me what I would do, and in my usual fashion, I asked him whether he really wanted to sell it or whether the opportunity had raised the idea. I asked him whether he was being offered a fair market price. With the idea of wealth accrual in mind, I asked him what his plans would be for the proceeds of a sale. I said something smart-alecky like, "What you gon do with the money? I spec the land gon' just be more valuable eventually; they ain't making no more land." I saw the land and land ownership as a commodity—a way to perhaps build generational wealth. And I'm sure there were sentimental reasons for my reaction.

One fall morning when I was nine or ten, my uncle took me and his son and other nephew hunting on the property of an old army friend of his. My dad came along with us. We were hunting squirrels, I think mostly to get used to hefting and firing a real gun. Toy guns—cap, water, suction cup, and ray with flashing lights and sounds—were some of our favorite toys. We had shotguns that day. My uncle instructed us on how to safely be with the gun and with others. At the edge of the wood that ran off behind his friend's house, past the playsets and cars that were being repaired or used for parts, my uncle had us boys take practice shots at cans to get used to the feel of it, to shouldering the gun properly, to the idea of looking down the barrel at something. He wanted us to know the sound of the gun's report and the push of its recoil. When he thought we were ready, he reminded us again of how to handle the gun safely. Then told us how to rattle the squirrels' nests: "Find a clump of leaves up in the branches and send some shot up at it. If a squirrel's up there, he'll fall out."

I walked with a .410 double barrel, my father's, broken over my arm. I wasn't that eager to shoot a squirrel. Light sifted down through bare sweetgums. The brass butts of two shells stamped MADE IN U.S.A. shone up at me. We walked abreast into the woods and always in sight of each other. Under a cluster of trees, I stopped and listened for gunshots. The ground was littered with dried sweetgum fruit, spiky brown balls. I kicked a few off into the underbrush before looking closer. They were hard and about the size of a ping-pong ball, with their spikes paired around holes that held the seed. The spikes dehisced, or gaped like a beak, to release the seed. They reminded me of baby birds. The summer before that fall, I had found a bird's nest tucked in Nana's scuppernong arbor. It was low enough for me to stand on tiptoe and see the bare and blind nestlings gaping when they somehow sensed me. Except for my great-aunt's yardbirds, I'd never been so close to birds before. These nestlings were different from chicks; wild, they would one day fly away, and I would never get this close again.

The other boys were successful in their hunts. I was not, but I was interested in the squirrels that had been rattled down from their nests. Even though they were dead, they fascinated me. Their fur, their paws—the pads and claws—their tails, all part of creatures that had only recently been animated wild things.

In a few years, I would end up attending the University of Georgia. The oak-shaded quads of north campus, the oldest part, was home to many squirrels. I remember seeing people feeding them to get them to come closer. Those squirrels would also rummage in trash cans. These habituated wild things weren't wild enough for me; I resented that, instead of being wary of me when in proximity, ready to scamper off if I happened to come too close, they would tentatively approach me as I walked by.

My uncle is a Vietnam veteran. He's a savvy and sharp mind. He loves gadgets and technology. He's handy with machines. He's an avid deer hunter, has been for as long as I can remember. He loves being in the woods and intimately knows the land he hunts. He enlisted in the army because he wanted some say in what happened to him—in determining his fate.

With the Japanese threat to the western coasts of the United States, Canada, and the Aleutian Islands in the US-held Alaska Territory, building a highway to Alaska was approved by the United States Army on February 6, 1942, almost two months to the day after the attack on Pearl Harbor. Congress and President Franklin D. Roosevelt authorized the construction. The Alaska-Canada Highway (Alcan) was a massive undertaking that became a national cause. Of the more than ten thousand men working on the project, one-third were Black, and in the then-segregated military, those men made up three "colored regiments." These Negroes, many of them from the South and with little experience building a road, much less doing so with the older equipment designated for them, started working at the northern end of the proposed route and built south, toward the white regiments that were building north. Given that for Southern Black folk held in slavery—the most extreme manifestation of white supremacy yet—north once represented freedom and being sold south, down river, was a terror, I'm struck by the direction to which these men were assigned. Nor was their more remote location an accident: the African American soldiers were to work away from Canadian towns so as not to come into contact with white people. When remembering how white officers drew their sidearms to keep Black soldiers from interacting with white Canadian women seeking to greet their train, one soldier said, "We were treated more like convicts than members of the United States Army." And yet they continued on their mission, to prove themselves capable, to carve a place for their race in this nation by carving a road through that northern wilderness.

There are photographs of these men working on the Alcan. One of these photos is kept by the Photographs and Prints Division of the Schomburg Center for Research in Black Culture, which is part of the New York Public Library. The photograph is of two young soldiers smiling at the camera from behind a motor grader. The caption on the back of the photograph reads: "Skilled mechanics are needed to keep the heavy construction equipment in good running order. Pvt. James A. Jackson of Kearneysville, West Virginia, and Pfc. Willie Lee Jell, of Baton Rouge, Louisiana make a few repairs on a motor grader. 1942." Their faces are framed by the tractor's arm. Downed trees and brush are just out of focus in the background, with the light and shadow of the forest even deeper behind. The oily grime of a well-used machine catches the light.

This photo captures a moment—records a blink of time—as all photographs do, and that act of preserving a visual memory is hopeful. Photos, like any recording, are for a future: there will be someone to appreciate the moment after the film is developed. Photos also accentuate pasts. There are the pasts of the subject and photographer before the two come together in the moment of exposure. There is the past that is the moments before right after the shutter closes. There is the past made up of all the moments that follow—all the myriad moments before I first viewed the image some seventy-eight years after the photograph was taken. I want to imagine the pasts that led up to the moment those men posed with the grader, the contexts of that moment and those pasts, the lives led to land them there. When I try to imagine James A.

Jackson in Kearneysville, West Virginia, and Willie Lee Jell in Baton Rouge, Louisiana, from what I know of that time and of Louisiana and West Virginia and southern towns and cities, I have to imagine that the natural world was a constant around them—framing their lives as they themselves were framed by the machine, and the woods, in the photo.

———

Kearneysville is in Jefferson County, West Virginia, and Harpers Ferry is also in Jefferson County. Harpers Ferry happens to be where—in addition to John Brown's 1859 raid—in August 1906, the Niagara Movement decided to meet for the first time on US soil after having to gather on the Canadian side of Niagara Falls in July 1905 because Black men and women were not allowed to use hotels on the New York side. I mentioned this connection between the soldier working on the Alcan and the Niagara Movement and Harpers Ferry and John Brown's raid to my wife, who is a historian, and she politely corrected me, saying it sounds like you're pointing out coincidences and not connections, and she was right, I am. As a historian, she doesn't really truck in coincidences; I think she's more interested in drawing causal relationships from past events to the extent that one can, or perhaps she's drawn to the work of chronicling (keeping) what one can for posterity—allowing those future minds to ponder what past bodies and minds did. As a poet and essayist, I think coincidence is fruitful. The fact that things happened on the same land, in the same space, even in different times, is enough to make me take note. If a photo contains many pasts and many futures, if it can preserve memories, then absolutely the land does as well.

The Niagara Movement's 1905 Declaration of Principles makes clear their stance on this nation's treatment of Black soldiers:

> We regret that this nation has never seen fit adequately to reward the black soldiers who, in its five wars, have defended their country with their blood, and yet have been systematically denied the promotions which their abilities deserve. And we regard as unjust, the exclusion of black boys from the military and naval training schools.

This quote speaks to the reality for African Americans at the turn of the last century, a reality that was circumscribed by "so far as allowed" parameters put in place by racist notions.

Because of his service in the War for Independence, Austin Dabney was afforded his freedom by an appropriation of the Georgia legislature, which purchased his freedom for him. Or, rather, the state purchased Dabney in order to emancipate him. I'm struck by the fact that money is necessarily involved in the manumission of an actual Patriot. Dabney fought and was injured in the Battle of Kettle Creek. This battle was a victory for the Patriots, those men who thought, felt, that this land should be theirs. But proving oneself worthy to those who maintain they have the right to withhold one's freedom wasn't enough. Because slavery in this land was about economic advantage, economic principles were always at play and had to be answered. As a child, I sometimes thought about those Black folks who had been enslaved and those who had been free. Somehow, I built the impression that once one's greatness was recognized one would be rewarded—simply granted one's freedom—that one's deeds or heroic actions would prove one's worthiness. But no. Slaves were wealth, and compensation to owners was necessary under that system. In my unthinking naiveté, I didn't recognize that I'd based this sense of things on the premise of enslaved folks being less than human. That they'd have to prove their humanity to be seen as equal to whites who, even if not owners, were above enslavement themselves.

There's a current and now-shifting understanding of nature and wilderness that views nature as something at a remove from the manmade—it's primitive, remote, pristine land; untouched land that those with the financial wherewithal, time, and "desire" can access. Going camping. Backpacking. Disappearing into the woods for days on end.

I want to posit that I grew up with nature and the idea that the human imposition on the landscape, our built environment, our habitation, is just that: an idea, a perspective, as witnessed by the growth of "weeds," vegetation that needs to be controlled or cultivated. I think about tall grasses trampled down for bedding or a termite mound or anthill eruption or the way a beaver dam interrupts the flow of a stream, about all the various excavations by animals endeavoring to make a place for themselves, and I wonder if they think of themselves as outside of nature. I'm not saying that our homes, hamlets, villages, towns, cities, metropolises, and conurbations are "natural," but that the thing that separates them from nature is a cultural perspective. The sprawl of us across the planet in the Anthropocene means we look for the pristine—the not "us"— to *find* what we declare nature. This seems to me to be about power and ownership—access to the "right" kind of places to hike, camp, and get away. (Not to mention hunt and fish.)

My son, who is five years old, has adopted my interest in birds and birding, an activity that's not often thought of as something people of color engage in. He recently identified the gulls in the park near his preschool as ring-billed gulls, and he identified the black-billed magpies in our neighbor's tree by their raucous calls. His world is entirely prescribed by human activity—by this school, that house—and yet he sees nature constantly on the wing.

My uncle's buddy's property, where I hunted when I was a child, is in Hancock County. Hancock County is adjacent to Washington County, where Austin Dabney's 1786 holding was located. And they are both adjacent to Baldwin County, where my hometown is the county seat. This was the territory I roamed when I was growing up in Milledgeville, these were the borders of my world.

When my son was one and a half years old, it was time to buy him his first shoes with real soles, shoes that weren't baby boo-ties. We were living in Fairbanks, Alaska, at the time, and this was in the spring, late April. It was surely below freezing, and there was plenty of snow on the ground and mounded at the edge of the parking lot at Sears as we turned off Airport Frontage Road. There aren't a lot of shopping options in Fairbanks, and I felt Sears was our best bet at finding a nice selection of shoes for him. It was around noon on a Sunday. The Sears was pretty quiet, as it always was compared to the relatively frenetic bustle of Fred Meyer and Walmart. Our salesperson was an older Black woman. She reminded me of the Black salespersons at the department stores in the small mall I grew up with in Milledgeville. Those well-dressed men and women presented as serious professionals there to assist customers. But they were also my parents' peers, and I would see that connection when they would shuck and jive with my dad or pull my mom in close to point her toward some deal. At some point, I decided to ask this woman, who reminded me of those people, how long she'd lived in Fairbanks. She was a retired schoolteacher, she told me, who'd come up from Mississippi in the 1960s because of her brother-in-law. He was in the military—Black service members have been going to Alaska and staying or returning to live and raise families since World War II, since before Alaska gained statehood—and convinced her things were different there, better than the Jim Crow South. So she came up to check it out and ended up staying. She'd had a good long career, she said, teaching in Fairbanks.

Austin Dabney was shot in the leg and sustained a disabling injury while serving what was then just an idea of a country in the violent throes of its birth.

75

My uncle met his friend at work back in our hometown a year or two after returning from Vietnam. His friend was in the Georgia National Guard and tried to convince him to join. It took five years of convincing, but my uncle eventually did join. And he served proudly. I remember going to a parade to see his unit and others from the area deploy for Operation Desert Storm.

———⌣———

Once, my uncle impressed upon me that I needed to use more of my senses when out in the woods. We were walking the land where he hunts, and he caught a whiff of tobacco smoke and knew someone who didn't belong there had been around. That was something he had learned while serving in Vietnam. They were told to be careful when smoking because the soldiers in the North Vietnamese Army would be able to smell their cigarettes from miles off. And they used their own senses of smell to detect the distinct aromas of Viet Cong soldiers' cooking on the breeze. His experience in the army instilled a habit of awareness and taught him a way of being present in nature.

———⌣———

My family didn't go on camping trips when I was a kid. Our vacations were mostly to the beach—Jekyll Island, St. Simons Island, Tybee Island, Myrtle Beach; we went to Pine Mountain once and to Sapphire Valley, North Carolina. We stayed in hotels and motels, not tents. But I still found nature in those places.

I went to the University of Houston for my MFA, and there I took an urban nature course with Professor Terrell Dixon. When I left Athens, Georgia, for Houston, the population of Athens was just over one hundred thousand. The population of Baldwin County, where I was born and raised, hasn't quite hit fifty thousand yet. So, Houston was my first time living in a metropolis. Navigating Houston on surface streets, as I did my first semester because I was fearful of the many lanes of traffic on the major arteries, I got the sense that the city had been built on a drained swamp that remembered what it was and was trying to get its identity back. And when I finally embraced getting around Houston on those major arteries, the elevation of the sweeping ribbons of concrete gave me another vantage of the lay of the land. And I began to see how nature found space in the built environment I negotiated. I saw my first black-crowned night heron in a fountain on the UH campus; I spent some part of an afternoon on my deck watching two male green anoles (American chameleons) display their dewlaps, bob their heads, and fight while airliners flew low overhead on their approach to Hobby International Airport. By fundamentally reframing how I think about nature—where nature can be found—and who can access it with essays like bell hooks's "Touching the Earth" and Rebecca Johnson's "New Moon Over Roxbury: Reflections on Urban Life and the Land," and books like Louis Halle's *Spring in Washington* and Edward P. Jones's *Lost in the City*, Professor Dixon's class affirmed my understanding of my engagement with nature.

I'm not the first to point out (and I'm sure I won't be the last) that Americans of African descent have fought in every major war this country has engaged in. We've fought for this land, and we continue to assert that it is our home. We are Americans; we are patriots; this is our land.

I'm going to posit that history takes place in space—a geography—and so this story is the story of land. This essay is about living on the land. I have a birding mentor and dear friend whose grandparents immigrated from Ireland, and now she's applied for Irish citizenship. One of her concerns is the toll that living in the United States, on stolen land, is taking on her emotionally, intellectually, and psychologically. Her solution to this problem brought into focus for me, once again, the ways history, identity, and race work to exclude possibilities for certain folks. As an African American, I don't have that kind of knowledge of ancestral place that is not on this land mass. According to the census records I can find of my family, my great-great-grandfather was born in Georgia in 1812, and his mother was born in Virginia and his father in Georgia. My people and I were born on this land. It defines our story as it does the stories of the Indigenous peoples, those begotten by this land, and certainly as much as it does those of the Pilgrims and other early settlers from Europe. This land was stolen, as were my ancestors. And like the land my ancestors, considered property, were used to create generational wealth for those who owned them. These facts and the fact that the military service—the fighting—at the center of this essay, the very thing that distinguished Austin Dabney for his courage, supported the theft of Indigenous lands and subjugation of Indigenous people pain and deeply trouble me. Our story is entwined with those stories. But the apparatuses of chattel slavery worked hard to make sure that here on this land is where we would understand our story began, save for the "Go back to where you came from" when our presence is too inconvenient for those who consider themselves and this nation white.

———

I have another friend who, in this recent political climate, was told by a white American that he was obviously not American because he's Chinese American, and so he's Asian. My friend's grandfather came here by boat around the turn of the last century. What is American identity? This friend of mine is a lifelong angler and avid hunter. He's taken me out on his boat on Lake Sinclair, in my hometown, whose many coves were created in 1954 by damming the Oconee River. One day, while motoring around the lake, we went by my cousins' house. Lakefront property is prime real estate in my hometown, and in the early 1980s, these cousins had "moved up on the lake." They were one of the few Black families (and perhaps the first) to live there. My friend remarked that they had one of the "big water"—more valuable—views; he himself lived on a cove. I hadn't thought about the value of the view that way before. When I was a kid and would sleep over at their house, I would wake up early, before everyone else, and creep downstairs to the two stories of windows in the living room to watch the sun rise and play golden rays on the expanse of water in front of me. I would sit quietly there for as long as I could before the others woke up and I needed to get about the day.

———

I started this essay while a global pandemic sent this nation into a lockdown, and even though the country eased into a tentative reopening over time, I didn't leave Montana, where I live with my family, for thirteen months. So I wasn't able to visit central Georgia as I wrote—the land where Austin Dabney walked, where I headed into the woods with a gun, where my uncle still hunts, where my father and I checked box traps, where I grew up squatting down in the yard to get cheek by jowl with flora and fauna. That's how I first encountered the splendor and beauty of the nonhuman world, up close and sometimes in the palm of my hand. Growing up in central Georgia, I didn't understand the sublimity—that awe-inspiring element of being attentive to, being aware of, existing in the world—I experienced around me. The sublime is feeling my body, my self, in the fullest context I can, from my immediate surroundings outward to as much of the extent of everything—the entirety of existence—that I can imagine. It is a pushing beyond the notion of boundaried space and time into all that inspires the awe; that's the sublime. Books, animals, what you can measure in just a few steps: these were the places where separations fell away for me.

Now I live in a different landscape, where the sublime looks very different. The town I live in, call home, in Montana began as a gold claim in the hills. The Continental Divide is to our west and on the east is the Missouri River. There are eighty miles of connected trails into the hills, all part of the city parks. The closest trailhead (and hours of hiking) is a ten-minute walk from our back door. Getting up on a trail in the South Hills and looking north across the valley opens me to the sublimity afforded by vistas. When I look out over the town to the far hills, I can see weather coming into and across the valley. That's one advantage of an expansive land-scape. In Milledgeville, even with the slight roll of the Georgia Piedmont, you hardly ever saw the rain-bearing clouds beyond the plentiful trees before they delivered the soak. As one of my grandmothers used to say, "It's done come up a cloud mighty quick."

Recently, one nice spring day, my family and I were enjoying some time on the walking mall downtown. There are usually kids for our son to play with and people my wife or I know. It's a great place to be social and outside. Our son and some of his friends were testing how close they could get to the strolling pigeons before the birds clapped themselves into the air, while my wife and I people-watched. In the steady trickle of folks walking by, I noticed the confident stride of one guy in partic-ular, a white guy; the majority of guys you see here in Montana are white, but what set him apart and left an impression was his T-shirt. Emblazoned on his chest were the words "Public Land Owner." I wasn't certain what statement he was trying to make, but it reminded me that since July 9, 1868, when the Fourteenth Amendment to the Constitution of the United States was ratified, granting citizenship to my ancestors and ensuring my citizenship as an African American, I'm a public land owner too. Austin Dabney was granted land and rights "so far as allowed" to a free Negro; he never saw the time in which his claim to this land, this nation, which he fought for and they of him could go unquestioned. But I think I have. This land is my land. This land is his land. This land is our land.

CONFRONTING THE NAMES
ON THIS LAND

Lauret Savoy

(Adapted and updated from an essay in
Trace: Memory, History, Race, and the American Landscape)

PROLOGUE

One Hualapai name is Wi-Nya-Ta-Lupa. Flat Black Rock.

Our twelfth day on the river, the current carried us in sight of what at first seemed a lone, dark sentinel standing in the middle of the channel. Each dory pulled into its lee, our guides pausing here—to breathe, to acknowledge this basalt mass they called Vulcan's Anvil, to prepare for what lay ahead. We had reached mile 178 below the launching point at Lees Ferry on the Colorado River. About a mile beyond roared Lava Falls, the largest rapid we would run.

The rock's patterns—blocky, columnar, contorted, massive—and its near-black color stood stark against the earth hues of canyon-wall strata rising three thousand feet above the river. Warm to my hand in afternoon sunlight this rock spoke of different origins, for volcanoes had once erupted in the western part of the Grand Canyon. In the days that followed we would float by remains of lava flows that had cascaded down from the northern rim—or had erupted within the gorge—to dam the river repeatedly over hundreds of thousands of years. Geologists tend to think Vulcan's Anvil is a basalt plug, remnant from the vent of a volcano long since eroded away.

There are other origin narratives. Hualapai traditions link the creation of fire to Wi-Nya-Ta-Lupa. The dark monolith has also been called Wi-Geth-Yea'a—Medicine Rock. For the Hualapai, for the Southern Paiute, and for other tribal peoples living in and around the canyon, here is ancestral homeland. The rock stands in reverence as a source of sacred power and knowledge, as a ceremonial destination of pilgrimages.

Photographs taken of the Grand Canyon region more than a century ago offered monochromatic glimpses to a privileged few of places most people would never see. Shadings in sepia and black-and-white accentuated lithic patterns.

So I immediately recognized the dark blocky rock in the photograph from the 1909 Galloway-Stone expedition. The print's brown tones were fitting. The high-water ring marking a time when the mud-laden river flowed and flooded on its own terms, long before major dams.

Then I turned to the two-line title. First, a description: "Monolith of lava in river." The general location: "Grand Canyon." Next, various names. Smooth reading stopped. "Lava Pinnacle, Nigger Head, Vulcans Anvil a mile above Lava Falls."

The weight of one name can be a heavy, malignant burden. Although years had passed since that dory trip, some residue of how I'd grown to experience the canyon remained. Names and facts had lost importance for me after the first days on the river. Beholding form and pattern, texture and light without labels mattered more. So, encountering such a name felt like an assault.

Naming is not innocent, passive, or neutral. Once the continent wore no names, having no need for them when the languages of water, wind, and ice prevailed. Yet without thinking one now says *Grand Canyon* or *Colorado River*, *New York* or *Arizona*—so embedded are such terms in the nation's vocabulary. It may be commonplace to consider place-names or toponyms as givens, merely distinguishing one piece of terrain from another. But to assume this is to see a reflecting surface and not what lies beneath.

Histories that mark our present lie in these depths. My search for them began in a young girl's enchantment by land-words. The path then led to historical accounts of place-naming on this continent. George R. Stewart's famous book *Names on the Land* has been hailed "a masterpiece of American writing and American history." But in his and most other works, it was the stories of those from Europe that formed the core. The toponyms of greatest concern either originated with voyagers and colonists from Europe and their descendants, or filtered through them from Indigenous tongues, sometimes much worse for wear. Most troubling to me is how people have embraced these namings as history, as "our" heritage, without asking if there might be other narratives, too. What of the indivisible ties between land and language in Indigenous traditions? What of names and other linguistic symbols left by those from Africa or Asia who'd come to this continent? What of names signaling hatred and disrespect?

The journeys that took me from a child's love to answers and understanding follow. I invite you to join me.

WHAT'S IN A NAME

Give me a story, and I'll give you one in return.

Anyone passing our yard might think the solitary child played with an imaginary friend. She'd twirl in place, arms outstretched, eyes closed. Each turn bringing a new word spoken with care. *Sequoia. Shenandoah. Cheyenne. Susquehanna. Mojave. Yosemite. Wyoming.* The words were names that rolled off her tongue. She'd stop, then spin the other way. *Potomac. Chesapeake. Narragansett. Appomattox.*

Once given breath, the names incanted spells, the turns crossing all distance between place and child. These weren't turns of fancy but a melding of sound and Earth *in* her—in my—mind's eye and ear, much as evening shadows overtook the house edge, then approached and included me. Soundings touched contours of mysterious stories that could be plumbed if asked. *Give me a story. I'll give you one in return.*

"Names are magic. One word can pour such a flood through the soul." Had I at the age of six understood Walt Whitman's words, I would have counted him friend. Word-moments could blaze with an intensity that seemed to concentrate all life. I placed myself by the compass of places sung aloud. That I hadn't yet set foot in most mattered little. There were other ways to travel to them.

———⌣———

I was born in the homeland of the Ohlone, which Spain claimed as part of Alta California. My parents and I lived at first in a city by a bay named for Saint Francis of Assisi. We then moved south to another city, grown around a river now confined within a concrete channel. That settlement was called El Pueblo de la Reina de los Angeles de la Porciúncula. One of the mountains in the range west of it came to be known as "Niggerhead," similar to the basalt block I had encountered in the Colorado River. Then we crossed the continent to what had been part of the Piscataway chiefdom and claimed by Great Britain. We settled in a capital city named to honor the first president of the new American republic. Few of the official names of these places, east or west, arose from the land itself.

I now live in New England, a half hour's drive from New Hampshire. On road trips south, I pass through New York and New Jersey. There are other "new" places. New Londons and New Bostons. New Brunswick and Nova Scotia. Names appear again and again. Cambridge, Bristol, Portsmouth, Newport, Plymouth, more—each having found at least two homes in the British colonies.

In the Chesapeake Bay area that became my paternal ancestors' home, English names paid homage to monarchs whose patronage voyagers either enjoyed or sought. Virginia for a virgin queen, Elizabeth. Jamestown and James, settlement and river, remembering a king. Terra Mariae (Maryland) acknowledging another queen, Henrietta Maria, wife to Charles, son of James. Then there are the Syracuses, Troys, Athenses, Romes, Alexandrias, and Philadelphias scattered across American maps to recall an older Old World. Other names spread westward, too, with Anglo-American settlers after the Revolution. They left the land, as H. L. Mencken put it, "bespattered with *Washingtons, Lafayettes, Jeffersons* and *Jacksons*." Columbuses, Columbias, Madisons, and, later, Lincolns joined them.

Colonial tugs-of-war left remnants in name-clusters born of other languages. I hear Dutch echoes on every trip by or to New York City: Haarlem or Haerlem, Jonkheer's (Yonkers), de Bouwerij (the Bowery). Streets named Breede Wegh (Broadway) and De Waal (Wall). Nassau, Flushing, Staten, Bronx. To the north, Poughkeepsie and Peekskill; across the Hudson River, Hopoakan and Hackensack. Breukelen's "broken land" a nod to Long Island's glacial debris.

I also hear lasting marks of Spain: California, Florida, Nueva México. Santa Fe, San Francisco, Trinidad, Santa Cruz, Los Angeles. Oasis meadows of Las Vegas. Sierra Nevada, the snowy range. Rio Grande del Norte, great river of the north. Colorado, mud-red river. *Cañon, mesa, arroyo, playa*—terms for dryland features that English didn't know.

"For name, though it seem but a superficial and outward matter," wrote Francis Bacon, "yet it carrieth much impression and enchantment." Names encode meaning and memory. I can understand the impulse to place the linguistic familiar about oneself. In stapling down small, created certainties, an overlain geography of home could then orient and transform a vast unknown into a knowable new chance. Naming and mapping would work as twin projects in the courses of empire, as semantic (re)defining fit a design that made sense to the ambitions of those men from Europe who made landfall after landfall.

Their linguistic claiming overprinted and appropriated older names, other views already there. Colonial maps and place-names reorganized space on a slate made blank—by drawing borders, by coding what (and whom) lay inside or out, by erasing. Columbus couldn't hear "Taíno" speech, or at least he rationalized that they had no language by which to embrace the Holy Faith. He shipped captives back to Spain "in order that they might learn to speak." The admiral then named and named and named, for God and Spain, islands, waterways, and coasts known by other terms.

The project of illuminating terra incognita's darkness made certain ways of inhabiting and relating to this place called "America" natural. It made particular points of view normal. In their place-making, these newcomers not only set out to possess territory on the ground. They also lay claim to territory of the mind and memory, to the future and the past.

The people who were already there—"Taíno," Powhatan, Wampanoag, and countless others—who now were discovered but still not seen, could and did look back.

Here lies a paradox. To become oriented, to find their way and fill their maps, venturers from Europe needed Indigenous peoples' knowledge of the land. Maps and names would then obscure that knowledge from its context, as Native people themselves were removed from the land.

A pot spilled. Perceptions and names spread inland from the Atlantic Seaboard, up from Mexico and the Caribbean, covering older names and ideas. Names come into view but sink from sight. Names metamorphose.

I look for those rooted in Indigenous languages. I look, too, for visions originating with newcomers from continents other than Europe. What I seek, of course, are linguistic seeds of my own presence.

Native place-names, or the names of tribal people living in those places, began to appear on sixteenth- and seventeenth-century European maps inland of the Atlantic Coast. It might be better to say that explorers and colonists transcribed into familiar symbols what they heard. Indigenous sounds twisted on European, then Anglo-American tongues. Words and phrases were often reshaped with little sense of original context or use. Maps and journals then carried forward clipped words, simplified renderings, and transliterated sounds. Mutating steps could result in an English version of a French interpretation of an Indigenous word that ended up as *Wisconsin*. In misreading hand-drawn sketches, mapmakers and engravers in Europe created more errors. One changed letter, once formalized in print, could make a name of great meaning become meaningless.

More than half of the country's state names originated, in some form, from Indigenous languages. Some began as records of tribal peoples encountered, either what they called themselves or what others called them. *Dakota, Illini, Kansa, Ute.* Some state names refer to specific elements of the landscape. *Massachusett*, to the Wampanoag, means "place of the foothill," but Puritan settlers used it for a bay and for their colony. Kwinitekw, the long tidal river, became *Connecticut*. And there is the convoluted origin of the name Wisconsin. According to George Stewart's *Names on the Land*, the French voyageurs Jolliet and Marquette heard and recorded Mesconsing (or Mescousing) in 1673 for a river flowing west to the continental interior. But Mesconsing became Ouisconsing or Ouisconsink on later maps, and finally Wisconsin in English.

Indigenous words for aspects of waterways, or of names of people living by them, also persist, even if in altered forms. *Potomac. Rappahannock. Susquehanna. Merrimac.*

Penobscot. Connecticut. Ohio. Wabash. Missouri. Mississippi. Chesapeake. All but one of the Great Lakes. Stewart described a shallow, braided river crossing the plains that was called Ni-bthaska in one Native language, *ni* for "river" and *bthaska* for its spreading flatness. Frenchmen in the 1700s translated this name to Rivière Plate but spelled it *Platte.* These waters became the lifeline of the Oregon Trail—and from Ni-bthaska, Stewart noted, came the name of one state through which the river flows.

Place-names that might or might not have been bestowed by Indigenous people for those places shimmer like mirages. I live in Massachusetts. I've swum in the Connecticut River. I've spent long hours by the Potomac and Susquehanna Rivers, by Chesapeake Bay. I've waded into the Platte, the Arkansas, the Missouri. I've crossed the Mississippi's headwaters on stepping-stones. And I've explored mountains. Adirondack. Taconic. Ouachita. Pocono. Wasatch. Absaroka. Uinta. Appalachian.

The long range stretching from Alabama to Newfoundland is ancient, its contours the worn roots of peaks thought once as grand as the Alps. For Stewart, its name began with a 1528 search for gold in Florida. As chronicled by Álvar Núñez Cabeza de Vaca, the ill-fated Narváez expedition found no gold but encountered Indigenous people and a village called Apalchen, Apalachen, or Apalache. This name would appear in various spellings on Spanish, French, and other maps as a marker for the mysterious interior. Even Mercator's 1569 map of the world placed Apalchen near a large river flowing between the two southern prongs of a long chain of mountains paralleling the east coast. Travelers from Europe and Anglo-American settlers would use various names up and down the chain, but by the late 1700s Allegheny (or Alleghany) and Appalachian vied for the entire length. After Arnold Guyot published "On the Appalachian Mountain System," his study of the range's elevations and structure, in 1861, that name's usage slowly began to spread. It could have gone the other way: Guyot's map, prepared before he finished the report, used Alleghany.

In my mind, though, Oregon and Wyoming offer the most telling examples of how far out of linguistic and geographic context American place-naming could reach.

The Oregon story George Stewart favored began with a coincidence of mistakes on a 1715 map, an old legend that hadn't yet died, and liberties taken by explorer-promoters who claimed and advertised far more than they knew. First, a map engraver misspelled the Ouisconsink River (already a mutated word) as "Ouaricon -sint," placing the hyphen and last four letters beneath the rest of the name. The crowded map showed the Ouaricon flowing west from the Great Lakes region. A later, more fanciful map applied the name to the fabled, mythical "River of the West," which legend had flowing from the midcontinent through the Rocky Mountains to the Pacific Ocean. Ouaricon passed into Ouragon and Ourigan, then finally to the name now used.

Wyoming also began as an eastern Indigenous term that migrated west. The name of a valley in northeastern Pennsylvania, it might be a corrupted version of a Lenape word for "at the big flats" or "great meadows." It became wildly popular among Anglo-Americans after an 1809 poem by Thomas Campbell, "Gertrude of Wyoming," memorialized three hundred settlers killed by British Loyalists and Iroquois allies in 1778. Ten Wyoming post offices sprang up between Rhode Island and Nebraska within six decades. The name was also proposed for a new territory organizing north of Colorado after the Civil War. Debates in both the US House of Representatives and Senate would prove the longest on the floor of Congress over land naming. Against the use of Wyoming was the obvious incongruity between name and place. Tribal names from the area were considered. Cheyenne received the most attention until one senator suggested it sounded too close to the French word for a female dog, *chienne*. We know the end of the story. The reasons that won the day? Euphony and poetic association, or as Wisconsin senator James Doolittle offered, "Because it is a beautiful name." So it is, one of my childhood favorites to sing aloud. Wyoming Territory was established on July 25, 1868.

The use of Native or native-sounding words as place-names grew ever more popular among Anglo-Americans through the nineteenth century. Washington Irving so favored them that he proposed the country be called Appalachia or, better still, Alleghania.

Walt Whitman, too, praised Indigenous names that "roll[ed] with venison richness upon the palate." He'd set out in the 1850s to celebrate the language of the United States in *An American Primer*. "All the greatness of any land, at any time, lies folded in its names," Whitman wrote. "Words follow character,—nativity, independence, individuality," elements that he believed set the United States and Americans apart. Being "of the national blood," Indigenous words that gave a "taste of identity and locality" contributed to this unique American character. "I was asking for something savage and luxuriant," he expanded, "and behold, here are the aboriginal names . . . They are honest words,—they give the true length, breadth, depth. They all fit. Mississippi!—the word winds with chutes—it rolls a stream three thousand miles long. Ohio, Connecticut, Ottawa, Monongahela, all fit."

Whitman never finished *An American Primer*. His companion and literary executor finally shepherded it into print in the *Atlantic Monthly* in 1904, a half century after its bulk had been penned, twelve years after the poet's death. But as Whitman had hoped, the primer went on to influence another generation of writers. H. L. Mencken acknowledged and matched Whitman's fervor in *The American Language*, his landmark study of the development of American English. He, too, was taken by "native" words. "Such names as *Tallahassee, Susquehanna, Mississippi, Allegheny, Chicago, Kennebec, Patuxent* and *Kalamazoo* give a barbaric brilliancy to the American map," Mencken wrote in the 1921 edition. "Only the map of Australia can match it."

Both men had researched toponyms in the official lists of post offices. Mencken also drew from the reports of the US Board on Geographic Names, whose mandate was to steer the country toward standardized place-name usage. Accented letters, names with multiple words, names with articles, suffixes, and apostrophes all fell prey as the board anglicized and simplified terms from many languages for the sake of "official" uniformity. La Cygne, in Kansas, became Lacygne. Portage des Flacons lost to Bottle Portage. El Dorado squeezed into Eldorado, De Laux to Dlo. "In its laudable effort to simplify American nomenclature," Mencken lamented that the board had "played ducks and drakes with some of the most picturesque names on the national map."

I stop to scan the master cartographer Erwin Raisz's hand-drawn landforms map of the continental United States, created in the mid-twentieth century. His pen strokes outline a sense of the land's texture. His lines are the paths of sinuous rivers, the edges of plateaus, the summits of mountain ranges. This map reminds me how the American landscape is palimpsest. Layers upon layers of names and meanings lie beneath the official surface. What came *before* colonial maps and names was vast and long. On the eve of contact the breath-taking diversity of Native languages exceeded that of Europe—at least several hundred distinct languages were spoken north of Mexico, perhaps thousands in the Western Hemisphere.

Imagine the names. Imagine their origins.

While many Indigenous languages ceased to be spoken over five eroding and assimilating centuries, hundreds survive in the Americas, even with the looming threat of silence as fluent speakers age and die. Some tribal groups, like the Wampanoag Nation, work to reclaim as a primary means of expression what had been nearly lost.

The land may be the "matrix" of linguistic meaning for oral cultures. Leslie Marmon Silko has described how "the continuity and accuracy of the oral narratives are reinforced by the landscape" for Laguna Pueblo people. In *Wisdom Sits in Places: Landscape and Language among the Western Apache*, Keith Basso notes that "place-names are arguably among the most highly charged and richly evocative of all linguistic symbols." A linguistic anthropologist, Basso had cowboyed with and worked among the Western Apache (Ndee) for years when an elder asked for help in making Apache maps of their land near the Salt River in eastern Arizona. Basso came to understand the sacred, indivisible nature of place and words for these people. Theirs is a language that situates ancestral knowledge (*nohwiza'ye bi kigoya'ii*) and traditional narratives, mind and heart, time and space in the lives of a person and a people. The Ndee word *ni'* means both land and mind, calling on the inseparability of place and thought. In *ni'*, Earth and thinking converge: "Wisdom sits in places."

Basso learned that the evocative power of place-names is "most forcefully displayed when a name is used to substitute for the narrative it anchors, 'standing up alone' (*'o'áá*), as Apaches say, to symbolize the narrative as well as the knowledge it contains." A place, its name, and other ancestral narratives emergent there cannot be separated. The land watches over and "stalks" the people as a cultural mnemonic of origins, of "purposive" behavior. What's crucial is to "think and act 'with' [landscapes] as well as about and upon them, and to weave them with spoken words into the very foundations of social life." As one example of "*sensing* of place," Basso recalls an incident while stringing barbed wire with two Apache cowboys. He noticed one man reciting a long list of place-names in between spurts of tobacco juice. Asked why, the man responded that he "talked names" all the time. "I ride that way in my mind."

N. Scott Momaday has referred to woven experiences of imagination, language, and place—and the relationships born of them—as "reciprocal appropriation." To invest oneself in the land while incorporating the land into one's "own most fundamental experience." Place-making is both a way of "*doing* human history," Basso offers, as well as "a way of constructing social traditions and, in the process, personal and social identities. We *are*, in a sense, the place-worlds we imagine."

"In contrast to the oppressed Indian," George Stewart concluded in *Names on the Land*, "the oppressed African left little mark upon the map. Pinder Town in South Carolina preserved the Kongo *mpinda*, 'peanut,' but white men probably did the naming after the word had become current in local speech. Doubtless many hundreds of small streams and swamps were named by Negroes, but their namings cannot be distinguished."

Left little mark upon the map. Their namings cannot be distinguished. A dismissal unlikely to be questioned by most. But as diaspora linguists like Annette Kashif have observed, languages and naming patterns from Africa crossed the Atlantic, too. Toponyms bearing their influence survive on the land and on maps, especially along the coast and tidewater rivers of the South. That these names have been overlooked beyond a few studies is, I know, part of the story.

Some place-names with at least partial roots in Africa were long thought either irresolvable mysteries or of solely Indigenous origin. *Suwannee* stumped William Read in his 1934 *Florida Place-Names of Indian Origin and Seminole Personal Names*: "The name . . . cannot be translated with certainty, the lack of historical data rendering futile all guesses at its etymology." Suwannee always summons to mind two songs I learned in childhood. Stephen Foster's "Old Folks at Home" from 1851 is still Florida's state song. It's easy to imagine Christy's Minstrels in blackface "a-longin'" for the old plantation." Quick on this tune's heels I hear Al Jolson singing, "Swanee, how I love ya, how I love ya, my dear old

Swanee!" Yet two possible African sources for the word include *nsub'wanyi*, for "my house" or "my home" in Kongo or Mbundu, and the West African (Mandingo) *Suwane*, a personal name.

Suwannee also hints at twining relations among southeastern tribal peoples and Africans, ties far more tangled than stories of harbored fugitives or enslaved workers imply. From their earliest presence in Atlantic and Caribbean colonies, enslaved peoples escaped bondage to establish Maroon camps in remote, inaccessible areas. The Great Dismal Swamp, straddling Virginia and North Carolina's low-country border, was one such refuge. Suwannee Old Town was a Seminole-African community along the Suwannee River sacked by Andrew Jackson's forces in 1818.

Though some findings have been questioned, Winifred Vass posited African roots for other American place-names. Combahee in Mississippi, from *kombahu* or "sweep here" (imperative). Ulah in North Carolina, from *ula*, possibly meaning to purchase or buy. Nakina, North Carolina, from *nuakina*, to hate or to be cruel. Alcolu, South Carolina, perhaps from *alakana*, meaning to long for, hope for, desire greatly. These are but a few. And hybrid words admixing tongues from two or more continents may be more common than once thought.

What disturbs me is how these names, if their origins bear out, may be commentaries on life *in* those places. Buy. Hate. Home. Deep longing.

There is no question, though, of linguistic agency with the many communities that free and freed African Americans established over two centuries. Parting Ways was settled near Plymouth, Massachusetts, by a small group who'd won their freedom fighting in the Revolution. "Black towns" grew in number with the great exodus north and west across the Mississippi River after the Civil War. Liberty. Freedmantown. Freemanville. Lincolnville. Independence Heights. Union City. Bookertee. Nicodemus. Blackdom. Some succeeded. Others succumbed within a generation.

A much more hurtful dimension lies in place-names that refer to African Americans but weren't given by them. "Nigger" once featured in at least two hundred American toponyms, according to the US Board on Geographic Names. "Dead Nigger Creek." "Dead Nigger Hill." "Nigger Canyon." "Nigger Slough." "Nigger Ford." "Nigger Lake." "Nigger Gulch." "Nigger Spring." "Nigger Head Peak." "Nigger Head Mountain." "Niggerhead Island." "Nigger Heel Bar." "Niggertown Marsh." "Nigger Prairie." "Nigger Joe Ridge." "Nigger George Draw." "Nigger Head" for Wi-Nya-Ta-Lupa or Vulcan's Anvil. On and on—in most states, from Maine to Alaska.

The NAACP and others petitioned the Board on Geographic Names for decades to remove the word. Piecemeal changes occurred, a name revised here, another there, until the board decided in 1963 to replace what it called the "pejorative form of Negro" with "Negro" on federal maps and documents. But so embedded was the "pejorative form" that it continues in pockets of local speech and on some maps.

I first encountered such a place-name on a journey across the country the summer after college. Erwin Raisz's map guided me by land texture. My Honda meandered with the Colorado River on Utah Route 128 between Cisco and Moab. On an afternoon in the high nineties, finding a wading spot was a high priority. Sheer sandstone walls flanked many small tributaries of the river. The Bureau of Land Management trailhead sign at one of them stopped me— Negro Bill Canyon. Who was this Bill? Why and when was he here? Sandstone echoed my questions. Later I learned that William Granstaff or Grandstaff was a man of mixed heritage who had come in 1877 as an early pioneer and grazed cattle. "Nigger Bill" featured prominently on an old map I saw in Moab. Only in 2017, years after my first visit, did the Board on Geographic Names finally approve Grandstaff Canyon as the formal name.

And the peak in the Santa Monica Mountains west of our Los Angeles home that wore the name "Niggerhead" also took a long linguistic journey. Its changing name stopped briefly at Negrohead, then, in 2009, it became Ballard Mountain to acknowledge this early Black homesteader who had lived there as a man with a name.

Other slur-names remain. Or they've only recently been changed by the Board on Geographic Names. "Chink Peak" or "Chink's Peak" near Pocatello, Idaho, became Chinese Peak in 2001. "Jap Rock," in California's Solana County, was renamed Japanese Point. But many are still the official names on the land: Pickaninny Buttes, California; Wop Draw, Wyoming; Darkey Springs, Tennessee; Wetback Tank, New Mexico; Dago Gulch, Montana; Dead Injun Creek, Oregon; Sambo Creek in Pennsylvania and Alabama. On and on.

Words of enmity and ignorance that had fallen out of general favor long ago persisted as the official, formal names on the land.

Names outlive the bestowers for many reasons. I think of the vantage point, the "appearance" of overwhelming difference in the eyes and ears of beholding namers for over five hundred years. Even the Linnaean system of binomial nomenclature (listing genus and species), so taken for granted as an international standard, began as part of colonial world trade that collected human beings as it collected exotic plants and animals.

Languages spoken by unknown ancestors converged toward me. But linguistic tributaries arising in Africa and Native America were cut off or diverted long ago. I speak and write in English, a language with no adjective form for *place*. My school rambles through Latin, French, and Castilian Spanish kept me mostly within Europe's realm. Sounds, gestures, rhythms from other lands, all were lost.

Yes, I am palimpsest, too, a place made over but trying to trace back.

⁓

Years ago, Barbara Ras invited me to research terms for a collection Barry Lopez was editing on a "vocabulary" grown from this land. The end product was *Home Ground: Language for an American Landscape*. My efforts played a small part in this community project, but their impact on me was immense. Old memories surfaced as I compiled a list of more than six hundred geologic, geographic, and regional folk terms for the continent's features. I began to call the words aloud.

> *a'a ablation hollow abra alamar alamo alkali flats . . .*
> *badland bajada bald bally banco baraboo . . .*
> *cajo caldera caleta cañada cañon candela cat hole catoctin . . .*

101

A current of language and imagination, dry for so long a time, could still rise and flow, entraining me as water would a grain of sand. Language of the land still worked on me.

What lies beneath the surface of maps and names? The answers, and their layers of meaning, of course depend on one's point of view. Whether what came before 1492 is considered prelude to an American story beginning to unfold. Whether participants from places other than Europe are seen as supporting cast or props. Whether *we* and *our culture* embrace a much larger changing whole.

If history can be read in the names on the land, then the text at the surface is partial and pieced. Readers might do well to look beyond "official" maps for traces of other languages, other visions. They might do well to acknowledge, and mourn, the loss of innumerable names born out of textured homelands that no longer reside in living memory. We all might do well to remember that names are one measure of how one chooses to inhabit the world.

Give me a story, and I'll give you one in return.

EPILOGUE

I first wrote "What's in a Name" in 2013, several years before seeing the 1909 photograph of Vulcan's Anvil. My first thought after reading that photo's title: *Not this place too.*

For "Nigger Head" to be associated with the dark rock seemed to violate so much, in particular the landform's sacredness to the Hualapai, Southern Paiute, and other tribes. The epithet was also an affront to my own experience as a Black woman. That the photo was taken and named more than a century earlier mattered little.

But I shouldn't have been surprised. The "pejorative form" of *negrohead* designated many things across the English-speaking world for centuries. The widest uses were in the United States. To refer to a kind of tobacco. A nob of coral. A wetland tussock or tangled mass of roots and decaying sedges. Spherical cactus of the genera *Ferocactus* and *Echinocactus*. The black-eyed Susan or *Rubeckia*. An advocate for African American rights before and after the Civil War.

And, commonly, any hard rock or stone, whether dark in color or not.

At least twenty-nine places in United States were once burdened by "Niggerhead" or "Nigger Head" as the federally recognized formal name. Mountain summits and hilltops in Alaska, California, Nevada, New Mexico, New York, North Carolina, Texas, Vermont, Virginia, Washington. A cliff in Texas. Capes and points in Florida and New York. Islands in Alabama and Maine. Streams in Alaska, North Carolina, Vermont, and Washington. Lakes in Connecticut, Michigan, Nebraska, Texas, and Vermont.

Wi-Nya-Ta-Lupa or Vulcan's Anvil doesn't wear that slur-name now. But other places still bear racist names that have long outlived the namers. They are intangible artifacts that still wound.

Yet there is a concerted effort to repair such language, thanks to the leadership of Deb Haaland. As a New Mexico congresswoman, and an enrolled member of the Pueblo of Laguna, she served as lead sponsor of the "Reconciliation in Place Names Act" in 2020. The bill sought to establish a process for the Board on Geographic Names to review and revise offensive names on federal land. It emphasized "place names that include racial or sexual slurs, or honor individuals who held racially repugnant views, committed atrocities against Native Americans, or carried out injustices against racial minorities[,] perpetuate prejudice, disparage racial minorities, and honor those who committed or supported atrocities." In July 2021, the bill was introduced again in both the House of Representatives and Senate.

As secretary of the Department of the Interior— the first Indigenous person in this post—Deb Haaland addressed the issue head-on in November 2021. DOI Secretarial Order 3404 declared "squaw" officially derogatory and set up a task force to consider replacement names for more than 650 geographic features bearing the term on federal lands. Secretarial Order 3405 created the federal Advisory Committee on Reconciliation in Place Names, which will actively review and recommend changes to other derogatory toponyms.

"Racist terms have no place in our vernacular or on our federal lands," Secretary Haaland stated. "Our nation's lands and waters should be places to celebrate the outdoors and our shared cultural heritage—not to perpetuate the legacies of oppression." She added that these "actions will accelerate an important process to reconcile derogatory place names and mark a significant step in honoring the ancestors who have stewarded our lands since time immemorial."

Both language and the land have always been contested spaces. And one may wonder when federal attention might shift again, with a future administration less attentive to the truths of this nation's history, or less committed to reconciling wrongs.

Yes, names are one measure of how we choose to live in the world—and a measure of just who *we the people* are.

Benjamin Bannaker's

PENNSYLVANIA, DELAWARE, MARY-
LAND, AND VIRGINIA

A L M A N A C,

FOR THE

YEAR of our LORD 1795;
Being the Third after Leap-Year.

BANNAKER.

—PRINTED FOR—
And Sold by JOHN FISHER, *Stationer.*
BALTIMORE.

AN URBAN FARMER'S ALMANAC
A Twenty-First-Century Reflection on Benjamin Banneker's Almanacs and Other Astronomical Phenomena

Erin Sharkey

The sun has one kind of splendor, the moon another and the stars another; and star differs from star in splendor.
(1 CORINTHIANS 15:41)

From the urban farm, the only light in the sky you can see most nights is the moon. Waxing and waning on schedule, the rest of the dark expanse and its messages obscured by the light from the city. The light of this city has waxed and waned, too, in the last two hundred years. Buffalo, New York, was nicknamed the "city of light" because it was one of the first to be electrified, to have streetlamps glow through the night. But that was long ago, and many lights have gone out since then.

There was a time before a city occupied the shoreline of Lake Erie. The land has felt lunar blue light on its face for many more years than artificial yellow.

Some say the moon's light helps plants regenerate and injuries heal. I myself was a big open wound when I moved to the Queen City. I headed for Buffalo after leaving a small Christian college in Minnesota, after my queerness got too loud for me to remain a student there under the weight of a "lifestyle covenant" signed at seventeen years old.

AUGUST 16

Best day to weed, to ween.

We harvested strawberries perched on the side of a wooden garden bed, its fibers eaten away by years of rain and snow. The little hearts bled on a teenager's palms as she moved them from fruit truss to basket. When the plant was only green again, we moved to the task of rescuing the bush from bindweed. The corkscrewing persistence, with its proud blooms, had silently snaked around and around the strawberry plant, which had braved buds and leaves and flowers, then hard white berries that ripened red in the sun and heat of July. But the weed was natural too, was growing earnestly and seeking the sun. Gently we unwrapped the spiraling insistence that had been strangling the strawberry for months.

Arica's parents were like that wild weed. Her mother, holding many responsibilities; her father, wheezing and tired; both ever present. Wrapped around her as she tried to get off this block with its crumbling sidewalk and slumped houses boarded with plywood, their paint peeling itself away.

She carried the molded-pulp berry basket home to share her bounty with them, to share the taste of her first harvest.

My parents are Christians. They read the Bible in a weekly study with some of their oldest friends; they attend church each week, volunteer in the nursery, teach Sunday school, help with funerals, deliver meals to homebound congregants.

They believe. But they aren't the kind of Christians who believe the world was created on a strict seven-day schedule, or that the Bible excuses the death penalty and requires we reject birth control and produce a huge quiverful of kids, the girls in ankle-length skirts. Socially progressive might be the most accurate way to describe their faith. They celebrate their gay children: me, my wife, my younger brother and his partner. They vote in support of civil rights reforms, public schools, gun control, and workplace protections.

When I was a kid, I loved church. Church was about friends and adventure. During the school year, church was gospel choir and the feeling of being full of sound. Connecting with my peers, sharing our feelings, failures, and hopes. During the summer, church was camp, paddling all day on bright clean water; the nights spent pushing cherry-red embers around a fire in the tall pines of northern Minnesota.

Earnest young adult leaders guided us in Bible studies by the banks of root beer–colored rivers, a chorus of insects vibrating around us, and in park pavilions, with squirrels chasing each other up a tree, jumping from branch to branch. Sometimes these volunteers had strong opinions about the faith, ones that I hadn't heard at home. The first time I heard, in a sincere, matter-of-fact tone, that being gay was a sin was from one of these volunteers. Another cautioned us against tarot cards and secular divination. Another said body piercing was bad, like premarital sex and swearing. I remember these seeds were planted vaguely, not embraced explicitly but burrowed to slumber near my subconscious, and that after each lesson we were sent into the woods to find a quiet private place to pray, to ask forgiveness for trusting something more than Jesus. The wind rustled through the leaves; the birds called to one another. And I thought about the order of things.

SEPTEMBER 27

*Best day to use your food stamps, to go downtown to apply
for section 8, to buy cigars at the corner store, to walk down to
the river to fish with your nephew.*

Summer's morning chores become fall's after-school chores.
The farm is quiet until the teenagers arrive bent-backed and
weary from their day, setting off on tasks, relieved for the familiarity of routine, for labor with their hands and the large
muscles of their backs, for taking their time.

Today, in the neighborhood, it might be the best day
to put the car up on blocks, to put your body between the
metal workings and the concrete, to drain the oil, to use tools.
Antonio always volunteers for chicken coop duty. He likes the
quiet. He used to be afraid, but now he pushes their stubborn
bodies aside and away from the heat lamp. In a hushed whisper, he reassures the brightly colored hens and thanks them for
the warm gift—Easter-hued eggs—their biological instinct.
Clucking, though now forgetful and unworried, the birds wander out of the coop and toward the compost pile.

The boy knows about duty. At home, he is responsible for
getting his sister to the bus after picking out the pieces of her
uniform, the khaki pants and navy polo with the charter school
logo embroidered on the chest, and brushing her ratty hair, forcing an elastic band around it. He sometimes takes a couple of
eggs home and cracks them in a big blue bowl and bathes slices
in it to make her French toast, but she drips syrup down her
front, so most days the menu is peanut butter toast or cereal.

Lately astrology is everywhere. As an artist and community organizer, I am regularly asked to offer not just my sun sign but my moon and rising (Sagittarius, Sagittarius, Libra) as an introduction at meetings. I know the answer because of Junauda Petrus, my best friend and collaborator, who believes deeply in astrology. Junauda can recall each member of my family's signs and uses them as a way of helping me navigate conflicts. When we sign contracts in our work, or collaborate with others, she insists we consult the stars. She invokes astrology when friends couple up. She suggests it as a theme for events we host. She loves astrology. And it's not just her. My social media feed is full of memes about what Scorpios think when packing for vacation or why Aries fear being alone, and my wall is filled with people bemoaning Mercury retrograde and their broken laptops.

Junauda is a serious student of astrology while most folks, in my experience, are not actually looking up to the stars and perceiving changes to celestial bodies and making predictions based on age-old observations. This period of public interest in pop astrology feels distant from a time when astrology was read on the map of the sky. Now, for many casual observers, it exists on the screens of our mobile devices. We aren't using embodied wisdom gained through our experience, but rather responding to a Co–Star app notification that cautions us against treating difficult feelings like hot coals in your hand.

111

JULY 3

Best day to declare your independence, to make a fire,
to show your colors.

The neighborhood starts to smell like sulfur back in June. Now the night is startled awake by the whirr and crack of a fountain of light. Kids throw explosives under the cars passing down Rhode Island Avenue. The city canceled their display downtown and in Front Park because of the cost of overtime for cops. So: lights on the next block, a green gash in darkness, a spray of purple and smoke on the horizon for weeks on end.

———

Most of the time, I don't feel the need to articulate or classify my spiritual beliefs. But at unexpected times, Christianity-tinged ideas, deep rooted from childhood, bloom. If I had to describe my quiet thoughts about astrology, it would be with some combination of suspicion and reluctant curiosity. I suspect this feeling comes from my Christian childhood, but I can't recall a specific lesson against astrology and don't know what my parents think of it. So I ask my mother.

"Well, to be honest, I just think it's baloney. Like fortune cookies or palm reading. And I guess it's harmless, but some Christians think it's an invitation to delve into the black arts." I start to hear her soft conviction harden. "And the Bible warns against divination, and I guess you could say they're in the same category." My dad yells from the background. I can picture him, looking at the screen of his cell phone over the top of his glasses.

He says I "should read Daniel or Isaiah. There are passages in Daniel and Isaiah." My dad has whole books of the Bible memorized for recall. I imagine him thumbing through the skin-thin pages in his mind.

So I go to the Bible, though it is not a text I tend to consult anymore. Its references to Chaldeans (astrologers) are all in the Old Testament. The book of Daniel chronicles Nebuchadnezzar, the king of Babylon who consults with magicians, enchanters, sorcerers, and astrologers to interpret his dreams. And later, this appears in Deuteronomy:

> *And when you look up to the sky and see the sun, the moon and the stars—all the heavenly array—do not be enticed into bowing down to them and worshiping things YOUR GOD has appointed to all the nations under heaven.*

And, at the very beginning, there's this:

> *And God said, "Let there be lights in the vault of the sky to separate the day from the night, and let them serve as signs to mark sacred times, and days and years, and let them be lights in the vault of the sky to give light to the earth." And so it was.*

With that, I am down a rabbit hole. Didn't the "wise men" follow stars to meet the baby Jesus? Didn't they show the way? Hadn't they been studying the stars for a sign, and hadn't they gotten one?

I was uninterested in astrology until I learned that farmers had used it. Or, to be more precise, that they used astronomy and wisdom gathered over many generations and recorded it in almanacs. *The Old Farmer's Almanac* predicted it would snow in July and August of 1816. And it did. In 1815, Mount Tambora erupted in what was then called the Dutch East Indies and is now called Indonesia, and the unusually cold following year, dubbed the Year Without a Summer, killed crops around the world.

Astrology has traditionally been a combination of long observation of the sky and its movements as related to the behavior of people and plants and other beings. Pattern marking or noticing, looking into the blackness and drawing visible lines between its points of light, making shapes out of the stars. One month the moon is large and blood orange, another it is far away and pale butter. The leaves of the trees begin to let go and blanket the ground before the snow or after. On the breeze, the smell of the dogwood tree sours, turning into a garbage odor before the round-petaled blossoms cover the sidewalk in another shade of white. The insects—cicadas and their hissing chorus—appear one year and then not again for seventeen. Benjamin Banneker recorded the cicadas' appearance in 1749, in 1766, and once more in 1783.

APRIL 15

Best day to get your edges laid, to wear your house shoes to
the curb while the babies board the bus, huge backpacks on
their tiny backs, to set traps.

Neighbors come at night and sit like they did in rice paddies, squat and low. They like the bok choy the best. As payment for this gleaning, they allow us to watch over the fence where they have fashioned, by hanging fencing pieces overhead, a suspension system for three-foot-long shiny green melons, fruit for which we do not have a name. Fruit not meant for this hardiness zone. Seeds gripped in palms, crossing the ocean, germinated.

And an old man who lives down the street walks past each day on the way to or from his errands, until one day he stops and waves over the teens to tell them how he carried seeds in his pocket when he came over from Sicily. How he still harvests those pears and apples in his backyard, even after his wife went to be with God. He crosses his heart and kisses his thumb.

───────

A Doritos bag tumbleweed rolls, end over end. The shiny flag holds tight a wooden paint stir stick that marks where the Black Krim heirloom tomatoes end and the black cherry heirlooms begin. Wrapped around the row marker is a weave, ratty black hair ripped violently in a tussle, the woman's face Vaselined and her earrings handed to a friend. The catalpa tree hurls her long spear-shaped seedpods toward the warm earth, ambitious and ill-prepared for childbirth. Most of her babies won't live.

Sure, there are squirrels and aphids and mites and lace-wings, and one summer there were days of bloated rat bodies, escaped after a meal of green foam poison to die belly-up in the sun. But the eight-year-old boys—who come wielding sticks, imagining, like boys do, other lands and other times, their feet trampling rows of beans—are the worst, because you can't blame them. The city park that sits across the street is not for them. The park is broken glass and condoms. It's not a place to imagine somewhere else.

———

Some believe Banneker was descended from the Dogon people, who knew of Saturn's rings, had counted moons, and had identified the Sirius and Digitaria and Sorghum stars. That perhaps his kin had survived the horrors of the belly of the ship from the land the Portuguese called Costa de Pimenta (Pepper Coast). That his name is derived from Bannka, for his grandfather, and from Banka, for a place in West Africa that would later be called Liberia, for its promise of freedom for America's formerly enslaved.

He wrote his first *Almanack and Ephemeris* in 1792, followed by five more years of almanacs, which featured natural and scientific writing such as tide tables, weather forecasts, and solar and lunar eclipse and growing schedules, as well as political commentaries, poetry, and proverbs.

———

A number of almanacs feature a best days calendar, chronicling in relation to the moon's phase which days provide the ideal conditions for different activities. As an example: the best days calendar in the *2020 Old Farmer's Almanac* notes that April 23 is a better day to cut your hair to encourage growth, to color it, or to harvest aboveground crops than any other day that month. The period when the dark face of the moon fills up with light to fullness is the time to do activities requiring strength and fertility, in order to make things grow. If you want to slow growth or to harvest a thing growing too quickly, the waning of the moon—April 23, say—is best.

The hood has best days too. Days at the beginning of the month when WIC comes through, and days when money needs to stretch, when we share our bounty without needing to be asked.

⌣

The Haudenosaunee, the longhouse people, the stewards of this land, looked to the sky and told of a woman there who took her sons, the moon and the stars, and nursed them on her breasts. She is the one who placed the light in the darkness.

How does time and observation work in the hood? Does an urban area have its own rhythms, its own calendrical energy? Measure the time between the Puerto Rican Day Festival—this neighborhood's own red, white, and blue; the teams clamoring over each other, climbing the grease pole, their race to the top, to the sausage—and the day snowflakes tumble after gathering in nimbostratus clouds over the lake. Blanketing the city in a quiet stillness.

You can't see stars from the urban farm. The moon shrinks and grows over the weeks, from a fingernail clipping to gone, a yawning blackness, a timid brightness, a plump glowing orb, only to yo-yo again.

Can you see the future in a starless sky?

⁓

There are twelve houses on the zodiac block, so to speak. My sun, Neptune, and ascendant are in the first house. My moon is in the eleventh. Different things happen in each house. In one you might learn communication; in another, the management of resources. The makeup of and movement through one's astrological neighborhood helps the student notice what parts of life are being called into focus.

In lots of areas in Buffalo, houses stand vacant. On Massachusetts Avenue, storefronts and houses were long unoccupied, and now they are ghosts. A haunted emptiness, missing teeth in the mouth of the neighborhood. A rotten cavity.

We sowed the garden in one of these cavities.

⁓

JUNE 10
Best day to string extension cords to your neighbor's house,
to tag your name on the vacant park building,
to graft, to pollinate.

On the first day of the summer, as they head out for their first tasks, to weed, to turn, to dig, these Black kids will inevitably say, "I ain't no slave, miss. I ain't no pickaninny slave." And who can blame them, really? Farmers wear overalls and ride horses and live in houses next to red barns. Their cows are named Millie, and the farmers eat fresh-baked apple pie that was cooled on a windowsill by the breeze that billows through white sheets on the line. Farmers are white. And these teen-agers know that people who were enslaved, aside from being beaten and raped and humiliated and sold and purchased and taken away from their mothers and crammed in the bellies of ships and forced to deny each other and learn the Bible and forget the language of their lullabies, slaved on farms. Enslaved people bent low and turned their backs to the blazing sun.

MAY 2

Best day to collect cans, to fill a shopping cart with one wheel
that spins, to push the rattling cage to Tops Market
to crush them for five cents apiece.

There are others who look more like them, who watched the fields dry up, crack in every direction, and run red with blood, before leaving the dream of subsistence farming for the refugee camp, for the plane, for resettlement in an ice-cold city here in another country, for a new name and a new birthday—January 1 on a green card.

One kid thought the Underground Railroad was really underground. Enslaved people like moles with squinting eyes; they would chug, chug, and scream the violence of metal on metal. And sing to a moon they could not see. A family of moles is called a labour.

JANUARY 12

Best day to do nothing, to rest. The snow is an unbroken shell.
There is quiet industry below. It does not need
to be tended. Sleep is its own labor.

Massachusetts Avenue is quiet today. Quiet because it is cold—quiet, except for the boys on the corner who kick snow and turn their backs to the wind that comes straight off Lake Erie. Steam swirls about them, about their heads, into plumes, turbans, fascinators. Their shoulders are sewed to their ears; they bounce on one foot, then the other.

Over their heads, and at their feet—a memorial. Plastic flowers, soiled stuffed animals, weathered and disappointed, slumped. Baby pictures, pictures with hands up and fingered signs, wrapped round and round the streetlight with clear tape. Ambers poured to quench the thirst of brothers sleeping on their backs under the earth. Triumph in commitment to brotherhood; glory in blood spilled for their set. "We own this block."

The air is cold, and the rest of the ground is hard; the hens stay close to one another like the boys do. Bantams, Plymouth Rocks, Red Sussexes. They peck and steam rises from the loam, black mounds. They peck in sight of Massachusetts Avenue.

Ceremony: a dirty blanket, downy, windblown, marked with salt (tears distilled) and sand (brown glass, not yet melted). Straw. Chicken shit, worm shit, some faraway cow's shit, delivered on a truck that came, bowed low, offered, and backed away slowly.

Then the dead, facedown, praying. Anointing for their more beautiful brothers long gone, brothers clipped, washed, chopped, dressed, forked, consumed, flushed. Forgotten. An offering.

———

The title on the cover of the 1792 edition of the *Almanack* is printed in a looping script; the paper is yellowing and brittle; the words describe the year—"being BISSEXTILE, or LEAP-YEAR, and the SIXTEENTH YEAR of AMERICAN INDEPENDENCE"—and from there the text fades with age. This edition features excerpts of British Parliament debates, Thomas Jefferson's writing, and abolitionist propaganda, as well as a plan to establish a peace office for the United States.

In the first few years of publication, Banneker's race is made explicit in the introductions. He is described as "a sable descendant of Africa" or "a free Negro," and these editions feature statements by prominent white men who cosign the powers of Banneker's mind. Statements like these were required to legitimize the work of Black genius. Banneker addressed this qualification of his skills with his own statement: "I am annoyed to find that the subject of my race is so much stressed. The work is either correct or it is not. In this case, I believe it to be perfect."

The 1795 cover is marked by Banneker's portrait; a banner wrapped beneath him conveys his name and ends in curly flourishes. Although he was not an officially enrolled member of the Religious Society of Friends, in the few portraits that exist of him, like this one, he wears the traditional garb of the Quakers. The Friends believe in quiet, in listening for a word.

———

OCTOBER 1

Best day to harvest, to play basketball on the broken hoop
that clangs and rings out across the park.

They listen to reggaeton on an old boombox while harvesting green beans, touching the flesh gently and flicking their wrists so the skin won't bruise. At sixteen, they know that we leave marks where we intersect, know how to carry a bounty of patience. The experience is not lost on them—the slow crawl from tiny seed in the cup of the palm to the painfully slow reach for heaven.

Magda is tiny, too. Can get lost for hours with her head low in the beans, palm, snap, palm, snap. But when she is directed to move a pile of earth, she looks even smaller. The handle of the tool barely fits under her chin and her arms spaghetti. She moans and her huffs balloon around her.

AUGUST 27

Best day to crack the hydrant and let water make rainbows in
the sun. Let it clean everything it can reach and leave
the pavement shiny and black.

NOVEMBER 2

Best day to take the man from a few blocks over up on his
offer to breed his blue-nosed pit bull with yours.

APRIL 17

Best day to braid hair on the front porch, to stand in line at the free clinic for a ham for Easter.

DECEMBER 14

...

⌣

The dilapidated house adjacent to the urban farm was a pale pink, its lead paint cracked and peeling. Rust-eaten railing running up to its concrete front porch and its crumbling stone walls. Inside, the floor had been cut open for its copper parts, leaving a wide, gaping hole duct-taped closed. There were two bedrooms in the peak of the house, one facing front and one back.

A family lived here. For a long time. Maybe it was the water bill, climbing and climbing, spilling over, sweeping the family away with it and toward foreclosure. Maybe they watched the neighborhood change and followed the Italian families when the block browned. Maybe they left in search of jobs when the General Motors plant closed. Or the Bethlehem Steel plant. Or the Tri-Co plant. Or the other plant, the place where they'd worked since they were teenagers.

Maybe they had been the ones to plant the rhubarb in the yard. Sent the kids out to break the stalks and bring in armfuls to sweeten for pie, though the kids would always dare each other to try the puckering sour juice from the end. Maybe they planted the raspberry bush that spread and spread without tending.

There was a family here before the house sat empty, before the electricity was cut, and the water. Before the scavengers came in search of stuff to pawn or scrap. Before the elements ate away at the building, nature doing its job, consuming the dead and pulling the remains into itself. There was a family living here before its ownership was acquired by the city, which then sold the house for a dollar to the nonprofit already doing work across the street, already occupying another building left empty when that same city had abandoned it.

An almanac trusts observation and prediction. The magic of its accuracy is in both the longevity of its observations and the faith that there is a pattern to observe, that waiting will reveal a design behind the phenomenon.

Nature isn't bad or good. Nature is a relationship, a big map of interconnectedness, of needs met, bodies transformed. The hood is a natural place. The hood was natural before the garden grew up in the middle of it. And above the garden, the moon is faithful, and it sits in the same sky Banneker looked to to make predictions.

When I moved to Buffalo, I didn't imagine a few months into the future, let alone predict I'd work on an urban farm or whether it would hurt or heal me. But after seven years on that urban farm patterns did emerge and clarify. Resilience and connection made shapes, the natural patterns of people in community. And I was healed by the way its people and animals and plants persist—and the moon and its cycles up there above it, looking down.

Many objects of personal significance and historical value have been lost to time because of a number of factors—lack of resources, lack of imagination, and lack of vision on the part of archivists and librarians. Incarceration has also erased many stories and their evidence. One of the ways the carceral system operates is dehumanizing people by invisibilizing them and the impact their absence has on their families and our communities. This erasure includes mementos and ephemera—evidence marking significant moments in the lives of those incarcerated within the "justice" system.

Ronald is presently incarcerated. Lack of access, to him and others, has been exacerbated by the COVID-19 pandemic, which left incarcerated people with little or no access to in-person visitation, programming, spiritual activities, recreation, or the library. This essay was written and edited over that period, crafted in a series of emails from Ronald, conveyed through a Minnesota Department of Corrections education department and a representative from the Minnesota Prison Writing Workshop. It was nearly impossible to access one another directly during that process, which additionally made the incorporation of an archival object challenging.

Please view this empty space as evidence of these narratives. Please view this empty space with an argument for the abolition of the prison industrial complex.

—ERIN SHARKEY

MAGIC ALLEY

Ronald L. Greer II

I cartwheeled and played hide-and-seek in the same place that the people who doubled over from wicked medicine walked in zombie-footed strides. In the same place faces peered from the edges of weathered windowpanes. Here, I built a clubhouse out of pieces of abandoned homes— these homes were empty of love but never of people—pieces patched together to create a castle for children who could never sit still or tame their free will. The place where I created my castle became my playground: a drab, drug-infested, gravel-paved alley in the heart of Detroit, along the main artery of the city—Woodward Avenue, between the streets of Pasadena and Grand. Out of artless life, in this narrow strip, my imagination created fierce and ferocious creatures, and it was there I learned the difference between a child's world and a young man's.

Wrapped in the landscape of crumbling structures and unkempt lawns, I disappeared in and out of garages and fields of orange-hued dandelions. I jumped from rooftops deep into dungeons and fought back the touch, the kiss, the sickle of death. I played my childhood games, participated in countless hours of roughhoused basketball, and found magic in what most would define as urban blight. Unbeknownst to me, I was heavily protected by my grandfather, Charlie Ramsey, and his shining light that sliced through darkness using nothing but compassion and generosity. In a garden attached to the alley, I witnessed my grandfather bend his tired body and pluck a red tomato from its vine. He walked to the garden's edge toward a man I had never seen before. The man, shabbily dressed, stood on the sidewalk. My grandfather handed the tomato to the man. They gave each other a head nod. The man proceeded along the sidewalk and my grandfather returned to a rusted metal milk crate that he had been sitting on before the man stopped to watch us garden.

I was barely ten years old in the mid-'80s, when I first started exploring Detroit's alleys. During this time, my childlike lens allowed me to see people and places for more than what they offered at face value. Every neighbor possessed their own variation of power; every animal was a pet, protector, or savage, and every building, a kingdom. The years I spent playing in the alley provided me with memories that only a child's imagination could create, but I also learned that the fun had in this alley could be equally deadly. Kick over an old Maxwell House coffee can, and you might find a four-finger set of brass knuckles, a small manila envelope full of powder, or Chuck's hidden gun. I'm not sure if there were always hidden weapons throughout the alley or if I just had a knack for finding stuff I wasn't supposed to find. However, I often found guns, drugs, knives, and I sometimes found a person.

Once, on a cloudy summer day in '87 or '88, on an expedition to cross the street, Ginard, Ronnie J, Chauncey, Harvey, and I found the body of a darkened man. He lay in the doorway of an empty, war-torn building that the land was reclaiming for itself; a tree sprouted into its crumbled walls. The man was twisted in death, his limbs pointed in unorthodox directions. We gathered around him and spoke in chant-like phrases: *Who is he? How did he get here? We should leave. Check his pockets. We're going to get in trouble.* We all spoke in broken unison until our words breathed life back into his being. He growled and cracked his body in line, then ripped a belt from around his forearm. It took me some time to learn why sleeping people always wore their belts around their forearms instead of their waists. The dead man erected himself from the doorway, dark and impossible, and as he arose, we ran from him in defeat. We were no match for his magic. We were experts at finding treasures, but we had no powers against resurrection.

We ran from him without looking back. Possibly, we were too afraid to face our fears, or maybe we'd come too close to a threat we had not yet experienced. Years later, I understood the importance of looking back and what can be learned when we pause. For a time after that failed expedition, we didn't attempt to travel outside our alley. We stuck to our narrow strip and searched for treasures that people lost in their travels, or for artifacts that were supposed to be hidden or cast off. We weren't ready to fend for ourselves past the war-torn building at the end of the alley, where danger lurked; in our alley, we found protection in our familiar landscape.

When my friends and I found certain things in the alley, such as Chuck's gun, we knew to leave his stuff alone because everyone knew: "Chuck will kill you." Though for some reason, I was never worried about Chuck killing me. I wasn't worried about receiving harm from anyone. I had magic on my side, and bullets had no effect against magic. The other young men I ran with, however, might have been a little worried about Chuck killing us—not from a bullet, but from being fed to his dungeon of Pit Bulls.

A few houses down from one of many small gardens my grandfather and I planted, the Pit Bulls lived. They were behind an old wooden fence with red paint that peeled, sharpened, and formed into skin-piercing little daggers. We'd tread lightly as we trekked past the Pit Bulls' fence. There were three of them that we knew of, and the slightest noise would drive them to violent scatters of madness. Our every motion around them would be in fright, except for the times when we wanted to witness the power they possessed. From the alley, we could climb on top of a garage across from the Pit Bulls' yard, and with accurate tossing ability we would launch rocks over the fence from the garage's roof. We couldn't see the dogs, but we could hear them slowly rumble about, sniffing for the source of their disturbance. I had witnessed them feed on each other and knew that if they ever caught me, my flesh was no match for them. We were smart to stay on the roof; they were evil and hungry, diabolical and insatiable. We tempted only enough to make them erratic, never more, for if they ever broke loose, that surely would have meant the end of our reign. There would have been no place to disappear— from them, or from Chuck's wrath.

A single instance occurred that made me, at least, stop harassing the bulls: the one with the large, gnarled head and red nose was halfway over the fence while we practiced how to defend our castle, if and when it was attacked. We could see the fence from our clubhouse and had no awareness of the danger we were in or of the disdain the Pit Bulls had toward us. But as I stood in front of our castle to defend it, the Pit Bull's front legs, head, and half of his body came over the fence. Foam flopped from his mouth, and his claws scraped across the top of the fence. It was evident that in seconds he would scale the fence and swarm us. I might have had magic on my side, but I was not a warrior, at least not yet. I did what I was great at: removing myself from the danger and replacing myself in my grandparents' home, a place that I considered to be the most protected place in existence.

I took one step from in front of the clubhouse, then appeared in my grandparents' bedroom. The room was empty when I arrived, but the hand-quilted comforter, the wooden chair I'd always sit in next to their bed, and a few hunting rifles stacked in the corner wrapped me in a force field of love and protection. I have no recollection of my transfer from the Pit Bulls to the bedroom, from one spot to the other: not how I made it through ankle-deep grass exploding with tobacco-spitting grasshoppers; not how I could have made it through pockets of bumblebees always protecting their queen; not how I climbed two mountainous flights of stairs. I do not know. All I remember is appearing next to a window, surveying yards overgrown with shrubbery, to see if the Pit Bulls had followed me. They had not, and I do not know if they ever made it over the fence, but I imagine that they did.

Although the Pit Bulls were deadly, they were not the deadliest animal in the alley. For an entire summer we heard laughing children, cicadas, and the shake of a serpent that was never found. The shake came from a rattlesnake, believed to be owned by Moo-Moo, who was one of the long-standing residents of the neighborhood. The snake, we learned through rumor, escaped from his house and was loose somewhere in the green grasses and gardens. We could hear its rattle shake wildly through the heat vapor lines that made the surface of the land move with the energy of the beating sun. The sound of its rattle was distant and immediate. Two houses down from Moo-Moo's lived people I called the Unknown; I never saw them arrive or leave, but they always came and went. This house of the Unknown had a twelve-foot fence around its backyard, where an authentic wolf and a Bouvier des Flandres, which we pronounced *boobie-a*, lived uncaged. Upon hearing that they possessed a wolf, I had to see for myself. Harvey lived next door and had a Juliet balcony on the back upper level of his home. I went there to see clearly into the backyard, to get a glimpse of the wolf. It was tall, long, and slender; gray and grayer, unlike any dog I had ever seen before. We played most of our basketball games in Harvey's backyard and sacrificed many a ball to the animals on the other side of that fence, balls that were never retrieved because they were attacked before they hit the ground.

Nothing that went over that fence ever came back, ever.

On a sweltering summer day, when one of the Unknown's pets broke loose, we learned that they sheltered more than human-sized dogs. As was to be expected, the Unknown was somewhere in between coming and going and were nowhere to be found. Everyone in the neighborhood always supposed that the wolf or the Bouvier des Flandres would someday escape and leave a wake of maimed body parts as they terrorized old folks and children. We didn't know what else lived inside the home of the Unknown, what also wanted to escape.

I used to think it escaped its captors from the window of a tower. It zipped across the rooftops and swung through the branches of trees, and we all listened as it attempted to get far away. Branches of hundred-year-old oaks and maple trees flexed and cracked from the animal's movements until it was no longer able to escape further; it found shelter in the largest tree in the alley, but instead of safety, the tree offered nothing but a dead end. In its moment of repose, we could finally see what had escaped. From a distance, someone might have thought it was a small, hairy man, but it was not. It was a spider monkey, sitting high in the trees, looking over a foreign land, a neighborhood that it knew nothing about.

Looking back on the incident, I realize the loose running spider monkey probably suffered from the shock, trauma, and confusion of new freedom. Most of the neighbors stood on their front lawns or huddled in the middle of Grand, pointing at the trees and looking for binoculars to get the novel view of a spider monkey in the trees. The Michigan Humane Society tracked the animal to its position high in the trees and shot it with a tranquilizer gun. No one moved from their spots during the pursuit and capture of the rogue spider monkey, its body limp and un-livid as it was hoisted down. The screeches of the rampant monkey still hung in the winds many weeks after it was captured, and they are forever recorded in my auditory system. Pit Bulls, a Bouvier des Flandres, a rattlesnake, a wolf, and a spider monkey—how could this alley not be magical?

Several houses around the alley contained different, powerful elements. Some sold little white pebbles that gave people super strength and speed; one sold a powdery substance that gave people the power to stop time; one was a watering hole where people held bottles tightly to their bodies. In the middle of it all grew my grandfather's vegetable garden, colorful and full of life.

The people who used the powdery substance alchemically transformed it to a liquid, then used a needle to escape to another dimension. They even had a ritual where they twitched and scratched while they stood in a long line resemblant of the ones at soup kitchens during the Great Depression. I saw them as the Lollipop Guild from *The Wizard of Oz*. They clucked their tongues, kicked their feet, and shucked their arms from side to side before injecting themselves with the liquid that provided them with the power to stop time.

Have you ever seen a soup kitchen line of Lollipop kids? I have, and they wore belts around their forearms and held conversations that they paused in the middle of. After their injections, they stopped moving: there would be tens of them standing like statues in a gothic garden, their movements no more noticeable than the rotation of the Earth. I watched these creatures' souls leave their bodies to find answers, then return minutes later with the answers they had gone searching for. Later, as a preteen in the late '80s, when I learned more about the substance that had made them seem magical to me, I would feel more sympathy for them than wonderment.

In the alley, several houses down from our clubhouse, was a three-car garage filled with stripped automobiles and rusted random pieces of cars long forgotten, dust covered, or tarnished by time. On the second level of the garage lived a powder person, and in his lair there was a kerosene lamp, a sleeping cot, and a milk crate that served as a nightstand. The garage was dilapidated at best but still able to stand strongly on its foundation. Surrounding the outside of the garage were light green, prickly weeds that grew to the height of my waist and dark green vines with waxy leaves that appeared to support the structure—nature took over where humans neglected. However disheveled this place looked, the second floor was meticulously well-kept. The space reminded me of my own family members' quarters: always clean and in order. On the milk crate sat the lamp; a burnt, soot-blackened spoon; and a needle. At eleven years old, whenever I laid eyes on a hypodermic needle I assumed the person using it was a diabetic or a doctor, because they were the only people I ever witnessed with one.

I stumbled upon this person's lair while I was exploring buildings I had not ventured into before, but when I found it, I was furious. I had allowed someone to move into our lands unscathed, to live and sleep and explore without us knowing about them. We had been infiltrated. Directly under our noses or in the dead of night, we had allowed what I took as a spy into our world, who had made themselves comfortable, and even possessed a genuine kerosene lamp. This lair had a lamp, and our clubhouse did not. This lair was clean, and ours was a box of mangy carpets and filth. This was an attic, and ours was a four-foot-high structure of particle board, old doors, and broken two-by-fours. I was infuriated that this person had items in their lair that we did not.

Chauncey, Harvey, and I assembled and advanced toward the powder person's lair. Once there, we stood in the space, not saying anything, just standing there. We didn't know what we were supposed to do, only that something needed to be done. I remember wanting to set the place on fire and claim the building as our own, but the mood hanging over us all grew somber. We were sedated by a force that I cannot describe or define. Finally, Harvey spoke up and said, "C'mon. Let's go. I think this is my uncle's stuff." His words felt like a confession. A damning statement, that his uncle, who we all knew as Bebop, was a powder person. We left that garage feeling a little older, a little more knowledgeable. I went there to take that lamp, but we all walked away with the ugly truth that our imaginations could produce only so much magic before reality choked out our creations.

We walked out of the garage into the alley, empty and empty-handed. We allowed Bebop to exist in our world, and even patrolled his lair for him when we weren't protecting our castle. But we could not allow our focus to rest on him when there were plenty of other things for us to worry about. Like the watering hole. The folks there were a ragtag, colorful group that came and went and rarely took refuge in any one place. They'd meet up in a field at the other end of the alley, opposite from the war-torn building, and sometimes they sat on an old wooden telephone pole that had been left to rot. They converted it to a nice resting bench; it was porous and had moss growing on it in spots that rarely received contact. The people appeared one by one, but always gathered into a cluster. When their water evaporated, they'd wander off into oblivion. As I encountered them, I imagined they were from a land called Wino.

I enjoyed the Winos more than any other magical creature that walked the alley. Some days I would talk to them and listen to their far-fetched stories, which usually made no sense. They regularly spoke through incoherent speech. On other days I would attack them by hurling rocks their way, or, when I got close enough, I'd kick dirt at them. A few times, one or two would come close to capturing me, and I would scatter off to safety before danger could catch me. I thought they would seek revenge when they encountered me again, but my magic was too strong for someone from the land of Wino—I possessed natural protective magic as well as supernatural. My most powerful magic was being able to erase grudges with a smile. It also helped that most of the Winos never entered the alley more than a few times. The Winos were fun to defeat.

When I kicked dirt at them, they'd try to chase me but always stumbled to their faces, while at the same time holding their bottles in their hand as if they were paying homage to some king on high. Most times when I approached them, though, they paid me no attention; they would already be occupied while talking to another Wino, the genie in the bottle, or an imaginary friend. I could never tell the difference. It's an uncanny thing to see a group of people talk to another group of people who can only be seen through the distorted view of a Wild Irish Rose bottle. I think the magic for them was trying to get the genie out of the bottle, and that's why they always hit each other in the head with the bottles.

When I was about ten, I witnessed a Wino drink a big bottle of Night Train with one continuous series of swallows. I went home and tried the same with a jug of Sunny Delight, only to learn that things done within the realm of a magical alley cannot be performed in a mundane kitchen.

There were many types of individuals that frequented the alley, but none of them were more memorable than the woman aptly named Crackhead K, who appeared pregnant for her entire existence. Folks in the neighborhood waited for her to deliver the baby, but, amazingly, one never came.

It saddens me to believe that the baby died inside her, and that K was too trapped in the effects of dark magic to commit herself to anything other than an escape from reality. In the early nineties, Crackhead K died from a heroin overdose, and when they rolled her away on the gurney, folks chatted about her then-pregnancy. All I could think about was how she had always been pregnant, and how I could not remember a time when her stomach wasn't rounded to its third trimester.

Sometimes Crackhead K could be seen dancing in a field—pregnant, barefooted, and inebriated—synchronizing her soul with the other creatures of the alley. She enchanted people with magic that was as dark as it was bright. I remember sitting with her on the mossy log by the Winos' watering hole. She was pregnant and wore dingy jeans, a T-shirt, and a shawl. I looked down at her feet as she spoke words that I could not comprehend except for "You're such a handsome boy," and "Don't get caught up in this world." She wore pink flip-flops; her feet were dirty, like when you step in mud and don't wipe them off, and I remember thinking: *Why won't you just wear shoes?* Now I wonder if she ever thought that the little boy she sat with on a log and called handsome would memorialize her in his words. She and I didn't talk often, but when we did, I think I learned what powers she possessed. I believe K had the ability to see the people who had died in the alley and directed what was left of them into realms that no one could see but her. Their souls, without her, would continuously trek in a loop over worn-down pieces of gravel, razor-sharp broken bottles, war-released empty shell casings, and hypodermic needles whose contents were used as a cure-all but were deadly as time.

To me, Crackhead K was part demon, part enchantress, part junkie, but, most importantly, a completely pleasant person. However, I was instructed to stay away from her and her kind because she, like many of the people in the Magic Alley, were drug addicts who, to my family, disturbingly only cared about the liquid they injected from a needle.

Have you ever seen a valley of hypodermic needles? I have. They look like deadly little dandelions with venomous, hidden stingers, waiting to poison their next prey. I think the souls of the people who died in the alley are trapped there forever, their souls forever asleep in those needles.

By the time I entered my high school years, I'd witnessed my share of what the alley had to offer: some things horrific, others morbidly beautiful, and some things fantastically unbelievable. Though instead of thinking of the alley as magical, I began to look at it through the lens of a growing young man. It was just an alley, an alley that held the troubles of most inner cities. Just another area flooded with drugs, violence, and buildings that could no longer bear the weight of the people who entered them. Those buildings no longer symbolized mystical, powerful places but rather crumbling structures that were smeared with the human stain. What once served as my playground became a few abandoned houses, garages, and apartment buildings that grew a reputation of housing mental and physical torture. Astoundingly, I never felt out of place in those structures; they felt as much home as my grandparents' front porch. No matter how bleak or deadly these places appeared, I walked in their murky hallways as easy as I could walk through air.

Next door to Harvey's home, where we played basketball, was a very large house that existed without a family for many years. The family moved away when I was eleven or twelve, and like every other abandoned structure I walked past, I held intrigue in the story of why it died. I was an explorer, and even though I didn't have my crew with me, I still wanted to know what caused these kingdoms to fall, their stories. In a sense, even as a teenager, I was still searching for magic in the alley. I entered the large house with no other reason than to climb to its attic and look out over the once-lively lands that had slowly died off. If my imagination still possessed the ability to paint phantasm over urban blight, I would have said that "the once powerful glowing kingdoms slowly died from the effects of a white plague." But, at the time, my imagination did not allow me to create that storyline. Though I was unaware of it, my imagination had experienced a deadening process, and the kingdoms were losing their color, paling compared to their previous moments of golden grandeur.

The colors were no longer vibrant but rather a faint hue of themselves. The life had been drained from the environment and my mind. I no longer felt like a protector or an explorer, just a teenager in a world surrounded by drugs. I did not partake, and I did not judge the people who used them; I merely watched those people's turmoil, their daily toil to find a way to procure their customary fix. Then, as heroin was replaced in the onslaught of the crack epidemic, the character of people worsened, and the alley became smothered by more tragedy and lush piles of green growth.

Backyards consumed by plants became hiding spots for shadows; at night, through the darkness, the flame of a lighter shone momentarily bright. The alley had become overgrown, but at least one area remained cared for, and when passersby walked along this small plot of land, merely the width of two city houses, they could not ignore the colors it emitted, the old man sitting on a rusted metal milk crate, or myself. On this small plot of reclaimed inner-city land, using our own two hands, my grandfather and I tilled the dirt and planted vegetables. And when the small green shoots of produce cracked the earth and grew green and edible, we shared the food with the neighborhood. Ms. Robinson, a heavyset, late-middle-aged woman who walked with a cane and a waddle, accepted our vegetables, and in return paid us in thank-yous. She never failed to give me a Snickers candy bar after I handed her a head of cabbage.

When I wasn't in the garden with my grandfather, I was either playing basketball at Harvey's or relaxing on my grandparents' porch. Though my imagination was much less active, and I found very little to explore, I still found the people and surrounding area of the Magic Alley satisfying. The one place I did need to explore was the large house. With the lack of a family, it had quickly fallen to waste. Even when a family lived there, the house had already succumbed to nature's reclaiming. The backyard was overgrown with prickly weeds and small leafy shrubs, and resembled a wildlife reserve more than a yard. I remembered imagining, as a child, that there were bear traps or land mines back there. I'm pretty sure, as I made my way from one border to the other, that I looked like a plain fool tippy-toeing through the backyard, like a cartoon jewelry thief. Soon after the house became abandoned without a family, the plants grew onto and into the house and reclaimed the structure for themselves.

Most of the time that the house sat abandoned, community children played in it as I had played in other houses a few years back, and drug dealers hid guns and drugs in its backyard

141

forest. Addicts squatted, finding a place to rest. No one seemed to care that it was overrun by verdant plant life. Then, in the early nineties, a tragedy occurred in the large, abandoned house, and most of the people who knew about it decided not to enter the house anymore; no one played, squatted, or practiced any form of magic behind the house's walls.

I was either never completely told what happened or I don't want to recall what happened in the large house; I only know of the solemn, angry temperament people spoke through when the story was brought up. The story was so inhuman that no one wanted to repeat it, so cold-hearted that it could make the cruelest cringe. I can't remember the story, only the community's feeling. If I had to venture a memory, the unspeakable event that occurred in that house involved a young girl, and afterward the story had the power to deny entrance into the house. I respected my community's wishes for as long as I could, but what happened there no longer existed there, and I wanted to explore, if for no other reason than to be alone.

When I finally decided to enter the large house, my ascension to the attic was arduous. The front walkway was broken into torso-size blocks; the roots from the trees fought their way through the concrete, compromising its structural stability along with the rest of the house and the community. The front porch twisted into an entanglement of early century colonial architecture and lush wildlife with a symbolic warning: *If you enter, you may not exit.* The porch moaned as I stepped on it. The wood felt moist under my feet, and every plank crumbled as the vegetation that grew from it tried to capture me for my invasion. I did not attempt to use the backyard—my muscle memory and imagination told me there were still bear traps and land mines there, but really it would not have been possible to fight through the plants without a machete.

I was standing in the doorway after I'd made it through the plants of the porch. The front door had been removed, along with every window, some of the walls, and the living room floor. Someone else had recently entered the house and had stripped it for its copper pipes, sinks, woodwork, and stained glass. I like to think they stripped it to leave it naked for the world to see, exposed to the elements without any protection, making the house suffer the same pains it had inflicted on others.

As I walked up the crumbling stairs, I could see directly into the basement. A small pond had formed, and dark green moss, or maybe thickened mold, had lined the walls. The house was so uncared for that only the growing plants gave it any attention. If it weren't for the brick structure, nature could have taken advantage of the house's frailty and leveled it with a gust of wind, flattening it to a pile of bad memories. The plants had waited many years for people to stay away so they could consume the evils of the house and cleanse it in the manner that only nature knew how. Along the inside of the house, vines and moss lined the walls, and squirrels, raccoons, or possums could be heard scurrying away when they recognized a human in their midst. For a moment I considered leaving, certain the rattlesnake that had never been found slithered around in there somewhere, waiting to strike invaders, or that a family of rabid Pit Bulls lived in the attic and that I would become a fat feast for them. The house was an uncharted forest in our neighborhood. That may have been the only moment I felt unsafe in such houses, the only time I felt danger near me.

I ascended to the attic, weathered and disintegrated, the roof opened to the sky. A structural collapse allowed golden sunlight to paint itself on the puckered walls. Spaces of the room were carpeted with splotches of dark green moss. Sparrows—dark and light brown, fat and agile—darted in and out of the windows. I was afraid I'd be pecked to death, that they understood I did not belong in their aviary. Then, for a moment, the house went dead silent. There were no animals scurrying about, and the sparrows flew out of earshot. In the silence, the room was magical, more magical than my imagination or words could create.

I took delicate steps toward a broken window and looked out over the Magic Alley, viewing it from this perspective for the first time. It served as an equator, a visible but unseen line that separated rows of houses. A calm, lazy river: sullen, violent, and providing. While there, looking out the window, I became one of the faces that peered from the edges of weathered windowpanes, seeming to play a game of hide-and-seek or peek-a-boo, and as I looked out the window my view of the world was changing. I no longer thought of the animals or people of the alley as magical or as beings with unrivaled powers. I only saw animals and people. The Pit Bulls were nothing more than a backyard full of dogs. Crackhead K no longer held my fascination; she was transformed to a dead junkie. I still looked at the Winos the same: people standing in circles, talking to another group of people through the distorted view of a Wild Irish Rose bottle. But as I looked out the window, I could see the ever-prevailing fortitude of goodness and calmer of calamity, a true force of protective magic. From the window I could see my grandfather, Charlie Ramsey, tend to one of our gardens. In that moment I reflected that all my protections came from his magical power instead of my own.

Since before I remember having a memory, my grandfather and I had grown and given produce to people. Next to a crack house, my grandfather and I planted and cultivated an urban garden that fed the neighborhood. We gave lima beans, green peas, tomatoes, and turnip greens to church ladies whose sons were dope dealers and whose aunts and uncles were drug addicts. In his own way my grandfather worked his magic on those people. They guarded me from the wicked magic that should have consumed me. "Mr. Ramsey's boy" is what they called me, as if I didn't have my own name. I feel because of my grandfather's magic, I was immune to the fate that befell occupants of the alley, but I was still witness to its effects, the shells of people left drained from wicked magic.

Have you ever seen a ghost bleed? I have. He walked past me while I played basketball; despite his sun-blackened skin, he was pale-faced and hollow, moaning a dreadful sound while blood trickled from his head. I didn't reach out to help or ask the injured man if he was okay; I recognized him as one of the people who had suffered in war, someone the Magic Alley had saved its worst parts for, to be released in dark vengeance. Once the golden youthful magic from the alley was drained, there were no imaginative moments of me being a savior, or some kind of imperial guard, but rather moments of being a gladiator, another body in a fight with time and misfortune.

The Magic Alley, for all the fun it provided me, took people's appearances, souls, or both, leaving nothing but ghosts of men and women. But in this story, in this world, my grandfather exists and burns brightly, always being reborn from the ashes. He survived and overcame everything between the Great Depression and the crack era, from rural Mississippi to inner-city Michigan, and it awes me to believe that a regular human could endure half of that: he was magical. And when the world and people around him were withering away or growing into some monstrosity, he used vegetable gardens to replenish the people as well as the land. He possessed the power to see the contents of people instead of the costumes they wore. I want to believe that all of mankind could be the same as him, but they are not, so how could he not be magical? And that alley, with all its lurking dangers, were no match for him or his metal rake, garden hoe, and seeds. His magic protected me at the times I thought I was fantastic; it was not me but the blanket of comfort and compassion that an old, weary king has on his lands and, especially, his kin.

CONCENTRIC MEMORY
Re-membering Our Way into the Future

Naima Penniman

It's no wonder the forest can be a terrifying place for Black folks. I don't even have to tell you. But my great-grandmother told me, "Herein lies the medicine."

"Light up a lantern in the forest," she said. "No flame, no fuel, just trust in your footsteps and memory, and a positive obsession with a future teeming with breath."

There are so many reasons we have been separated.

This is what I re-member.

Childhood in the woods. My brother, Allen; my sister, Leah; and I would spend hours exploring the terrain around our home: a trailer down a dirt road that Dad reinforced with pine milled from the trees he cleared to bring light around us.

Black mother, white father, three kids the color of earth.

The years Mom couldn't be around, I think she assigned the best babysitter to watch after us: Mama Nature herself. We were lucky to have such a dynamic and ubiquitous caretaker, to be schooled by the marshes teeming with tadpoles, held by the cushions of moss, watched over by the shape-shifting sky.

I remember the way buds burst open in spring, witnessing their immaculate freshness unfurl from tightly clenched tips. I tied pieces of pink yarn around maple and ash saplings and returned every week to register the patterns of their growth in my spiral-bound sketchbook.

I remember the enchantment of July, when the fireflies would blink their glow-in-the-dark spectacle, a stunning rendition of stars spilled out before us. We chewed on sprigs of sassafras, gathered wintergreen leaves for sun tea, and foraged spicebush and huckleberries to make tarts.

Autumn was regal and mature, paper birch white against copper and gold. I remember a warm-on-the-inside sensation, relishing the mushrooms rising throughout the forest floor. I'd nestle in the sweet musk of fallen leaves and revel in the multicolors twirling down around me.

Even January, when so much went to sleep, was animated. We saw the footprints of fox and cottontail in fresh snow, sucked on icicles, and watched meteors streak the crisp indigo sky.

Being raised in the woods wasn't easy. An anomaly of Blackness, we were told at our school that we did not belong. Kids sneered at our handmade and hand-me-down clothes, scorned our untamable hair, cursed our skin made of clay not porcelain. But we saw our complexion reflected all around us in the tones of tree bark and fallen oak leaves. We didn't have an abundance of toys, but we had jungle gyms of trees and front-row seats to ponds and tributaries.

Sometimes it was piercing cold, and one time our wood-burning stove sparked a ravenous fire that expelled us into a wintery night before devouring every last splinter of our shelter. We lost everything we owned that night, but our home extended far beyond those walls, into the forest that did not burn. There were forces that separated us in the time we needed each other most, but nature ensured our connection across those impossible miles.

Mom taught us about being independent, making things from scratch, speaking up, defending what we love, being proud of who we are, about not giving up. Dad taught us to revere all life, how to work hard, how to listen to nature, how to make up our own songs, how to be resourceful, that there are many paths to God.

And Mama Nature taught us to be generous, loving, co-operative, multidimensional. That we are part of something so much bigger. We are no accident. We are never alone.

⸺

The trees are breathing too.

When Leah, Allen, and I were the size of saplings, we were enchanted to learn that trees take in carbon dioxide and release oxygen in direct complementary contrast to our inhale and exhale as humans. How meaningful to know that we had something to offer, something that came so naturally and of necessity as breath.

A ferocious love for the Earth arose in us from being in relationship to the ecosystem around us, and with it came the innate response to defend what we belonged to. Allen and I would walk through the cool spruce forest, counting the wild pink orchids after we learned they were endangered due to loss of habitat. Seeing one was a stroke of hope that it was not too late to defend the wildness against all that would try to erase it.

I remember learning about global warming in third grade. I think it was 1988, when Leah and I turned Dad's shed into our clubhouse, the Junior Ecologist Kids Club. We etched a chalk mural on the side depicting planet Earth with a thermometer in her mouth and ice pack on her head. Inside we strategized how we would mobilize to defend our collective future. We patrolled around on our Huffy bicycles to pick up litter from the roadsides and held up our magic marker protest posters against the school bus windows.

The word on the street in the eighties was that recycling was the way everyday people could pitch in for the planet. We didn't yet know how it masked greater systems of capitalist extraction, so we marched into the principal's office at JR Briggs Elementary, determined to convince Mr. Gould to start a school-wide recycling program. Unsuccessful, we took it upon ourselves to set up a barrel in the cafeteria to collect our classmates' empty soda cans and juice bottles.

Every day, we dragged an oversized bag full of salvaged glass, aluminum, and plastic home on the school bus, and sprayed the contents down with a hose in the yard. Dad would take our collection to the dump for us, and we'd be rewarded with handfuls of coins we'd use to buy stamps to send envelopes to people we selected at random out of the phone book. Remember back when everyone's addresses were published in public directories on yellow and white pages that doubled as chair boosters when you were too short to reach the table?

We folded up our ten prescriptions for protecting the planet, enclosed our handmade S.O.S. (Save Our Sphere) stickers, and marked the outside URGENT. We knew it was imperative to get everyone on board to defend our singular, sacred Earth.

You know that feeling, the heat that rises in your belly when someone or something is threatening what you find most precious in the whole wide world? For us what was most precious *was* the whole wide wondrous woven world, exceedingly precious and unspeakably threatened. We heard Mama Nature crying out from every curve and corner. The fires were raging. Our home was burning. We were gasping for oxygen.

—

We opened every Junior Ecologists Kids Club meeting in the backyard shed, with a prayer:

> *God, grant me the serenity to accept the things I cannot change,*
> *courage to change the things I can,*
> *and wisdom to know the difference.*

It was important, in the face of the immensity of the threats posed to our planet, to grasp what it was that we could control. The more we learned about the sheer magnitude of the catastrophe—how quickly the forests were being clear-cut, how many rivers ran toxic, how plastics never biodegrade, how much the insatiable machine of capitalism guzzled and dumped to fuel its endless expansion—the more overwhelmed we became. No matter how many hundreds of cans we collected from school and from the roadsides to recycle, how could we ever repair the damage that had already been done and halt the nightmare yet to come?

We reached out to the forces beyond what we could see. We knew there was a Divine Force all around and in us, responsible for this animate universe. We knew we were connected to underwater beings that lived on the other side of the world that wanted to survive.

How imagination gathers, fills the pail with moonlight.

One day, Leah and I found an abandoned shack in the woods and turned it into a shrine to honor the Spirits of Creation. We decorated it with boughs of cedar, curls of birch bark, and a collection of hawk feathers, snakeskin, and robin eggshells. And that's where we had church. We'd go there to make offerings, to pray for the strength to overcome the challenges in our lives, and to sing our grief for a burning world. That's where we made promises to do everything in our power to protect the sanctity of all Life.

We knew the rain that fell upon us was the same water that quenched our ancestors' thirst, that fed plant life before humans existed. We knew that complex exchanges of mutual reliance were playing out in the forest constantly, above and belowground, in extraordinary ways. And we knew for certain that we were part of that interdependent infinity.

What we did not know as children was just how far-reaching and meaningful forests have been to our people's resistance and survival across space and time. A perception beyond senses of a pervasive, mysterious power, palpable all the way from our forest shrine in the backwoods of Massachusetts to the potomitans of Haiti.

———

The forest was a place of spiritual power and physical protection, vital for the liberation of Grandaddy's ancestors in Haiti just as it had been for Grandmommy's ancestors in the American South. The cover of the woods was essential for the Underground Railroad, as were the natural medicines Harriet Tubman harvested from the wild to quiet the babies and heal wounds along the journeys to freedom. Plants, too, were key to defeating the enslavers in Haiti (then known as Saint-Domingue), and forests became the sites for autonomous communities forged in resistance to the exceptionally sadistic slave system that operated for centuries on those lands. "Those whose boldness of spirit found slavery intolerable and refused to evade it by committing suicide," wrote the Trinidadian historian C. L. R. James, "would fly to the woods and mountains and form bands of free men—maroons."

Needless to say, for any spirit, the heat was too much to bear. The boiling point of cane syrup, the ceaseless toiling, the brutal thirst, the sun-scorched earth, the searing whips, the deranged torture of being slowly burned alive. If you could, you would run out of the flames. By 1751, there were at least three thousand Maroons who had escaped the sugarcane plantations and lived shaded in the forests of Saint-Domingue.

Do you know about François Makandal? He was a healer, orator, and Vodou priest from Guinea who had been enslaved in the district of Limbé. He had revelations and claimed to predict the future. A lifetime before the Haitian revolution, Makandal sensed the possibility of creating a center of organized Black resistance in the forests of Saint-Domingue, and for eighteen years he presided over a free Black village hidden in the trees.

After escaping the plantation, "he conceived the bold design of uniting all the Negroes and driving the whites out of the colony." Makandal used his knowledge of plants to craft powerful poisons and distribute them among enslaved Africans to destroy their oppressors. He traveled from plantation to plantation, enrolling people in his plan for a simultaneous, calculated poisoning—a secret kept for six years, while he summoned mass solidarity. "Wait patiently until you hear the call."

In 1757, Makandal led the first organized revolt of enslaved peoples in Saint-Domingue. The fabric was ripped. The colonial order was threatened. It is estimated that Makandal's forces killed over six thousand during six years of insurrection. Makandal was captured and burnt alive, but his fire would help ignite the revolution that birthed the first independent Black nation in the New World.

A statue of Makandal gleams in the capital of Haiti, wrought in bronze, in a deep warrior lunge. Have you seen it? The chattel and chains are broken on his left ankle. His right hand brandishes a machete, and in his left hand is a conch aimed toward the sky. His face is turned upward, throat open, heart to the sun.

Have you heard it? This is not a silent statue. It blares through the atmosphere like an incessant shrill, signaling ceremony and insurrection. The declaration of freedom before it is attained. The determination of breath to break open sound. Makandal blows the conch to announce, "It is time."

Freedom, as Alexis Pauline Gumbs writes, is "a basic need and a divine imperative."

This is the moment to reorder the world.

Thirty-four years after Makandal's burning, the revolution commenced from a ceremony in the thick forest known as Bwa Kayiman of the Morne Rouge. On a stormy night in August 1791, more than two hundred enslaved Africans representing distinct plantations gathered on a mountain overlooking Le Cap. They convened in secret to plan an insurrection against their enslavers in the colony's wealthy Northern Plain. A ritual took place under a very large mapou tree, presided over by two prominent Haitian Vodou spiritual leaders, Dutty Boukman and Cécile Fatiman.

The revolutionaries must have recognized that the only way to overcome the arsenal of their rulers, backed by the strongest army in the world, was to call upon the forces of nature, backed by the strongest gods in the universe. "This God who made the sun, who brings us light from above, who rouses the sea, and who makes the storm rumble," said Boukman, "will direct our hands, and give us help. Throw away the image of the god of the whites who thirsts for our tears. Listen to the liberty that speaks in all our hearts." Boukman summoned the courage of their aliveness, the truth of their humanness, and the power of the Divine Force that moves through the natural world to claim an impossible freedom.

In direct opposition to the one-God, one-race religion that called for the pillage and enslavement of non-Christian, non-white nations, the revolutionaries combined the influences of a pantheon of gods from their multitudinous traditions across the African continent to support their quest to define their own destinies. Soon after, Cécile Fatiman led a blood oath that they would not give up or give in. "Be free, or die!" they shouted to a storm-pulsing sky.

In the following days, the whole Northern Plain was in flames as the revolutionaries rose up against those who had enslaved them. They murdered their masters and burned the plantations to the ground. "For nearly three weeks the people of Le Cap could barely distinguish night from day, while a rain of burning cane straw, driven before the wind like flakes of snow, flew over the city and the shipping in the harbour, threatening both with destruction."

Destruction was the goal. To destroy all of what they knew was the cause of their suffering. Without ammunition, they forged their way to freedom with machetes, agricultural implements, sticks pointed with iron, plant poisons, fire, fire, fire, and their pact with the Divine.

Thus commenced a twelve-year revolt against the greatest market of the European slave trade, which rested on the unpaid labor of half a million people. The revolutionaries overcame not only the plantation owners, local whites, and soldiers, but also the successive invasions by French, Spanish, and English expeditions, to form the first independent nation in the Caribbean.

———

Haiti wasn't the only place. Makandal wasn't the only one.

All across the so-called "New World," our Black forebearers resisted the institution of slavery, the colonial order, white supremacy, and the exploitation of their labor. And all across the so-called "New World," the forest was an ally in this quest for self-determination.

Tens of thousands of Maroons escaped enslavement to the mountains and dense brushlands of the Caribbean islands, the humid swamps of North America, and the rainforests of South America to build autonomous, close-knit communities. As oral histories of the Matawai Maroons in Suriname recount:

> And so, right before the arrival of dawn, Mama Tjowa took a bundle of the rice that her people brought with them from Africa, and carefully braided the grains in her hair. And then, they ran, far, far away from the plantation, tééé (until) . . . they arrived at a hidden place, deep in the forest, where a lot of trees had fallen. . . .

They burned the trees, Mama Tjowa loosened her
hair, and shook the rice seeds on the ground. Some time
later, rice seedlings grew from out of the fertile soil. Then,
they took the harvest even further upriver, and did the
same thing again. And today, we plant and eat from the
same rice, that Mama Tjowa brought for us to survive.

Wherever they settled, the Maroons carried seeds with them,
organizing to grow their own food and raise free children.

They also descended on plantations to liberate those
who were still enslaved, obtain machetes and other tools,
steal the fruits of forced labor, and poison the drinking water of the enslavers. Colonial troops embarked on raids into
the wild lands to locate the Maroons, burn down their settle-
ments, and return the fugitives back to the plantations. It was
a theater of perpetual war and perpetual fleeing. But having
tasted freedom, the Maroons were determined, at any cost,
to preserve it.

Our forebearers called upon spiritual forces (through
Obeah, Palo, Vodou, Lucumí, and Hoodoo) that forewarned
them of the approach of the white soldiers, disguised them as
trees or rocks, and let them go for long periods without food.
The forest helped to protect the Maroons from the soldiers,
who were trained in conventional combat in open battlefields.
They laid traps for the troops in the dense underbrush and
ambushed the colonial armies from behind hilltops to defend
their right to exist in peace.

While many communities were destroyed, there were
many that survived. In many places, whites were far outnum-
bered by Maroons, not to mention their allies in the natural
and supernatural worlds, and the colonial administrations

had no choice but to surrender. Treaties were signed in exchange for a ceasefire and parcels of land, allowing many Maroon communities to be more rooted instead of always in flight.

Can you imagine what it must've been like to root in a new place after all that displacement? What would it have meant to rebuild a relationship to land, and to your own body? What would it have meant to reclaim agency over your own sexuality and reproduction? What would it have meant to bear your own children?

The Maroons developed their own dynamic cultures to make sense of their entirely new realities, far from their homelands and far from the homelessness of enslavement. They preserved and adapted their traditions, practiced and mingled their languages, spiritualities, and ways of healing. They fashioned a new tree of life, like a rootstock grafted through creative adaptations of their distinct African heritages, guidance from the indigenous communities they befriended, and aspects of social life on the plantation they carried with them.

Through deep listening and experimentation, they learned which plants cured their ailments and which trees were favorable for constructing boats. They developed the best methods to grow food, not for someone else's profit, but to nourish the new generation they birthed into freedom.

We are descendants of persistent quests for freedom.

And despite the blood, tears, sweat, and seeds we've spilled upon their soils, the lands and forests that are indispensable to our sovereignty as Black peoples have been systematically seized, stolen, sold off, sequestered, and wrested out from under us.

The newly free Black Republic of Haiti was forced to pay France the modern equivalent of $21 billion as compensation for the "property loss of slaves" and its slave colony. There's a twisted irony of the formerly enslaved paying reparations to their enslavers: buying back their bodies as if they hadn't belonged to themselves in the first place. To pay off this indemnity, the Haitian government was forced to export timber over the course of six generations, driving deforestation.

Meanwhile, the newly freed Black people in the American South, who collectively amassed sixteen million acres of land within forty-five years of the formal end of chattel slavery, were driven off their plots by the White Caps, the Ku Klux Klan, White Citizens' Councils, and the United States Department of Agriculture (USDA) discrimination. Millions left the soil behind for the asphalt of the urban north because of legal trickery and racial terror.

How do we reconcile the contradictions of the sacred— where the lands that were the source of our dignity and sovereignty were also the scenes of slavery, sharecropping, convict leasing, and cross burning; where the trees that bestowed the fruits that nourished us were also the limbs that bore the unbearable weight of our murdered bodies; where the forests that held our medicine and housed our gods were also the landscapes cleared and burned by missionaries intent on destroying our sacred groves?

There are so many reasons we have been separated.

Granddaddy was raised in Haiti, where mountains undulate, magic abounds, and mangos ripen and rain the juiciest, most delectable sweetness on Earth. Where tropical storms, cholera epidemics, deforestation, debt, violence, and a vicious colonial history ravage the nation unabated.

In 2010, a 5.0 magnitude earthquake devastated Haiti, toppling homes, swallowing cities, and turning three hundred thousand living loved ones into ancestors overnight. In its aftermath, my dreams were crowded with voices and faces calling me to a home I'd never been to before. I was full of doubt whether I, this scattered seed, had anything meaningful to offer my kinfolk once-removed. But my dreams were incessant. "Come home now!" they shouted. This cataclysm of unimaginable scale required every drop of care available.

Months later, I traveled to Haiti for the first time, with pockets full of handwritten prayers I had collected from people in Brooklyn and Detroit, who participated in an installation ritual I created to raise support for survivors of the earthquake. My first stop was the ocean.

Knowing well how water listens and transmits and travels, I read out loud those prayers in hopes the currents would carry the messages of love and solidarity all around and through the island. As I finished the final words, a conch shell washed up in the tide and anchored itself right between my feet. I slid my hand into its smooth cavity and lifted the shell to the sky. Right away, it reminded me of Makandal and his pact with nature to overcome the unthinkable. I opened my broken heart to the sun.

For the next seven years, I devoted myself to forming teams of Black healers, artists, and farmers from the African and Caribbean diasporas to join forces with earthquake survivors in the village of Komye, Leogane. Leah and Allen were part of the effort, and our endlessly inventive grandfather, who became an ancestor twenty years prior, was ever present too.

Our goal was collective healing, and there was so much to heal from. Not just the most recent trauma of the earthquake, but the generations of pervasive structural injustice that seeped into every corner of the psychic and solid worlds. Healing would require sourcing from within and around us, collaborating with the Earth and each other. It took shape as co-counseling, vermicomposting, community gardens, and clinics. It looked like drumming all night to honor the ancestors born in the earthquake, digging irrigation trenches, establishing a fruit-tree nursery, sculpting river stones, offering acupuncture, passing along remedies from wild plants, and putting on uproarious comedic theater in the mango grove.

One day, we gathered together to write our dreams for Komye's future on long, colorful strips of fabric and then tied them to the climbing tree near the community center. By night, it was aglow with lanterns that a group of children made by hand from twigs, twine, and candles. And in an instant, a dream I'd had months before flickered vividly before my eyes. Without question, I'd seen this before. I held my conch shell to my heart and fell to my knees as the moon crowned the horizon. The earth caught my tears that night. Not of sadness or of joy; these were tears of trust.

The trust deepened between us and spread through us. I will forever be astounded at what we accomplished together. But by year five of our collaboration, the river that had been the primary source of water for everyone in Komye—to wash, cook, bathe, drink, and irrigate the growing fields— was drying up. The banks were sinking into the riverbed, due largely to deforestation, and the dry season kept getting longer. We worked together to plant thousands of trees on the hillsides to guard against erosion as a long-term solution, but until those roots took hold, where would folks source water?

Water was, is, and will always be essential for all things.

We'd just lived through the hottest decade on record, and the symptoms of planetary fever were manifesting in incalculable ways all over the Earth's body. We were already experiencing how communities with direct relationships with the land, rivers, oceans, forests, ecosystems, and rhythms of nature for survival were hardest hit by the record-breaking heat waves, unyielding droughts, supersized hurricanes, and receding lands. And while there is no escaping the inevitable impacts of this universal conundrum, we know there are those who have the means to escape and recover from disaster, and there are those who are displaced, deceased, or unable to walk for water anymore.

On the dusty path back to the Komye after a day of planting on the slope above the river, Dimmy looked solemn as the sun gave us reprieve from behind the mapou tree. A school teacher, community leader and visionary, Dimmy's words were judicious and far-seeing, "Somehow, we will need to install a well before the next dry season, or it will not look good for us."

"Yes," all of us walking together agreed. "Whatever it takes. We must find a way."

And so, after a few months of research and resource mobilization, I returned with my siblings, blood and chosen, to help make it happen.

Before we began digging into the earth for water, we had to ask permission. On the eve the drilling was scheduled to begin, we held a ceremony to make our intentions clear. The houngan drew a vèvè with wood ash on black dirt: a symbol to open the gates between Earth and the realm of Spirit, a beacon to invite the presence of the Divine. Elegba accepted our offerings. Grandaddy transmitted his blessing. The next day, water was flowing.

I can still feel the cool currents filling our palms, the eruption of joy overflowing, a long-held longing quenched, a promise opened.

The cement enclosure around the well was painted with vivid colors and symbols, in celebration of this fountain of life force. One artist painted Makandal right there, beside the well, in memory of the ancestor who remembered us long before we were born. How appropriate, I thought, that Makandal would guard what would soon become the only water source for miles.

A stone's throw away from the presidential palace that was decimated in the earthquake, his statue survives—conch shell on his lips, throat open to the sky.

The perpetual echo of his trumpet alerts us to the need to assemble.

It's time to come together.

―――――

There are so many reasons we have been separated.

This is what we are re-membering.

Our relationship to land is bigger than the trauma that took place on it. Our histories and futures with forests extend beyond the grip of oppression that transpired within them. We are finding our way back to our rightful relationship with the Earth that we belong to.

In 2006, Leah purchased the deed for eighty acres of mountainside land with her partner, Jonah, determined to start a reciprocal farm to feed both the earth and the people. Despite the degraded hardpan soil, they could feel the pulse of aliveness below its crust and the protection of the encircling forest. Their children, my beloved niblings Neshima and Emet, were toddlers when they began building their home from the timbers and clay around them. In an act of defiance to the USDA, who deemed the land unsuitable for agriculture, and an act of faith in the Afro-Indigenous farming techniques our people have always employed to cultivate abundance from marginal lands, Leah and Jonah began the passionate journey of remedying the soil so it could produce life-giving food and medicine for their community.

Soul Fire Farm grew and grew and grew from a seed carried in the crown of our ancestors, braided for safekeeping through generations of displacement until it could put down roots on fertile ground.

The destiny of a seed is to multiply.

I joined the team when Soul Fire began passing seeds into the palms of others ready to re-member. As the earth transformed into lusher depths and darker tones under our love, Black and brown people came to the land to take part in week-long immersions we called FIRE: Farming in Relationship to Earth. Together, we learned and practiced regenerative agricultural techniques from our lineages and invested in healing from the many reasons we've been separated.

We'd spend our days waking with the dew and sun, carrying feed to the animated chickens, crouching close to the earth to transplant squash seedlings, sifting the rich soil for gold and purple potatoes. We'd skill up on soil science, poly-cultures, propagation, and the fundamentals of raising vegeta-bles, fruits, healing plants, and honey. We'd take turns stirring up giant pots of hoppin' John and collard greens just harvested from the field, while bopping to the hypest playlists. We'd walk through the forest together, speechless and listening, and share stories and laughter around the evening fire. We'd voyage into the past to study our ancestors' brilliance and resistance, then start to reimagine our own relationships to land far into the future.

⌣

Those experiences of stoking the FIRE rekindled my vision to cultivate community on land as a site for creativity, col-lective healing, and cooperative economics for those of us who have been dispossessed of our rightful relationships to it. I knew that the sense of belonging I felt as a child, being in kinship with the natural world around me, is everyone's birthright. But through generations of division and dis-placement, so many of our people have been denied it. After learning how Fannie Lou Hamer built a cooperative farm in Mississippi with Black farmers who had been expelled from the lands they sowed, the flame grew brighter. I could almost see it. Could we create a liberated zone for Black, Indigenous, and other people of the global majority to practice inter-dependence and sovereignty together?

Before long, I acquired forty acres through an act of Spirit, faith, and reparations, at the halfway point between my con-stellations of Soul Fire and Brooklyn, and it was the perfect spot on the aboveground railroad to freedom.

WILDSEED Community Farm and Healing Village became the ground in which to plant our wildest dreams. In the first five years, we established gardens, tapped sugar maples, threw parties, produced art, wildcrafted herbs, foraged mushrooms, made medicine, held ceremony, played capoeira, housed our elders, erected childcare spaces, built shrines, composed poetry, and watched fireflies flash and meteors streak across the big dome sky. We grew African and Indigenous heritage foods like Lenape blue corn, sugar baby watermelons, and Carolina ruby sweet potatoes. And we learned how to make medicine from the yarrow, burdock roots, red clover blossoms, waterlily, mugwort, nettles, and wild callaloo growing around us.

We hosted people of all ages and shades, from as far away as Puerto Rico, Mississippi, Arizona, and Alaska, and as close as Harlem, Hudson, and just down the road. Community organizers, movement leaders, radical healers, spiritual practitioners, former political prisoners, family members whose loved ones are incarcerated, veterans for peace, revolutionary artists, Black farmers, queer farmers, and young activists came together on the land for retreats, trainings, workshops, workdays, and celebrations.

One of the clearest visions and one of the first to bloom at WILDSEED was a rites of passage program for teenagers who, like us, came of age in a time of change with skin the color of soil. Eighteen youth and a squad of mentors shared a week together, rising on the land as the sun spread over the horizon. We filled our days with making music, planting amaranth, playing burdock tag, shaping vessels out of creek clay, harvesting medicine, cooking up heritage recipes, learning about social movements, swimming in the quarry, drumming and dancing in the grass, and stringing beads while we shared our struggles, doubts, and determinations.

One night, after dinner, we were all reflecting on times when we'd felt stuck or hopeless in the face of what seemed unchangeable. Each of us thought up the message we needed to hear in that moment—a truth, a reminder, a promise that would have soothed us in our spell of despair. Half the group circled up, sitting with eyes closed on the floor of the Unconditional Love Room. The other half stood behind them, one by one whispering their affirmation into each person's ear. By the time we finished the rotations, many of us were in tears and everyone's hearts were watered.

Our week culminated in a ceremony that centered around the commitments we were determined to embody, the drive to conjure what we longed for in the worlds around and within us. The initiates climbed the nearby mountain with their intentions scribed on folded paper in their pockets—a practice in self-elevation, determination, and long-distance vision. Not without struggle, disorientation, or doubt, every single person made it to the summit. We lay our deep-breathing bodies on the sun-warmed rocks that pressed us up against the sky, pledging our pumping hearts to life.

At the base of the mountain, we were immersing ourselves in a spring water quarry, when the sky broke open in a sudden downpour. Water bouncing off water, a cleansing, cool surrender, no part of us untouched.

That night, we set light to a blazing fire in an open field hugged by the mountain we had just climbed. Each initiate burned what they didn't want to carry into the next chapter, and then came to the shrine in the amphitheater of night. It was the grown-up version of our sanctified childhood forts: cedar posts in the four directions, woven with vines that spiraled up to the stars.

It was healing for me to witness my niece unfurl throughout that journey. When it was her turn to enter the shrine, Leah and I greeted her with open palms and faces. Neshima was regal in the torchlight. She pounded the earth with her staff, calling our ancestors by name. The ones who loved us both into existence.

We made a gift of song and water. We made a request for guidance and protection. "Please guide Neshima to her fullest expression, down a path that enlivens her spirit, satisfies her purpose, and fulfills her destiny. Please protect her from harm, and support her in overcoming adversity with courage, creativity, and interdependence."

Beads tied around her wrist. "I am no accident."

An offering placed on the earth. "I am part of something so much bigger."

A wash with herb-steeped water. "I am never alone."

We all came back together on the other side of the passage and spoke our gratitude in all seven directions: East, West, North, South, Above, Below, Within. "With the Earth as my witness, I devote my life to truth."

We became more of ourselves, in service to the world we were determined to create.

WILDSEED wasn't the only place. I wasn't the only one.

The people who have gone through the Soul Fire farming immersions have gone on to seed an array of beauty and power. Green Acre Community Garden has transformed an underutilized lot into a flourishing farm and green space in urban New Jersey. Catatumbo Cooperative Farm is a worker-owned farm raising vegetables in South Chicago. Love Fed is a community of Black and brown neighbors growing their own food and supplying gardens to the folks who need it most in New Haven. Percussion Farms is providing employment for people leaving the prison system to grow healthy food for folks living in Seattle. Seeds of Osun is centering Afro-Indigenous folk medicine and rootwork for healing mental, emotional, physical, and spiritual imbalances resulting from generational trauma.

Chef Fresh, who participated in a FIRE immersion in August 2018, said,

> I sat in this living room at Soul Fire and dreamed about what Fresher Together could be. Dreamed about what it would look like to create a space deeply rooted in my people thriving together where all of me could show up. I pulled together all the things I had ever dreamed about and had a new sense of clarity and urgency that this work could not wait.
>
> I first formed the sentence, "A collaborative food project for healing, economic development, training and retreat," the night of our Action Planning workshop. It was like a seed braided in my hair for my journey back to a different unknown. A seed . . . One that the earth has been making space for, that has been planted and watered, and given sun. I've been finding the supports and community to nourish it . . . And it is starting to germinate . . . A new beginning . . . It's coming . . . We are who we've been waiting for.

Fresh quit an exhausting, abusive job and got to work on their dream. It's happening. As I write this, they are on their way back here to Soul Fire, to teach others what they learned along the way.

This is what gives me hope.

We will protect what we love. And she will protect us.

We are reclaiming our dignified kinship with land as Black people. We have inherited the seeds that are ready to grow. We have knowledge in our ancestral memory that is rehydrated through practice—being with the earth, breaking out of isolation, coming back together. Like our ancestors at Bwa Kayiman, we are synching our strategies, uniting our spiritual forces, and committing to interdimensional collaboration. Like the Maroons, we are asserting our sovereignty by partnering with nature.

We are practicing ways of living that rely less and less on extractive and harmful systems. We know how to nourish our communities without abusing the planet. We are saving and passing on seeds, co-building the soil, growing our food, producing our fuel, devising our medicines. We are healing and expanding our families and kinship networks. We are forming our own freedom schools, cooperatives, land trusts, sanctuaries, mutual aid networks, gift economies, and lending societies. We are organizing authentic communities connected through purpose.

And there is so much to do on purpose. The magnitude of the crises we have inherited cannot be overstated.

When I was a child, I thought that if people only understood that the way we were living was causing immense suffering and disruption to our planetary relations, they would surely want to fix it. Perhaps we want to but don't know how. After all, recycling will not offer water to the beloved neighbor approaching an arbitrary and heavily militarized border, to leave behind the lands that raised them, now void of sustenance and safety. Picking up litter will not stop a small handful of people intent on hoarding the profits of pillage and criminalizing anyone born poor.

There are no ten simple fixes for saving the Earth. But there are prerequisites for our collective preservation. We are called to shape the future now. At this crossroads of peril and promise, the natural world is our beacon and compass. Our ecosystems offer templates for resource sharing and proto-types of pollination. The forest gives us archetypes of interde-pendence and frameworks for evolution.

Instead of ten prescriptions for protecting the planet, I will offer up ten lessons our devoted babysitter Mama Nature taught us—handwritten and sealed with love. May we apply them on the path ahead.

1. TRANSFORMATION IS INEVITABLE.

Change is happening on every scale. Change, including devasta-tion, creates openings for new ways of being and ordering our rela-tionships and systems.

Wildfires are a destructive force necessary for regeneration for many species. Wild lupine, for example, requires fire to maintain an ecosystem balance in which it can flourish. And the endangered Karner blue caterpillar relies on wild lupine as its sole food source, needed to undergo metamorphosis and become a butterfly.

Spruce, sequoia, cypress, and pine cones are encased with a resin that must be melted for the cone to open and release its seeds. When a fire moves through the forest, the cones' scales spread, and the seeds are distributed by winds and gravity. These freshly cast seeds thrive best on the burnt soil available to them, the recent flames providing reduced competition, increased sunlight, warmth, and nutrients from the ash.

What catalysts have been essential for your own metamorphosis? How might destructive forces make way for new possibilities in our lives and societies?

I think of how the COVID pandemic has inspired mutual aid and closer networks of support. That it made possible a pivot to remote work and, with it, drastically reduced travel and fossil fuel consumption. After natural disasters, we have seen both the exploitation of crises to advance neoliberal free market policies, and the opportunity to build back more equitably and sustainably.

How can we partner with transformation to arc the world toward justice?

2. ADAPTATION IS ESSENTIAL.

Change requires growth, new tools, and new ways of being. Like how dolphins evolved dorsal fins across generations to withstand the wild movement of the ocean. Like how plants partnered with fungi to migrate out of the water and grow roots in order to survive on scorched and desolate land.

What are ways that we can mature to respond to what is required? What could be an evolutionary adaptation, for instance, to attend to the immense and imminent climate refugee crises?

When we realize something isn't working, how do we reassess, reroute, and make different choices, for example in how we distribute resources, produce our food, and deal with violence in our communities?

3. EVERYTHING WE NEED IS HERE.

The Earth is abundant, prolific, and brilliant. If we practice equitable resource sharing and let go of excess, we have more than enough to go around.

Take a tree growing on the south-facing slope on the edge of the forest, with all the sunlight it could ever drink available to it. With all that light energy, it could grow twice as big as all the others. Instead, it sends its surplus sugars and nutrients to boost its neighbors through a vast underground network of mycelium.

How do we let go of excess and practice fair distribution of sustenance regardless of what slope we were born on?

What wisdom in our lineages can we draw on for examples of ways of ordering society and existing beyond colonialism and capitalism?

4. WE ARE STRONGER TOGETHER.

Interdependence, mutualism, reciprocity, symbiosis—again and again nature demonstrates interspecies collaboration whereby each species plays a crucial role in the health and development of another. In order for a forest to mature, a variety of life-forms need to learn how to share nutrients and protect each other.

Masting trees organize regionally to synchronize the production of their seeds every two or more years, so that seed predators can't possibly eat them all. Timing this superabundance of seeds allows birds, chipmunks, and insects to feast while ensuring the trees' off-spring a chance to establish.

The interkingdom marriage of algae and fungi creates an entirely new organism called lichen, which allows them to inhabit and me-tabolize rock and survive extreme conditions.

How can we join forces across difference to protect and strengthen our communities? How can we weave our powers in the midst of unthinkable circumstances to discover how to flourish together?

What can we learn from masting trees about having reproductive control over when it is safe and desirable to give birth, and how we raise the next generation in coordination with our community?

5. DARKNESS IS TEEMING WITH CREATION.

Soils are the most biologically diverse places on Earth. Three-quarters of our planet is covered with a layer of seawater two miles in depth, providing a deep dark habitat to the greatest number of organisms on Earth. And the blackness of night is one of the most important influences on the biological world.

Artificial light at night disrupts the livelihoods of nocturnal species, confuses our circadian rhythms, plays havoc with sea turtle navigation, alters how insects pollinate and animals reproduce, interrupts our sleep patterns, and is downright bad for our health—just like white supremacy.

So love your Blackness, respect your shadow, tend to your womb and gut and blood and bones, even more than your skin and what we can see. Let your eyes adjust to the dark. Therein lies the miracle of starlight, of fireflies, of bioluminescent fungi on a moon-dappled night in the moist oak woods.

How can you protect the Blackness within and around you?

How do you value darkness? What does it make possible?

6. NOTHING, AND NO ONE, IS DISPOSABLE.

Nature doesn't waste anything; it all goes back into the cycle. There is no such thing as "away"—not for our waste piled high in landfills or accumulating in the Pacific, not for the people society has deemed throwaway, who are warehoused in cages or open-air prisons. There is no escaping the totality of this single beating Earth, and the inseparable webs of our limitless relationships.

Are you down for a challenge? Carry around any landfill waste you create in a backpack, for a week or more. What do you notice about how this affects the choices you make about what to take and consume?

Are there things in your own life you just want to do away with? What would it look like to decompose, recycle, reassemble, or reintegrate, rather than bury what's unwanted out of sight?

What are the social systems that exist nowadays that perpetuate disposability culture? What are ways we can practice seeing who has been hidden from view?

7. EVERY MEMBER IS INTRINSIC TO THE WHOLE.

Everything is in relationship. All of us belong. As we study nature, we see evidence of repeating patterns on multiple scales of existence, echoed in our own beings. The particles of stardust are the very elements in our bones. When we were first born, our bodies contained the same proportion of water as all the lakes, glaciers, rivers, and oceans constitute the surface of the world. We are part of something exceedingly vast, and we are individually unmatchable. We all have a unique contribution to offer to this existence.

You are no coincidence. You are a series of miracles crescendoing into this moment, here to express, generate, activate, what only you can. You are right on time to help usher in evolution.

What are the roles, attributes, and innovations you embody and offer the whole?

How do you express your purpose in the ecosystems you are part of?

8. EVERY STAGE IS INTRINSIC TO THE CYCLE.

We need all of it: the still winter, the dormant grief, the sap flowing, the gestation, the tender shoots, the budding, bursting, unfurling, the ripe-on-the-vine abundance time, the dried-stalk-papery-husk seed time, the milkweed in the breeze, the dissolution of the chrysalis, the storm, the calm. All of it.

As you reflect on your life a natural cycle, what stage do you find yourself in now? How does this frame help you understand the function of what you are experiencing?

What stage would you ascribe to our current realities as a species?

As unnatural as so many of the disasters we are enduring are, what can Mama Nature teach us about the role of destruction in the larger pattern?

9. REGENERATION IS THE NATURAL ORDER OF EXISTENCE.

Even amid devastation, the animate force of existence is pulsing all around us, doing everything in its power to regenerate life. We have the opportunity to team up with that vital energy toward healing, flourishing, and co-evolution. All that dies is reborn in a new form.

How will you partner with the infinite power of renewal to nurture evolution?

How do you represent both the human ancestors and the extinct species that we have lost? How will you carry their legacy into the future?

10. DEATH IS NOT ONLY A PART OF LIFE; IT IS INTEGRAL TO LIVING.

Dead trees stay around for generations as part of the life of the forest. Snags are dead trees still standing. Their decomposing bodies provide food and shelter for a multitude of species. The insulation of a tree-trunk home makes perfect dens for foxes and porcupines. Starlings raise their young in nests in the hollows. Squirrels use tree cavities to store their acorn supplies, sapsuckers and woodpeckers feast on the buffet under the bark, and deer and caribou eat the lichen growing on the trunks. Snags are lookout perches for owls, hideouts for bats, hosts for mushrooms, fodder for ferns. And after they fall, these dead trees continue to serve their interspecies community, releasing their nutrients slowly into the soil and streams, storing water, preventing runoff, nourishing mosses, and providing nurseries for new seedlings to grow.

On a transcendent level, our ancestors too are still among us, here to shelter us, nourish us, nurture us, support our procreation, and supply our regeneration. If we are going to find our way out of self-destruction, we cannot do it alone. What a gift that we never are.

In what ways do you feel your ancestors' love? How is their eternal energy activated through your aliveness?

What role do our ancestors play in shaping our futures? How might we be even more available to their presence and partnership?

⁓

Love is a force, formidable like windstorms and waterfalls, transforming landscapes, shaping stone. We the living are the result of countless love stories and unnumbered feats of overcoming: the rice seeds braided into hair, the baby carried through the woods, the love stretched across borderlines.

This is what I re-member.

I ran and ran and ran until my heart pounded so loud and all I could do was let the Earth catch me. She held me still. My blood kept running, coursing through the rivers of forever. The trees supplied me oxygen and I could smell the sweetness of decomposition transforming the earth below me.

With my ear to my conch and palm on the ground, I could hear my great-grandmother whisper:

"We belong to each other."

THERE WAS A TREMENDOUS SOFTNESS

Michael Kleber-Diggs

First, the hard thing: about a month before my twin brother, Martin, and I turned nine, our father was shot and killed at the dental office he owned.

That was about forty-four years ago now. It isn't unusual for people to know me for years without knowing that my father died or how. When I speak about it, I feel a need to soften the news, to comfort the listener, to protect them from my hardest loss.

When my father died, I was not yet old enough to consider the possibility that such a thing might happen. I knew people died, maybe even that children died sometimes, and I'm pretty sure my thinking on it stopped there.

Which is my way of saying that all of it was shocking, a real disruption, a reordering, a shift in my thinking and in my connection to people and places, a shift so large that I did not notice it until decades later.

Now, as I look back on it, I imagine the day differently. I see it a bit more from my mother's perspective: the call that came to her, who she called in response, the team she assembled, all the people leaving their day to help us, everyone thinking *what to do about the boys*, the plan to come to our school, to pick us up, the decision on where to take us to deliver the news.

And after that, what to do *with* the boys, what to do *for* the boys.

All the decisions that had to be made; all the tasks that had to be completed.

I'm too ashamed to tell you how old I was when I first considered how lonely that time must have been for my mother, how devastating and exhausting and sad.

Eventually—after a few weeks, I think—it was decided that my brother and I should leave Kansas City and go to Wichita to live with our maternal grandparents, Arthur and Grace, while our mother did all the things she had to do associated with her hard loss. Arthur and Grace, who every single grandchild called Granddaddy and Grandmommy, even when we were all well into our adulthood.

They had a small home on a standard lot—a buttercream-yellow house on East Eighth Street, in the northeast quadrant of Wichita, Kansas, but just barely northeast, more central to the city (eight blocks off Central, in fact). Grandmommy's Oldsmobile, a gift from the family she worked for as a housekeeper and nanny, was always in their one-car garage, and Granddaddy's older, green-and-white Chevy truck was always in the driveway, off to the side on a parking pad he'd added himself. Company entered through the front door, but in the many years they lived there, I don't think I ever did. We entered through the garage or, more often, the side door. From there, the basement stairs were straight ahead, the garage was to the left, and the kitchen was to the right. As you entered the kitchen, up a stair or two from the side entry, there was a small pedestal ashtray with one of those push-button trays that would sink and spin to send spent ashes into a container below. The ashtray usually held three or four tobacco pipes, plus yesterday's ashes and that day's too. Atop the pedestal there always rested a can of Prince Albert tobacco.

Their house was a fragrant house: pipe tobacco and smoke, Folgers in the morning and Sanka in the afternoon, bacon and brandy, cocoa butter and inexpensive aftershave, Polident and Fixodent. Mothballs in the basement, detergent on the sheets, hot food on the stovetop every morning and every night. Bacon, wheat toast, and eggs scrambled for us in the small bit of bacon grease that was not poured into a used coffee can and kept around for cooking. Red meat, some kind of potato, a green vegetable—mustard greens or collard greens (always with a ham hock), spinach or green beans—with a roll and a small dessert—homemade ice cream or cake, the best peach cobbler ever made—we ate something sweet every night. Lunch was usually cold meat on plain bread with yellow mustard, a few chips, and a piece of fruit. Sometimes, Granddaddy would make what he called "choker sandwiches," so named because its three ingredients—bread, peanut butter, and honey—were difficult to swallow.

Beyond the kitchen, there was a small living room (to the left) and a small dining room (to the right). Through the dining room, there was a year-round porch my grandfather had also added himself. Beyond the living room and dining room, there was a bathroom and two bedrooms—theirs was off to the right a bit, and ours was off to the left. We had two twin beds with old plush mattresses and dense, durable pillows, and both beds were quite high off the ground. In the basement, there was a family room with a few recliners and a television. Past that, there was a bedroom where our mother's only brother, our grandparents' youngest child, had slept before he left for college a couple of years previous (he had a collection of *Playboy* magazines and more prurient periodical temptations in a wooden chest at the base of his bed). The rest of the basement was unfinished. There was a room where Grandmommy kept canned goods and her preserves, another small room with a shower Granddaddy had installed at some point, beyond that the washer and dryer, and, off in the far corner, things they stored—coins in coffee cans, documents in cardboard boxes, a couple of rifles, my granddaddy's fishing equipment, his golf equipment, and lots of things I cannot remember, not even generally.

Perhaps now is a good time to tell you I am an unintentionally unreliable narrator. Sometimes I say, "I have a terrible memory," but I'm not sure that's right. I remember some things quite well: the smells of my grandparents' house, what I watched on television the night I learned my father was dead (*The Man from Atlantis*), who starred in that show (Patrick Duffy), what I did the morning of my father's funeral (played tetherball with Martin), and riding in a limousine for the first time.

There are lots of things I do not remember well: my father's funeral service is a blur of general images. I don't remember the interment at all. I don't remember the names of most of my grade school, junior high, or high school teachers, even those I loved and admired.

Every once in a while, things come back to me. When they do, I wonder if my memory is terrible or if I've cultivated a selective memory. I read or heard that when traumatic things happen, human beings respond in particular ways: fight, flight, freeze, fawn, forget.

I'm pretty sure I chose to forget. When I try to remember that time, I notice I can recall things that were pleasant or soft, things that kept me from falling apart. A few hard things endure: my mother's face when she came to tell us the news, my brother's face as she told us, and the first night without my father, trying to get to sleep in the bottom bunk, worried about nightmares, imagining I might disappear too.

I think my brother chose something besides *forget*. My theory is *fight*. He remembers a lot, especially in comparison to me. Because we are twins, I wonder sometimes if my ability to forget (or sequester hard things away) depends on my brother's ability to remember. Comforted in a belief that a record of that time could be kept without me, I deleted my files or hid them away and conveniently forgot where.

I don't know how long we lived with our grandparents. Sometimes I try to piece it together: we left Kansas City not long after the funeral; we enrolled in school in Wichita the following fall. There was a winter that we lived at Grandmommy and Granddaddy's. We had a birthday there the following April, I think. We moved out of the house in Kansas City the following summer, I think.

Time was a blur back then, so let it be blurry here.

I could ask Martin or my mom, and they would tell me. I could ask them to fill in the gaps for me, but I want this to be my story, and I hope something like truth will come from how I felt and how I feel. Anyway, as you read this, assume the facts are close, generally correct, true in emotion and tone.

My grandparents moved from Watonga, Oklahoma, to Wichita when my mother was quite young. I think they wanted to start a family and needed to be near work that would allow them enough income to do that. Before the house on East Eighth Street, there was another house, a bigger house. My mom mostly grew up there. I don't know why they moved to the house on Eighth. I don't know if they downsized by choice or circumstance.

The lawn at our grandparents' house was perfect. Granddaddy worked on it at least a little bit every day. There was a produce garden in their backyard. You accessed it through a chain-link fence just past the side entrance. There was a small patch of pristine grass between that garden and a small metal shed where Granddaddy kept his tools and his lawnmower. As I remember it, he worked on other people's lawns and hauled things in his truck, and, by that time in his life, primarily did odd jobs here and there. Grandmommy worked part time, which I probably imagined had more to do with her age than with the unexpected presence of two nine-year-old boys in her house.

My grandparents seemed quite old to me then. They weren't. I did the math. They were around sixty, seven years older than I am now. They both had many years of life left—my grandmommy died in 2015, almost forty years after I lived with her. Granddaddy died in 1997.

My grandparents moved at a precious pace, never watched television back then, mostly drank decaf, and listened to Paul Harvey and the Kansas City Royals on AM radio. They had dentures and rarely ate at restaurants or after 6:00 p.m. They had chifforobes and davenports. They had slipcovers. There was a small marble-topped table in the living room with one of those glass dishes on it filled with sublime ribbon candy that was so old it had gone soft.

Grace and Arthur were shaped by the Great Depression. They kept almost everything they received and oriented their lives around enough, not abundance. My grandfather whittled and got his hair cut at a place where old men got haircuts and played checkers and looked at naughty magazines we were not allowed to touch. Grandmommy was in the Ladies Auxiliary at her church and attended long services faithfully every Sunday. She wore spectacular hats and knew her way around the kitchen at the church too.

That's where I see her, standing in the kitchen, cooking or cleaning. Grandmommy was soft and short—5'3" or so. She had medium-brown skin and wore wigs sometimes and spectacular hats (it bears repeating). Grandmommy wore polyester pants and bright-colored shirts to work but simple, bright-colored cotton dresses besides. I think she made most of them herself. She wore sensible shoes and inexpensive eye-wear. She had arthritis in her hands. She was quiet and hugged us often. She had five kids. By the time we arrived at her house, she'd mastered a balance between expectations and space. We were expected to go to school and that was pretty much it. If we weren't acting right, at home or at school, she'd ask a calm question like, "where did you get that idea?" Or, "where did you learn to use words like that?" She was never angry or upset with us, except one time when I was rifling through the refrig-erator and rested my shoe on the inside frame, appalling her to tears and prompting her to remove all the contents and scrub the interior with bleach and water. She was frustrated with Granddaddy sometimes, but she had just cause. Our grand-mommy was a church lady. She made and served food at wed-dings and funerals. She encouraged the family's attendance every Sunday. If she had any vices, I didn't know about them.

Our grandparents didn't do many things together. As far as I know, Grandmommy found joy in society at church; I'm certain our granddaddy found joy in the society of men and games with varying ranges of skill and luck—golf, cards, dominoes. Otherwise, they worked in the house or on the yard.

They also worked their garden. Their house was on a standard city lot, not much land at all. The garden sat just behind the back porch, and, working from memory, it was just a bit longer than the porch, twelve feet or so, and eight or nine rows wide. There must have been two plantings each season. As I remember it, the garden produced lettuce, tomatoes, cucumbers, spinach, peas, beets, and watermelons. Both of our grandparents tended the garden, not often together. We helped like nine-year-old city kids would help. We learned to hoe. We moved weeds in a wheelbarrow the twenty-five feet or so to the side of the shed. We picked things that were clearly ready and left everything else alone. With my grandparents' garden, whatever could be eaten was. What could be canned or pickled was; those things were always eaten too.

I had not gardened before I gardened with my grandparents. I likely helped my mom pot or plant a few flowers, but we did not have a vegetable garden in Kansas City.

So the summer after my father died was the first time I really gardened. I gardened a lot that summer. We watched some TV shows (*Ultraman* and *Davey and Goliath*) but not many. There weren't many kids in the neighborhood, so we didn't go outside to play very often. We took the summer off from football and baseball. I probably wasn't much of a gardener. I imagine now my dirty hands and knees. I feel like I remember watching things grow and ripen. I'm sure I carried things into the house. I know we ate things fresh off the vine. I distinctly remember hoeing and getting calluses on my hands. I know Granddaddy used his pocketknife to cut fat slices of tomato and eat them while standing at the kitchen sink.

I'm sure I was bored at the time, but when I look back on it, I remember those days with pristine fondness; the images are hazy and soft like a dream.

My father was in the kitchen, talking on the phone. For a moment, I wondered if I should say "good morning," as was expected, or allow him to have his call without interruption, as was also expected. I don't remember what I decided or what the outcome was. I remember kissing my father's cheek. I remember his tight morning scruff and the smell of his aftershave.

From there, I fill in the moments with assumptions. The assumption is that Martin and I did what we usually did. We walked down a small hill from our house, then up a big hill, to Silver City Elementary. Other kids would have been around. Maybe I had to carry my 3/4 size cello with me that day. We would have arrived at school. The day would have started as it usually did.

I know we were taking a standardized test. I confirmed this with Martin. I remember analogies, fish : fisherman :: pheasant : _____ . Martin and I were in fourth grade because we had skipped second grade. I don't remember if it was morning or afternoon or how far into the day we were. But at some point, while we were at school, a man went to our father's office, where he worked as a dentist, asked for drugs, and then, when our father said he didn't have any, shot him twice.

Later, responding to a provocation I sensed beyond sight or sound, I looked up from my test to see my teacher. I saw her looking at the classroom door in a way that compelled me to look there too.

I remember seeing my mother standing in the doorway, and I remember understanding from her face—

something terrible happened

something terrible happened to our father

we would not see our father again

We walked to a home nearby. The home belonged to our parents' closest friends; their children were Martin's and my closest friends. In the master bedroom, where, a week earlier, we'd watched *Charlie's Angels*, our mother, speaking in short clear sentences, told us our father had been killed and how. I remember she asked if we had any questions. I remember the expression on her face and not having any questions. It was about six weeks before our ninth birthday. I remember my brother had a question, but I don't remember what it was (even though he has re-minded me several times over the years). Death was more theoretical to me then than it is now. I understood only that we would not see our father again.

We left our friends' house and went home. There: visi-tors and care packages, lots of desserts and very few rules. I remember wishing I could breathe underwater and talk to fish. Family arrived, friends. Not much else. The passage of hours and a couple of days. The passage of time beyond the clock or

calendar until the day of the funeral, a day with its own specific occurrences—Martin and I dirtying our new suits playing
tetherball in the front yard, how upset that made our mother,
her tears. I remember the limousine ride to the service, looking out the window instead of inside at Martin or Mom,
noticing familiar landmarks that also seemed brand new. I
remember a somber gathering at our Presbyterian church,
where they played songs my father liked: "Bridge Over
Troubled Water" and (I think) "A Whiter Shade of Pale." I
remember the church was packed. I remember the reception,
where I understood for the first time that, in the eyes of those
assembled, I was both pitiable and pitied.

In Kansas City, we played outside with kids around our age,
built ramps for bicycles and forts with the deepest "dungeons"
we could dig. We threw dirt clods and water balloons at other
kids while they threw them at us. We shot BB guns (which our
parents forbade us to do) and squirt guns (also not allowed).
We played wiffle ball and tried to wander past our boundaries, as far as the TG&Y, without getting caught. If we made it
to the store, we'd pool our meager money for something to
share, usually candy or pop. Sometimes we stole cheap things.
I remember boosting a plastic compass—not a real one, but a
useless spinning dial with no true north.

For the most part, time outside was scheduled time: re-
cess, compulsory after-school playtime, Cub Scouts and then
Webelos. We engaged in intentional activities, the kind of
things you planned for and built in, exceptions to our largely
indoor lives.

In Wichita, we played with cousins sometimes, but we were usually with our grandparents. We ran errands with Granddaddy. We sat in the truck while he did his work. At the end of each day, he'd give us some money so we could buy candy at a candy store. Many many days passed before I understood that my brother purposely dragged his feet choosing his candy so Granddaddy had enough time to buy a pint bottle at the liquor store next door. We had left most of our things in Kansas City—our bicycles, board games, puzzles, and books. We didn't finish the school year. During the week, one grandparent or the other watched us or took us with them as they went about their day. After errands and work, we helped in the garden or played dominoes. The summer passed by pretty quickly. So it seemed that not long after we arrived, we started school.

Near their garden, I swung one of my granddaddy's golf clubs for the first time. Granddaddy showed me how to grip the club, how tightly—"Hold it like you would hold a bird"—how to draw it back and bring it down and through. He said things like, "Pure is better than hard," and, "If you can par with a seven iron, hit a seven iron off the tee."

But most weekends, Granddaddy took us fishing.

———

I was born at 10:00 a.m., and my brother, Martin, was born at 10:07 a.m., on April 15, 1968, eleven days after Martin Luther King, Jr. was assassinated, twins in twin cities. Our house was in Kansas City, Kansas—always a free state—but the hospital was in Kansas City, Missouri—formerly a slave state. I always say I was born in Kansas. There were riots in both cities, and a curfew was in effect. I know my parents drove to the hospital after curfew, when it was dark. I know they were stopped by the police. Martin Luther King, Jr. was born Michael King, but he and his father changed their names to Martin when Michael King was young. I got MLK's first name, my brother got his second, and we both share a middle name with him. When we were born, we lived in what I remember as a small, light-green house. We moved when my brother and I were pretty young. The only thing I remember about that green house is the black-and-white, four-slice toaster we had there.

Not long ago, I was talking to my mother and brother on the phone. I asked my mom if I could try to describe our second house in Kansas City, the house we lived in when our father was killed. I wanted to test my memory against my brother's, against what really was.

As I remember it, we had a wide driveway and a two-car garage leading to the basement, where there was a storage room, straight ahead; a laundry room, off to the right; and what we called our playroom across from there. Outside, a set of stairs with a wrought iron railing led from the driveway to the front door. There was a small entryway, and, beyond that, our living room. It had a window out to the backyard. I remember we had a green couch with slipcovers on it and a safe hidden behind a painting on one of the walls. To the left of the front door sat our kitchen, on the way to a dining area with two sliding-glass doors that led out to the backyard. To the right of the entryway, there was a hallway with two bedrooms on the right and a bathroom on the left. At the end of the hall, to the left, there was a family room where we watched TV—*Donny and Marie, Hee Haw, The Man from Atlantis, Barney Miller*, basketball, football. My parents' bathroom was along one wall, and their bedroom was at the far end, recessed a bit, down a stair or two.

In the front yard we had a weeping willow tree and a tetherball pole. Along the side of the house, leading to the backyard, there was a small hill that supported a little sledding. Just as you entered the backyard, we had a Sears swing set, where wasps took up residence in each end of the top pole. Then, the backyard itself: a concrete area where once there was a swimming pool. A generous stretch of grass, and, beyond all that, along the back and side, a wooded spot all the neighborhood kids called the Okefenokee Forest.

When I finish describing the house as I remember it, my mom explains that I have the rooms in the hallway a little bit wrong, and that I forgot a room. Beyond the master bedroom, behind accordion doors that were held closed with a magnet, there was another room—our father's den. My brother remembers not only the room and the order of all the rooms in the hallway, but other things, like a woman standing next to our mom in our classroom doorway when she came to school that day, and what the woman's name was (Georgia), and what her nickname was ("the ice cream lady") too.

I remember general things: our father was busy getting his dental practice going. He also had an ownership share or a majority share or was the sole owner of a new restaurant that wasn't doing well. He was taciturn and mercurial. I remember fearing him sometimes and trying to stay out of his way.

General things: like our mother was the wife of a hectic man, raising young twins while working herself. Our parents had desirable obligations in the small, tight-knit social circle of Black medical professionals in Kansas City. Our mom was a registered nurse, and she was social too (still is). She was also in The Links, an organization for Black women professionals; our father was active in the Missouri chapter of the American

Dental Association and another national association for Black dentists. Busy. We seemed to be concerned with appearance and appearances. All our friends and their parents seemed to be too.

General things: sometimes we played baseball or wiffle ball with our dad in the backyard or went jogging on a 440-yard track nearby. Our dad was fit and trim. He usually ran in khaki pants and pristine sneakers. We watched football on Sundays sometimes. My dad grew up in Boston and liked the Celtics and JFK. He also loved the TV show *Barney Miller*—it made him laugh. I remember his laugh. I remember he liked ice cream and had it almost every day, usually vanilla. He liked blueberry pie too. He wore a small mustache, cut low, like his hair. Both were impeccably maintained. He had a five-o'clock shadow every night when he came home. I still remember how it felt to kiss his cheek—sharp and rough. He tended to his appearance with care. He was fond of Hickey Freeman suits and stylish loafers. His shirts were thick cotton and expensive. He favored French cuffs, held fast by ornate cufflinks. He wore Aramis aftershave, the brand I've worn my entire life. He had a black Volvo coupe with leather seats; our mom had a Volvo sedan with cloth seats. He liked music, but I don't think he danced. We went out to eat at places like Red Lobster, and we were always allowed to order whatever we wanted (at Red Lobster, we always added hush puppies). Our dad drank whiskey from crystal decanters he kept in the family room. I remember how it smelled on his breath. As far as I know, he did not drink to excess.

There are things I've been told many times over the years, what I call the mythology of my father, all of it true. He was an outstanding student his entire academic career. He spoke

French fluently and knew Latin. He was a talented baseball player. He was fastidious. He never wore jeans and rarely wore sweatpants. It's a silly memory, but I remember once he bought me and my brother each a small toy boat for the bathtub. They came from the Avon catalog and were little barges big enough to hold a bar of soap. They had paddles you could wind up with a rubber band so the boat would travel across the tub. They were a spontaneous gift, which was unusual. As I look back on it, the distance between him giving us those boats and his death was very short, a week or two.

I vaguely remember playing checkers sometimes and learning a bit about chess from him. One year, for Christmas, our parents gave us an expensive and elaborate knowledge system for use in learning math and geography, history and science. I knew our father wanted good things for us: good schools, good outcomes there, and good lives. I know he cared a lot about what and how we were doing, and I know we were loved.

We had an edgy house, an eggshells house. Order was maintained with abundant rules: rules for breakfast and rules for dinner, rules for outdoor play and for returning indoors, for homework and housework, for clothes, for bedtime, for how to act when our dad was on the phone, for how to act when he came home from work, for when we had company, for when football was on. When liver and onions were served, you ate liver and onions, or else. You ate whatever was served, and you would not be excused until your plate was cleared. When the streetlights came on, as you hurried home, you made sure not to leave your sweater underneath the weeping willow tree in the front yard again. It was wise not to ask to stay up a little later. Fibbing was a felony. All consequences were certain and swift, unless they needed to wait until our dad got home.

Punishments were furious, fueled by frustration, fatigue, and fear. We had Black parents in the '70s; spankings were forceful and common. People were trying to keep their kids safe, alive, and out of the unjust criminal justice system.

———

Kansas is blessed with sky, not water. We usually fished in creeks or large ponds. Most of the time we drove away from town a bit, east toward El Dorado or west toward Goddard, to fish at Works Progress Administration lakes. The quiet and pace of our grandparents' house prevailed at the edge of each body of water. Not much happened and what happened took its time. We had rods that were just the right size for our bodies, simple reels, and blunt sturdy lines. We fished with lead weights and bobbers. My brother and I had lures; Granddaddy usually fished with bait. We mostly practiced casting and reeling. Granddaddy fished. Every so often, he'd point out that one of our bobbers had gone under. If our catch was too big, he'd help us bring it in.

Granddaddy was about my father's size—5'8" or so. He had medium-brown skin and a thin, straightish afro, mostly gray. He was wiry and strong. His hands were huge. His fingers were huge too, and his knuckles were angled and amplified by arthritis. I never saw him run or move above a saunter. I rarely saw him sit down until the day was done. As far as I know, he never ate margarine or drank skim milk. He was a protein man, though he wouldn't say it in that way. He worked at a packing house for most of his career. Dinner, as I've said, was usually red meat. We had poultry sometimes. Pork accompanied breakfast. We ate fish on weekends after fishing. Granddaddy never held a gym membership or lifted weights, but he moved without stopping from when he got up until he laid himself down, from when he was born until he died.

Like my father, he had a mustache and shaved around it every day. He wore inexpensive aftershave—Aqua Velva or Skin Bracer—and almost always wore a hat or cap if he was outdoors. He had simple, generously sized wire-frame eyeglasses, with visible bifocals or trifocals. Grandaddy usually wore jeans or overalls, and he was fond of patterned shirts. He smoked tobacco from a pipe throughout the day but not all the time—Prince Albert from a pouch when we were out and about and from a tin can when we were home. Brandy was an issue; I remember that. It accompanied every afternoon and affected the evening sometimes. There was a point when he needed to stop, so he did. That was years after we lived with our grandparents, when Martin and I were in high school or maybe even after that. Granddaddy was kind to me and my brother. He wasn't slow to anger; as far as I know, he never angered. Whenever I was around him, he was unfailingly quiet and patient and kind. If we were doing something we weren't supposed to do, he would shake his head disapprovingly. If we were not doing some chore we were supposed to do, he usually did it—the task needed to be done. In both cases, I'd feel terrible.

Sometimes, when we fished, Granddaddy let us take a sip of his beer. He drank Coors from cans. He kept the come-away pull tabs, crushed each can with his hand or foot, and, when he had a bag full, took them, along with any other cans he found, to sell for scrap. I remember the beer as carbonated and a bit warm. It was the first thing I drank that wasn't milk or water or sweet. I never had enough Coors to feel any way in particular, and I didn't like it as much as my brother seemed to.

I don't remember specific fishing trips, except one. I'll tell you about it later. I remember general things: the summer heat, very long outings that were probably quite short, the sound of a transistor radio at a low volume, usually playing a Royals game. I remember his small cooler, filled with beers, a little juice, and a little ice. I remember an ellipsoid red-and-white bobber he had; a round orange-and-yellow bobber; old, dented lead weights of various sizes and amounts; a chain we hooked our catches to; and a rectangular cuboid ruler with a scale at one end, used for weighing and measuring fish. All of it kept in a small metal tackle box that had bounced around the truck bed a bit and was in line with Granddaddy's general tendency to favor function over form.

I recall the joy of casting out and reeling in, even when nothing was on my line. I remember my grandfather's skill and wondering how it was I could stand ten feet away from him while he thrived and I starved. I remember waiting. I remember the waiting punctuated—rarely for me—by the shock of a sudden pull against my line, the dramatic down arch of my rod, the fast clicking sound of my reel spinning, the work to bring the line the other way—in.

At some point during the time that my brother and I lived with our grandparents (or perhaps a few years after), I learned about Verna Mae. My mother was the oldest sibling her entire life, but Verna Mae was my grandparents' first child. She died when she was two, I think, of the flu; I vaguely recall a medical error associated with her death. There was a small plaque in her honor in our grandparents' basement. When I talked to Grandmommy about it, Verna Mae had died thirty-nine years before. Around the same amount of time between my father's death and the writing of this essay.

grief : people :: water : rock

So, by the time each of us told our story, we had acquired an ability to speak about our losses without losing our voice, without a tremble. And yet, for reasons that are mysterious to me and will remain mysterious, I feel like my relationship with loss was shaped over time, while my grandmommy's relationship with loss was shaped by the times.

It's a theory I have. Losing a child was more common back then, I think. Women's loss was. Black loss. Black families' losses.

Please don't understand me to say that what my grandmommy carried was small or light or unsurprising. I know it was shocking and heavy. I was a child when we talked about it. A child with his own loss; a child who needed sheltering and received it.

With the benefit of time, experience, and perspective, I wonder now if the love and care our grandparents offered us was shaped by their loss, if they extended to us in our grief what they would have wanted in theirs. It is possible they had been supported and sustained by a loving community, but I was too young to ask. So I am left to wonder what or who—if anything, if anyone—was, for them, salvation.

At the time, I don't think I thought about it, but as an adult, I have come to understand that my mom stayed in Kansas City for a lot of reasons. She sold our dad's dental practice and his stake in the restaurant. She likely dealt with insurance companies and lawyers. I think she attended the criminal trial and met with police officers and prosecutors. She grieved. She got back on her feet. She got the house ready for sale and sold it. Martin and I went up with our grandparents to "help" load the moving van. I have come to understand that my mom spent the time when we lived with our grandparents getting ready—administratively, physically, mentally, and emotionally—to join us in Wichita.

Our mom. She is short like her mom was, 5'4" or so back then and shorter now, at eighty-two. She had short, straight dark-brown hair back then and has a short carob-and-gray-colored afro now. When we were young, she was fond of patterned dresses, and I've always known her to care about her appearance (like my father did). I think of my mom as many things. She could be stern or playful. She has a broad emotional range and an expansive willingness to share how she feels, even when how she feels is hard to consider. Related to that moment in time, here's how I think of it now. After an excruciating loss, our mom reunited with us in Wichita. We got an apartment, then a condo, then another. My mom went back to school. She got a master's in psychiatric nursing, then taught at Wichita State University. She sent us to summer camp, took us on modest but wonderful vacations, exposed us to art and ideas, invested in our projects, encouraged us, and scolded us. My mom is a woman of uncommon endurance. She is among the more vulnerable people I've ever met and among the strongest.

At some point after we lived with our grandparents, my brother and I got Ronco Pocket Fisherman rods and reels for our birthday or Christmas. By then, we lived in a condominium community called Country Lake, "lake" being a generous term for what it was. It was more like a pretty good-sized pond. There was a creek nearby where we grabbed crawdads only to let them go, but the lake of Country Lake was stocked with catfish and smallmouth bass. Martin and I fished there several times a week—catch and release unless we grabbed something grand. We took big fish home for our mom to scale and gut and cook.

In high school, we lived in a condominium community called Chisholm Creek, which had a real creek that was wide enough and deep enough to fish in. We fished there too. We usually fished alone, but I sometimes fished with a Vietnam vet who lived nearby and told me stories about the war.

We were moderately skilled by then—not Grandaddy good, but good. We affixed our own night crawlers. We graduated from the Pocket Fishermans to full rods and reels. We had tackle boxes full of equipment, lots of lures, thoughts about test lines, and ideas for fishing in different kinds of water. We didn't use bobbers. We could sense when a fish was nibbling, could usually tell what was on the line by how it fought, and knew when we were snagged or encountered a catfish. We knew when to fight and when to let the fish run. Sometimes, we woke early to go fishing. We went fishing after school plenty of times and most weekends. We knew how to fish. We knew where to fish. We had grown more patient. We had learned how to be still and wait.

A specific memory from when we lived with our grandparents: Granddaddy took me and Martin fishing at a catfish farm outside of town, a rectangular pond overstocked with hungry catfish. There weren't many trees. We checked in at a shed without air conditioning, and the man who worked there sold us a few things—bait, etc. He was an older man, at least Granddaddy's age. He had white hair and a medium-length white beard. He was a mostly outdoors man, and his skin was rough and red. I don't remember specific conversation, but in my memory the man was Kansas kind: colloquially conversational, social regarding the business we were there to transact.

There were no clouds around, and there was no shade to seek. It was summer in southern Kansas, and the sun worked on us real hard. When I think back on that day two things stand out, and the first was the almost unbearable heat.

It seemed not to affect Granddaddy at all. This wasn't fishing, really. Our cast-to-catch ratio was comical. Almost no technical skill was required. The things it's helpful to have when you're fishing—smart equipment, sensitive hands, knowledge of the water, a feeling for where the fish are biting (connected to time, season, temperature, weather, and knowledge or experience), patience, a solid hook game, and a sense for how to bring the catch in—these things were not needed at this catfish farm. I'm sure our excitement was purchased by Granddaddy's boredom.

Catfish stay low in the water, down near the muddy bottom, where it's cool. They don't move around a lot. When you catch on one, it feels more like a stop than a fight. I used to think I'd hooked a log or a boot or got tangled in a mess of weeds.

And so it was that day, catching on my first catfish. I'd been reeling my line in slowly, then everything stopped. I thought I was snagged, and in the effort to get unstuck, I realized I'd landed a fish.

I brought it in gradually, like you would work a wrench in a tight space: turn a bit, reset your hand, turn a bit, reset your hand. I remember Granddaddy watching me, but only a little—if this one got away, there'd be another one soon. There was a sudden silvery thrash near the pond's surface, and there it was, an ugly whiskery thing, probably both bigger and smaller in reality than it appeared to me back then.

It was not my first fish, by the way, even though it was my first catfish. I'd caught fish on other trips with Granddaddy. And there'd been fishing of a sort back in Kansas City, through Cub Scouts—little guys, crappies and sunnies and such. I remember reaching for the catfish, wanting to do it on my own, to be a fisherman, and getting whipped and stung by its barbels, and feeling hot and hurt and elated. I know Granddaddy set his rod and reel down, came over to me, took hold of the fish like a person would hold a bird, unhooked it with casual ease, and put it in our bucket. I imagine he said something affirming.

I know Martin caught fish that day too. I remember that, but I don't remember whether he unhooked his own. If I had to guess, I'd say he did.

I don't know how long we stayed—a very long time that was actually not long at all. We put our bobbers and weights and bait back in the tackle box. We hooked our hooks on one of the eyes on our fishing poles and tightened the line to hold them in place, then carried our catch back to the shed, where we paid by the pound.

The second thing that stands out: pouring the fish into a metal pan that sat atop a scale. The men somehow accounting for the weight of the water. The fish thrashing about wildly, beating against each other and the sides of the pan, trying to flip out and get away. The proprietor reaching up to a light switch I had not seen, connected to the pan and the scale, flipping it on—then off—with a single finger. I will never forget how suddenly the fish stopped moving at all, how still they were, how calm.

After our mom joined us in Wichita, we visited our grandparents occasionally, not a lot. In the summers we'd visit the family farm in Oklahoma. It had a pond too. We would leave at night. Granddaddy would put a mattress in the back of his truck, and we would drive about four hours (back then) to our land in Watonga, a bit northwest of Oklahoma City. I don't remember doing much at the farm—a few light chores. By the time I was old enough to remember going there, it was primarily a space for family reunions. We'd gather with Kansas cousins and Oklahoma cousins and Florida cousins—outdoors, playing and working.

My mother and her siblings still own the property, and someone checks on it from time to time. We rent it to a farmer nearby, mostly for grazing. The land we own sits atop the Anadarko Basin, a massive field of oil and natural gas. Once a month, the family gets modest compensation from an oil company that leases the mineral rights. Dividends for the land paid for Grandmommy's last years, when she lived in an expensive memory care unit.

I live in Saint Paul, Minnesota, now. My wife is a horticul-
turist, and we live near a park about a four-minute walk from
a city lake about 1.3 miles in circumference. It has two docks,
one for launching canoes, kayaks, and paddleboards, and one
mostly for fishing. The lake is home to channel catfish, north-
erns, bluegill, largemouth bass, walleye, and a few other kinds of
fish. Quite often, even in winter, I see people fishing there, from
the dock or shore or on top of the ice. I am not among them. I
don't own a rod or reel or tackle box anymore. Sometimes, if I'm
up at a friend's cabin, I'll cast a few unlicensed lines, but even
counting that, I haven't gone fishing in years.

I'm a writer, and large parts of my life are spent indoors,
hunched over a Moleskine or laptop. I read a lot, and I'm more
likely to go to a poetry reading than a pond or a creek. I love
the outdoors though. I took up one of my granddaddy's
other passions—golf. It's a rare round that I don't consult his
wisdom. Quite a few of his golf clubs are in my basement; a
cousin in Texas has some too. I have all but one of the golf balls
he gave me. They're hard, like rocks, and have a wide red stripe
around them. The one I don't have, I placed near Granddaddy's
hand as he lay in his casket.

I don't have any of his fishing equipment. My aunt Joyce
has it at her home near Dallas. She told me his tackle box was
passed down to him by his own daddy.

I enjoy cycling and try to go camping with my wife and
our family and friends at least once a year. I love scenic hikes
by day and sleeping on the ground. I love the ritual of looking for flat land, putting a tarp down, raising a tent, looking for
wood and kindling, building a fire, making meals in a Dutch
oven, never hurrying, never running but never resting, moving
all day from one joyful task to the next, quiet and calm.

Often, when I'm outdoors, I think of my grandparents and how connected they were to the land. Their connection was organic and unscheduled. They began their married life in Oklahoma. My mom was born in a small town called Geary. My grandparents grew up Black at a time when being Black was even more difficult than it is today, when acquiring and keeping land was more difficult, so you cherished it. You mowed and planted flowers. They lived at a time when you made use of everything you had to help you survive. You farmed the acres your parents fought to get and keep; you grew enough food in your backyard. Except for my granddaddy's passion for golf and clubhouse games of chance, my grandparents didn't seem to have hobbies. They didn't watch television until later in life, and for vacation they went to the farm—and worked.

But I think of them when I'm outside. When I'm golfing or camping or on the rare occasion when I go fishing. I think of them when I watch my wife work in the garden or when I'm hiking along a quiet trail.

Black people alive today can see their parents and their parents' parents and all of their ancestors in almost every blessing they have. It's true for me, as well, and so are these facts that persist beyond memory, that maybe even obscure my memory: just before I turned nine, something happened that was very hard. The kind of hard that reshapes a life immediately and gradually, over time; the kind of hard some people never overcome.

And soon after that hard thing happened, there was a tremendous softness:

Arthur and Grace . . .

. . . in their fragrant home, in their home with its purposeful cadences—constant and calm. We were parented there by grandparents with grandchildren who needed abundant care.

If I close my eyes, I can comb my grandfather's thin, gray afro between my fingers or feel again my grandmommy's pillowy bosom against my face. I smell Sanka brewing on their stovetop and hear a radio, mostly catching the AM station they wanted, cracking and humming in the background.

If I close my eyes, I can travel back in time to when I traveled back in time and lived for a certain number of days in what will always be my favorite home, the home of my salvation—a buttercream-yellow house on East Eighth street, not far at all from the center of Wichita, Kansas.

WATER AND STONE
A Ceremony for Audre Lorde in Three Parts

Alexis Pauline Gumbs

INTRODUCTION:

"MISS LORDE, ARE YOU A NATURE POET?"

Audre Lorde is the best-known Black lesbian poet of the twentieth century. In the twenty-first century, we seem to quote her essays more often than her poems. Activists, theorists, and even football coaches invoke her words in their social function, the work of collaborating across difference, the need to address multiple forms of oppression simultaneously, the importance of raising our voices against oppression's insidious silencing.

Over the decades, other readers have attempted to add other descriptors before the word "poet." After her first reading on campus as poet-in-residence at the historically Black Tougaloo College, a student asked, "Miss Lorde, are you a nature poet?" Lorde was surprised. "What are you talking about?" she recalled thinking, later. Contemporary discussions of her work, after all, concentrate on the relationships between groups of people, not on natural imagery. A significant amount of her work occurs in the hyper-urban setting of New York City.

But even though most discussions of Audre Lorde don't focus on her poetic imagery, she consistently references nature. Even in her poems about New York City, she focuses not only on the smells and movements of the city's human

213

animals but also on its rivers, her own garden on Staten Island, and one of the most prolific and important animals in the city: the cockroach.

Her fascination with the natural world began early. In high school she was inspired by the romantic poets, so much so that her high school literary magazine said her work was too "sensualist." The imagery she used in her poetry followed from an erotic intimacy with the earth that she found in the work of her favorite poet during her adolescence, Edna St. Vincent Millay. Millay's "Renascence" was Lorde's favorite poem, a poem that describes the speaker experiencing all the seasons and changes of the earth in her body, being overwhelmed by that amount of feeling and therefore burying themselves in the earth, and then, just as quickly, missing the sensation of being connected to life and so surrendering to rebirth. Lorde said she loved the poem so much she had it memorized, and it is not a short poem.

Lorde's breakthrough about the purpose of her own poetry came while she was a college student studying in Mexico. A field of birds and wildflowers came alive and taught her that the true function of her poetry was to be able to deeply inhabit and transport a moment, to bring together feeling and imagery. The content of her poetry focuses on seasons, solstice, equinox, the ocean, the work of growing plants, the Yoruba orisha as representations of the elements, bees and stones and snow and deserts and fire and cuttlefish and birch and snails and serpents and so many bodies of water. Given all this, I'm not surprised, unlike Lorde herself, by that Tougaloo student's question; I would argue that she is a Black feminist nature poet.

Others have disagreed. In his review of her first book, Dudley Randall, Lorde's future publisher at Broadside Press, says explicitly, "Audre Lorde is not a nature poet." He explains

his assessment: the use of nature in her poems is about "feelings and relationships," and her focus on the cycles of the seasons is about the "inner weather" of human emotions. Randall,
writing in the early 1970s, felt that he was affirming Lorde's
poetry. To call her a "nature poet" in that moment would have
been to suggest that her poetry was apolitical, characterized
by white naturalist nostalgia, and irrelevant to the Black Arts
Movement, within which he was a central institution builder
and within which Lorde would soon become an important
and controversial voice. Her attention to nature had everything to do with the possibility of revolution, he wanted to
suggest. I can agree with that. Especially in this moment, when
environmental racism, climate change–induced disasters, and
new viruses disproportionately impact oppressed people. And
also in the 1970s, '80s, and '90s, when Audre Lorde thought
of the natural world as important, not only as a representa-
tion of inner life but as a terrain on which those relationships
Randall referenced would or would not be able to continue.
Lorde wrote specifically about the problems of nuclear energy,
the correlation between fossil fuel use, oil drilling, and the rise
in natural disasters, including Hurricane Hugo, which she
survived on the island of St. Croix, in the Virgin Islands. She
would follow her many public statements about the political
work we needed to do around difference with the words, "We
do not have to become each other in order to work together,
but we do share an earth that is in danger." For Lorde, the relationship between the people and each other and the people
and the planet could not be separated. Ultimately Randall's
statement was more a critique of white nature poetry than it
was a true misunderstanding of Lorde's work. Randall, and
Lorde herself, did not have the benefit of Camille Dungy's

powerful reclamation and contextualization of the genre in her groundbreaking 2009 anthology, *Black Nature: Four Centuries of African American Nature Poetry*, which features Lorde's work five times.

Though Lorde was surprised at the student's question—just as I was recently surprised to be included by the Sierra Club on a list of Black "eco-poets," and even momentarily confused when I first learned about this book you're reading—that sense of surprise indicates more about how the colonization of writing categories mimics the literal colonization of planet Earth, and about how iterations of nature writing that are in no way accountable to the lives of oppressed people have taken up most of the discursive space for the exact reasons that make poetry "not a luxury," as Lorde would say, for those of us whose accountability to all life is clarified and nurtured by our love of our own oppressed communities. Despite powerful interventions by poets like Dungy, Ed Roberson, Erin Sharkey, and the other contributors to this book, this tendency has long outlived Audre Lorde. If someone like me can write daily about marine mammals and never think to call it "nature writing," then an argument can be made that Black feminist poets are experiencing a completely different natural world than the writers for whom these marketing terms were invented. By the same token (I'm going to leave that word there), it is Lorde's approach that holds the most potential for this writer to reexamine what is natural, what is possible, what is here?

Almost twenty years after that Tougaloo reading, during an interview with Louise Chawla, a doctoral student writing a dissertation on nature poets, Audre Lorde explained the profound influence of the few green spaces her mother, Linda, took her to as a child growing up in Harlem; the rivers surrounding Manhattan and her mother's own descriptions of her childhood in Carriacou, in the Grenadines, led her to focus very much on nature in her poetry. As James Manigault-Bryant suggests in his essay "Journaling the Body into Nature," Audre Lorde does not conform to the idea of nature poetry presenting a pristine Eden that is sacred because of its distance from the impurities of modern life. Instead, he argues, she activates a relationship to nature that empowers readers and generates alternatives to the consequences of industry, particularly its cancerous outcomes and climate disasters caused by oil drilling and transnational corporate profiteering. I agree. Lorde's poetry presents an encounter with the natural world that is as dirty as our relationships to each other, and yet she allows nature to serve as a teacher for how we could relate to each other differently.

I would go even further, to say that Audre Lorde is a Black feminist *speculative* nature poet. She writes about grass and puddles from the perspective of a vampire in the poem "Prologue." She incorporates West African stories about animals into a depiction of her multi-lifetime goddess-self throughout her 1976 collection *The Black Unicorn* and beyond. And her poem "The Brown Menace," from the perspective of a New York City cockroach, models an interspecies intimacy—not only because it situates roaches where they are, in the kitchen, on the white pillow, and not only because it could be used to challenge the hypocrisy at the core of systems of racism against people of color in New York City, but also because it uses the first person; the speaker is a cockroach looking the reader in the eye. Audre Lorde doesn't bring mere observation to nature; she brings queer Black desire. Her very first inspiration to become a poet was her mother's unexplained use of Caribbean sayings and turns of phrase in the context of their Harlem apartment. They conjured for her the lush idea of home in Grenada, which her mother spoke of wistfully and to which they never returned. Lorde explained to Chawla that it was the love in her mother's voice as she described the fruit trees of her childhood and the dew on the bucket of water her mother would go fetch in the morning that made Lorde become a poet. She focused on those few green spaces in her own life as portals to her mother's inaccessible reality. Lorde had to imagine speculative landscapes beyond her knowing as she chased after her mother's desire to return to a home that remained out of reach. She used words as a way to imagine herself at home in the world, sometimes in a deeper way than she felt in her actual home. And for Lorde, that required engaging something older, wider, than a single human life or institution. That reach, or what she called *renewal*, taught her that the witnessing energy that moved through her would continue to live through others who encountered the same rivers she wrote about, long after she herself was gone. Or who, like her, would need poetry as a way to move across a distance they otherwise could not bridge.

As she says in *The Cancer Journals*, renewal "means trout fishing on the Missisquoi River at dawn and tasting the green silence," which she describes as part of "knowing that my work is part of a continuum of women's work, of reclaiming this earth and our power, and knowing that this work did not begin with my birth nor will it end with my death. And it means knowing that within this continuum, my life and my love and my work has particular power and meaning relative to others."

And this is what I myself do as a speculative poet. I reach. I speculate. I ramble. I renew. I make myself into a relative of Audre Lorde, part of the continuum of women she invoked in

order to understand her own life as eternal and meaningful beyond the constructs of oppression. In this essay I will practice
this work of reclaiming this earth and our power, especially in
relationship to water, stone, desire, and home. I am focusing
on Lorde's relationship to water and stone in three contexts:
Carriacou and Anguilla, our respective ancestral homes across
diaspora; St. Croix, her final home and resting place, guided
by a group of stones I collected during two weeks I spent living in her former house there and walking daily to the beach
she also visited; and Krumme Lanke, a lake in Germany, contemplating an iconic series of photographs of Audre Lorde on
the water, taken by the feminist activist and filmmaker Dagmar
Schultz over several years. This essay speculates, using artifacts, so-called historical facts, and the capacity for memory in
water and stone themselves as technologies of reclamation and
access points to Audre Lorde's eternal life.

I. THE BLESSING OF MISRECOGNITION

In 1986, Audre Lorde and her companion, the Black feminist
scholar and activist Gloria Joseph, went on vacation to the
island of Anguilla, my ancestral home. While she was there,
Lorde enjoyed being mistaken for a local. It affirmed the
Caribbean sense of self she craved as a daughter of Caribbean
parents in exile. The healing impact of the sun and the sea on
her during her time there is part of what convinced her to
move permanently to the region, to St. Croix, with Joseph.
While she was in Anguilla, she wrote a poem about Crocus
Bay as well as many journal musings about how the island felt
like "a piece of home."

I have my grandmother's journal from her first visit to Anguilla, made after years of hearing vague references to the beauty of the island from my grandfather. The journal has a page for every day of the year, but all the pages are empty except for the single week of their trip. Anguilla is the center of my concept of home and of my connection to the natural world. It's a small island and everyone there is a close or distant cousin of mine, and since it was the site of our annual family gatherings, we went there almost every summer and several winters as well when I was a child. As a college student, I began visiting on all my breaks from school, to listen to my grandparents talk about their lives and their roles in the Anguillian revolution of 1967.

When Audre Lorde and Gloria Joseph first visited Anguilla in February 1986, I was four years old. Joseph told me she had vague memories of meeting my grandfather Jeremiah Gumbs, who would sit on his porch and hold court, although she was not sure if they had met during one of her trips with Audre or before. Maybe Lorde and my grandfather, who memorized every poem he loved—these two people who were both born on February 18—got a chance to talk about poetry or about Crocus Hill, where Jeremiah was born, overlooking the bay that Lorde wrote about. Maybe they celebrated the fact that it was, right then, the season of both their birthdays. Or maybe not. I like the possibility, the blur, there, though. Audre Lorde loved it in Anguilla, and in Grenada and St. Croix, where people mistook her for some local relative, and I love allowing the places where Audre starts and I end to get mixed up. When I walk the beaches of Anguilla, a sixteen-mile-long, geologically unique island made from a coral reef that was born in the mouth of a volcano, I feel a kinship with my oldest relatives, with the cyanobacteria that oxygenated the earth, and with the small bones and shells of those ancestors who are now sand. With the heat at the core of the earth. With the deep breathing of the planet. When I sit quietly in Anguilla, place of Arawak ceremony, where archeologists have found evidence not so much of settlement as of prayer, I hear my inner voice clearly. This is how I have learned to listen to myself, the "it feels right to me" discernment that Audre Lorde calls *erotic power*, which has been at the root of all my major decisions. I like imagining that while Lorde was being mistaken for one of my cousins, she was hearing the same voice I hear, encouraging her to trust her desire, to know that she could have what she wanted: to live the rest of her life in a place of sun, ocean, and what she called Caribbean "Blackfullness."

It wasn't until my second trip to Audre Lorde's maternal homeland of Carriacou that I thought to wonder if Lorde and I actually were cousins, not on the Anguillian paternal side of my lineage, but on the maternal Jamaican side. I visited Carriacou on a short day trip in 2008, when I was visiting Grenada for the first time, for the Association of Caribbean Women Writers and Scholars conference. As soon as I got off the airplane in Grenada, I recognized the smell. Not like Jamaica, not like Trinidad (where I had been stranded for a day on my way), not like most other islands I had been to, but *yes*—just like Anguilla. I wonder if it was, in part, the particular similarities in plant life and the smell they generated that caused Lorde to feel a similar resonance with home when she was in Anguilla. When I took the ferry to Carriacou, the sea grape trees, powder beaches, and rustic shoreline structures made me think of Anguilla even more. They made me want to come back.

A decade later, in 2018, I had the opportunity to spend a full week in Carriacou as part of the "Take My Word for Jewel" retreat, created by the Black feminist artists and healers Karma Mayet Johnson and Shelley Nicole. The retreat took place in a house owned by the Belmar family. (Belmar is Audre Lorde's mother's maiden name.) At the last minute, one of the retreat participants had to cancel, and her spot was offered to a local writer, Cindy McKenzie. (McKenzie is my mother's maiden name.) During one of the few-and-far-between moments when my phone had a signal, my cousin Andre, on my mother's side, sent me two hundred years of birth records of the McKenzie family in Jamaica. Meanwhile, I was seeing the name McKenzie on the gravestones in the cemetery on the way to the beach, and residents were telling me that there was a long history of McKenzies on the island but that most of them had migrated. It seemed as if a web was tightening. Finally, likely exasperated with my questions, Ms. Clemencia Alexander, the woman who runs the museum of the Carriacou Historical Society, took me by the hand. She and her little nephew walked me down the street to the gate of the house where the McKenzies lived. No one was home.

On a small island, everyone is presumed to be cousins in some way—or, as my elder cousin Hudson (also exasperated with my questions) said, "All Anguilla people is the same people." On Carriacou, several unexpected signs seemed to point to the possibility that I have a deeper connection to the island than I suspected. But my connection to Audre Lorde does not need to be one of lineage or ancestry. It could just be the grace, the blur of possibility and calling. And the openings, like the mouths of coral, wrought by letting the water move us and by building upon the breathing of our dead.

II. JOURNEYSTONES, SEA GLASS, AND SHELL

In the film *A Litany for Survival: The Life and Work of Audre Lorde*, by Michelle Parkerson and Ada Griffin, Audre Lorde speaks of her connection with the ocean, as a portal through which generations of ancestral love can move. Walking on the beach in St. Croix with her daughter, Elizabeth, she theorizes that being near the ocean must be a mental health resource for Caribbean women, including her mother, including herself. In this film, we get to see Lorde explaining to her daughter, who had recently graduated from Harvard and begun teaching in New York City, why it was important for Lorde to live in St. Croix, beyond the cold and combat of the city. She needed the healing presence of the ocean.

By moving to St. Croix at the end of her life, Audre Lorde fulfilled her mother's desire to return to the Caribbean. That desire had been interrupted by the Great Depression, possibly even by Lorde's birth, as the third child the young couple was responsible for in the financially precarious time between wars. That dream of returning was finally rendered impossible for Linda after her husband's early death. If Lorde is right, and the ocean, the Caribbean landscape itself, was a necessary mental health resource for her mother, it was a resource she was only able to access through language and memory. The images of Grenada and Carriacou that her mother offered were a passage- way to an alternate reality, an idea of home beyond the struggle days of Harlem and the racism of the United States. Let's call it a diaspora technology: a form of nature poetry spoken out loud in the kitchens of the metropole, where migrant mothers tempt their children with a relationship to the natural world that defies the separation between them and the urban landscape they are navigating daily. A multigenerational mental health practice that lets a child know this way of being in the world is not the only way, even if the glorified homeland and nostalgic references become increasingly outdated as the same systems that forced parents to migrate ravage the natural resources in their home countries. Lorde started early on to emulate this use of language.

When Audre Lorde moved to St. Croix to live with Gloria Joseph, she had years of healing oceanic proximity to catch up on—generations to catch up on, in fact. So she visited a beach near their house every day. I went to St. Croix in 2011 to live in that house for two weeks and to assist Joseph with her "bio/anthology" of Lorde, *The Wind Is Spirit*. Every day, I worked in Audre Lorde's office, which was mostly as she had left it. It was in that room that she took her last breath in 1992. I felt awe. I felt gratitude. I felt guidance. Every day, before sitting down to work in that office, I took a morning walk and greeted the ocean. Every day, I chose a stone, piece of sea glass, or shell from the shoreline, and allowed it to speak to me. When I went back to the house of the Lorde, I wrote the word that I heard most strongly in my spirit directly on my treasure. It was not until the very end of my trip that I learned Audre Lorde had had the same practice—not the Sharpie part, but that she visited that exact same piece of shoreline for her peace of mind before getting to the other work of the day.

I brought these stones home as an oracle. First as a small offering to my partner, an archive of my days away, which had led right up to our third anniversary in love. Then as an oracle for my brother Seneca who, like Audre Lorde, deeply explores his dreams and creates comic books and game designs based on them. When he turned seventeen, I wrote him daily poems based on these stones and my waking memories of my dreams.

Audre Lorde dreamt often of stones. Moonstone and ebony opal for nurturing and love. Turquoise, amber, and malachite to soothe the heart. She used stones in her poetry to describe how she felt: "those stones in my heart are you." In her series of short poems "Journeystones I-IX," she released the resentment she was holding from relationships with women in her life who she felt had betrayed her. In *The Cancer Journals,* she wrote of a dream she had about a class on "language crazure," a course where she could learn the edges and faults in words as if they were rocks. And so, nine years after I collected these stones, I want to drop nine of them into your hands as an oracle for this point in our journey. And to honor the fact that Audre Lorde, daughter of Oyá, represented by the sacred number nine—who connects the ancestors to the living, and transforms us all through the wind—is here with us, light as air and grounding as the stones she left for us to follow.

1. Trust.
(A small porous stone, maybe coral, almost pink)

I am learning to trust something bigger than me to hold what I cannot hold, so I can truly release the patterns and habits I have outgrown. Those patterns let me tell myself I was safe enough in the moment, but the cost was huge. In fact, the cost was exactly the size of this bigger trust that I am ready to cultivate now. I think about what it took for Audre Lorde to trust herself and her own body in her diligence to survive cancer as long as she could. In a context where American surgeons were biased and believed only in surgery, where the published research was sexist, and where the entire medical system refused (as it still does) to trust Black women about their own bodies, she had to distinguish between fear and wisdom. She had to dig for the places where her fear of her mortality was blocking her ability to make decisions about her life. She had to decide who she could trust for her medical care and to access and create systems of nonsurgical treatment beyond the United States. She had to listen to what her body said about what foods, climates, and practices would support her. Lorde's daughter, Elizabeth, now an award-winning doctor at Mount Sinai Hospital, says that her mother added years to her life and improved her quality of life immeasurably by trusting herself to take on "alternative" practices that are now standard for cancer treatment in the United States. She had to trust the small voice on the wind that told her, while on vacation in Anguilla, that it was time to move to the Caribbean permanently. Can I trust myself to live? Can I trust whoever I will be without the constant work and distractions I use as defense mechanisms to avoid full surrender?

2. Write.
(A rough gray stone, flat enough to skip, but not at all smooth)

Good point. Writing *is* the most consistent way I tap into trust. And although it is the center of my work, it is where I procrastinate the most. According to Lorde's journal, she procrastinated in her writing too—but for her, journaling itself was a practice of tuning in to her inner voice. Audre Lorde journaled consistently and allowed her writing to bring the dream images that she sometimes could not understand into discourse as ceremonies that she could share with her community. In 1988, when Lorde, Joseph, and their whole

226

community survived the devastation of Hurricane Hugo in St. Croix, Lorde turned to her writing practice, rewriting her life's work. The power was out for months, but she sat by lantern light every evening after eating a dinner cooked on a makeshift driftwood fire in the driveway, revising the poems in *Chosen Poems, Old and New*, one of the books that survived the flood. I have it here with me, thanks to the generosity of Gloria Joseph. In the preface to *Undersong*, the collection that came out of that process, Lorde explained that this ceremony was a ritual of intimacy with her younger self. A time travel within, as she not only faced the bleak circumstances of the long aftermath of the hurricane, but also reckoned with the knowledge that the tumors in her liver had returned. The form of accompaniment that she offered to both her younger self and her oldest self came through the intimacy of a repetitive practice of writing. One of the major differences between the poems as they appear in the two books is that Lorde introduces more space within and between lines. I wonder if revising poems that she had written throughout her life in the crowded context of New York City, in a Caribbean landscape made even more rustic by the slowness with which the US government responded to the destruction of the island's infrastructure, offered something to the spaciousness of the revisions. Right now, I am in the process of revising my younger self through the photo albums my mother left with me last year, when she moved across the ocean. I am writing revisions, not of earlier poems but of stories about separation that I hold like stones in my heart and my mind. I am allowing the younger self in these photos to teach me that something else is possible, now that I have the space and inclination to look back.

3. Play.
(A speckled brown stone, like a lopsided egg)

This is the word that comes to mind when I think of Audre Lorde in, on, or around water. Play! I love witnessing the record of the true playfulness between Lorde and Joseph in St. Croix as they ate fresh coconuts, swam in the ocean, harvested honey, and debated every topic under the sun. And this is what my younger self would tell me to do. Play! That activity where I trust myself again and again to do what feels right. The freedom to experiment and switch it up if it turns out something I try is not as fun as I thought it might be. In her poetic work, Audre Lorde was not interested in what she called "sterile wordplay," but her flirtation, teasing, and joking with her friends and lovers, using language, movement, and facial expressions, all invited play. I can release the heaviness I often impose on my life by remembering that it is all a learning experience, shaped by how exuberantly I can lean into my desires, release the outcomes, and try again. Is there an area in your life where you can introduce more play?

4. Transform.
(A multicolored stone, some places white, some places brown, one bright red mark)

Once this stone was smooth, but a long piece immediately under the word "transform" has chipped off after almost a decade of this rock banging around in a bag with other rocks. So now the word is underlined in 3-D. The rock itself has transformed from what it was when I first dared to bring my pen to something so perfect. Is that the message? That I must allow myself to transform, not just in word but in structure, in the physical shape I make of my life with my days? When Audre Lorde had a radical mastectomy in hopes of stopping the spread of breast cancer, she celebrated the asymmetry of her body, despite doctors and even other breast cancer survivors strongly suggesting she wear a prosthesis to avoid "disturbing" other people with her appearance. Instead, she practiced stonework, creating her own jewelry to wear on her transformed chest, embodying what she thought of as a neo-Amazon warrior aesthetic. Am I resisting my own transformation in order to keep other people from being disturbed by how I am growing and changing? How can my creative process celebrate the beauty of my changes? And you?

5. Dance.

(A shell shaped like a boomerang, but rounder,
bull horns but curving in on themselves)

Audre Lorde loved to dance. She describes the erotics and politics of the 1950s lesbian dance scene in her biomythography, *Zami*. The film *Audre Lorde: The Berlin Years* begins with her dancing in a living room filled with women. And beyond physical dance, she also danced between worlds. *The Black Unicorn* is an artifact of a ceremony through which Audre Lorde began to understand herself and the hyphenated dance of being an African American or African in the United States as part of a multilifetime diasporic movement between worlds, mythologies, and forms of consciousness. My dance practice is one of my most vital listening practices, but I am writing this essay during a pandemic where the three-times-a-week, community-based West African dance classes that I attend and the social dance parties and events that I enjoy are all canceled indefinitely. The dance I am doing more right now is the dance between worlds. This morning I had a vision of myself, my father (an ancestor), my godfather (living), and my brother Jared (also living). Before I closed my eyes to meditate, I could see the waning moon, Venus, and Mars out my window, and in my vision, I saw the four of us dancing and playfully holding and spinning with planets. Maybe the dance that allows me to trust is a cosmic dance across oceans, across time, across anything that I imagine separates me from love.

6. Dig.
*(A layered stone that looks like the desert
or an archeological site)*

And stones can be made. In Audre Lorde's poem "Digging," she writes about a stone machine and a stone museum. What do I need to learn about the making of stones, the keeping of stones, or both? The poem suggests that underneath the situation we dig through, there are useful stones, medicine for our melancholy spirits. Amber is crystalized tree resin petrified over millions of years. Under extreme pressure over time, coal becomes diamond, a metaphor Lorde uses in one of her most remembered poems. What is the pressure and petrification, stress and fear, that have contributed to the heaviness, blocks, and stone places within me, down deep? Do I need to release these stones or are they becoming medicine?

7. Fly?
(An off-white triangle with rounded edges,
and a round depression in the middle)

I guess this means I need to take the stones out of my pockets. Audre Lorde often wrote poems while in flight, in airplanes looking over familiar and unfamiliar landscapes. One of my favorite in-flight poems of hers is "On My Way out I Passed over You and the Verrazano Bridge," which Lorde wrote while a flight she was supposed to be taking to California circled, stuck in a holding pattern, over Staten Island, where she and her family lived at the time. The poem starts with the repeated words "Leaving leaving" because Audre Lorde is considering taking flight in more ways than one. Ultimately, she would leave Staten Island and the life she created with her longtime partner Frances Clayton for the island of St. Croix, but in the poem she writes across centuries and continents, concluding at the end of the poem that the "flights of this journey" are "mapless uncertain / and necessary as water." What do I need to leave behind? What do you need to leave on the ground while you soar?

8. Watch.
(An almost rectangular piece of glass, every edge softened by sea)

I wonder what this piece of sea glass was. A beer bottle? A window? Could it have been debris created by Hurricane Hugo that had grown soft and smooth and almost clear by the time I got to St. Croix decades later? In "Hugo Letter: Of Generators and Survival," Audre Lorde writes about humility. Human beings build structures as if they will last a thousand years, "but the wind is our teacher." Now, kept indoors by a narcissistic government's failure to protect the public from a global pandemic, I am watching through my window the slow return of airplanes to the sky while death counts rise. In "Hugo Letter," Lorde critiques the oil profiteers, the troops sent to St. Croix to protect the interests of Hess Oil while terrorizing the majority Black survivors of a deadly storm. She warns that if we collectively do not learn from that particular unnatural response to a natural phenomenon, history will repeat itself. It already has. I have to learn. To learn, I have to let go of the blocks I hold, the stories that I use to distract me, and really watch what is happening where I am. Even if it's through a window.

9. Breathe.
(A flat brown stone like a coin, or a cookie)

When I stand next to the ocean, I can feel the moon breathing. The planet's saltwater gravitationally pulled across space. When I'm quiet, I can hear Audre Lorde breathing. Laughing at me. Sometimes sending her voice high to sing her poems like a prophet ringing the bell of her own life. I take these stones as instructions for how to continue this journey that did not begin with my life and does not end.

III. *CRUMENSE* MEANS CROOKED WATER

As I mentioned previously, Dagmar Schultz took a series of portraits of Audre Lorde on the water in Germany, rowing an inflatable raft in an asymmetrical red T-shirt, or just floating while eating a peach. What characterizes these pictures? Joy. I hear her laughing through the clear air, the light of her being reflected in blue. The chronic pain of cancer taking a backseat to the practice of pleasure.

I have never been to Germany, but recently Schultz let me know the name of the lake where she took these photographs. During different visits Lorde made to Germany, first at the invitation of Schultz to teach at the Free University of Berlin and then to access those revolutionary (at the time) cancer treatments, she loved to get on the lake. There were so many things that were healing about Lorde's time in Germany. The community of feminists who embraced her, especially the young Afro-German women who found each other and the language to describe themselves through their admiration and attraction to Lorde's literary readings, in a country where they felt invisible and attacked at the same time. The food: fresh produce, which she needed for her rigorous healing diet, free from the carcinogenic pesticides used in the United States. And the water. This particular water. Krumme Lanke.

What do I know about this water without visiting? I know it was never straight and that the people named the land after it. Crumense, crooked water. I know archeologists identified the pottery they dug up nearby as Slavic. I know it has a nude beach where Lorde once ate ice cream while joking about the particular Berlinesque nature of the practice of nude sunbathing. But its role within Berlin's history is not at all laughable. When Audre Lorde was four years old, there was a community for Nazi officers on the shore of this lake. The street names told a story of racial superiority, pure blood, and the intention to breed generations of Aryans. All but one street name has been changed since. The Nazi officers and their wives and children believed they deserved these scenic homes on this beautiful lake because they were part of an Aryan future. Nature loved them more. Did Lorde know that history and intentionally defy it with her joy? Or did she simply gain energy from this lake, once conscripted into another story, for her years of work challenging what she saw as the resurgence of Nazism in Germany?

Judging from the length and shape of her afro, this photo must be from 1984. Her first visit to Berlin. Teaching at the Free University. Audre Lorde is representing joy. Embodying the ethos of the red T-shirt with Emma Goldman's words: "If I can't dance I don't want to be part of your revolution." She does not know, except for the part of her that knows, that we will one day wear T-shirts bearing her words and her face. We will try to live as loud and brave as we should, since we are the ones who get to have her breath and likeness in ink across our chests. Our backs. I, too, often cut out the necks of my T-shirts, daring my shoulders to free themselves. Dagmar Schultz says Lorde was not athletic, but she loved to get on this inflatable boat and pretend to be an athlete when she had the energy. I once had inflatable water wings the same yellow as the boat. It is hard to remember that life is hard when you can feel water and air supporting you. On this water, Audre Lorde dances. The sun touches every part of her. This is not the clumsy girl who feels too fat and too dark around her sisters. Not the aloof intellectual, so much like her mother, looking seriously over her glasses on the back of *Sister Outsider*. This is simply the genius at play, who will read her sexiest poems at the beginning and the end of the night on purpose, groove to the music in rooms filled with women who adore her, laugh and sing while cutting beets. Hands becoming as red as this very shirt.

This is the anarchist Audre, filling the moment with blood, desire, creation. This is the anarchist Audre, secretly dreamt of between the lines of *Mother Earth,* the radical journal the insistent dancer Emma Goldman founded in 1906.

My red shirt has black words by Lorde's friend and colleague Toni Cade Bambara. On my back it says: "The role of the revolutionary artist is to make revolution irresistible." In her early seventies letter-poem to Bambara, "Dear Toni Instead of a Letter of Congratulation Upon your Book and Your Daughter Whom You Say You Are Raising to Be a Correct Little Sister," Lorde corrects Bambara with the words "our teaching means keeping trust / with less and less correctness." Maybe she means that Bambara's daughter, Karma, should have more freedom, fewer strictures, should be able to dance, if indeed we are having our revolution. Lorde says that Bambara, like her own daughter, Elizabeth, has "deep aquatic eyes." Pools of wonder and curiosity. Maybe it was her own mother's stern training that Lorde was really protesting in this poem. Or maybe it was a version of the same possibility of peace, on a different scale, that she saw in Toni's eyes, Elizabeth's eyes, and this water.

Another photo. It is eight years after the first picture. Head shaved now, she has let go of the silver dreadlocks I will find in an unmarked box on my first visit to the archives, next to the box containing her prescription snorkel mask. And she looks relatively light, right? She is literally floating on air. The compressed air of the blue-and-yellow inflated raft, less dense than the oxygen in the water. Less thick than the liver tumors Lorde is trying to dissolve with infusions and fresh fruit. She wears a bright Black History sweatshirt, also blue, and water and sky are darker blue, and one day she will be all of this to me: water, sky, tight and specific breathing, history, and blues. Now she is all of this.

On her knee, light denim and a quilted bag made from patterned fabrics representing those she might call the global majority of non-white people on the planet. The hyphenated people always in relation. Her relations. Us. Over her eyes? A shade attachment clipped to her strong prescription glasses. She can see the trees on the shoreline and remembers how, when she was a young child, trees were as impressionistic as children's books illustrations until she got her glasses and could acknowledge each leaf for herself. These are the years where she bravely acknowledges that she is leaving. But not yet. On her wrists? The watch that reminds us that "none of us have 300 years," and bangles bent to hold her even as she loses weight. In her hands? A knife. And a peach she has already cut open. On her face? The biggest smile. Do you want some?

I am eating a peach as I write this. And a nectarine, just in case that's what is actually in the picture. And also a pear and blackberries—who knows what is in that bag? Who knows how long I will have to enjoy the fruit of what I am just now opening? Which is air, and its density, and how it supports me and when. Which is shade, and what I see. Which is my smile, and what it is for exactly. Which is infinite innuendo. The peach has a womb, and this is it. The seed lives here. The flesh around it is sweet on purpose, so a living being will want to break its skin and bring the seed somewhere the tree cannot see it. And yet the tree can dream. Yes. Trees can dream that one day landfills will be orchards. That she who wields the knife will love herself enough. To share.

One of the places that Audre Lorde's ashes were scattered, by her directive, was Krumme Lanke. A strong deviation from the eugenicist purity path of the Aryans who once named the streets here. Lorde was among the first and most outspoken

voices to call out the vestiges of white supremacy and geno-
cidal action that remained in Germany, and one of the first poets from the Western world to read her poetry in East Germany
after the wall fell. In her final months she and Gloria Joseph
coauthored a public letter to the German chancellor about the
Nazi tendencies emerging in the violence against immigrants
post–Cold War. Audre Lorde would remain part of this place.

According to Dagmar Schultz, she and several of the
women Lorde influenced—including the writers and activists
May Ayim, Ika Hügel-Marshall, and Ilona Bubeck—scattered
a packet of Lorde's ashes, along with flower petals and shells
from St. Croix, all around the lake, rowing in this same inflatable boat. And so, the water holds what we can no longer
touch. The sound of laughter, defiant triumph, unapologetic
pleasure. Grace.

HERE'S HOW I LET THEM COME CLOSE

katie robinson

I practice fear with bugs. Specifically, stinging bugs. I sit on my cracked concrete stoop on humid Minneapolis summer days and notice the behavior patterns of bees and wasps at different times of day. In their dewy waking hours, they stretch their wings and clean their delicate legs. As the sun rises higher into the sky, they take flight, investigating the daylilies and dandelions, yellows and oranges punching out of velvety greens. Later in the day, when the dew has burned off and you can smell the heat coming off the sidewalk, they turn their attention to me—my brightest clothes, the bubbly water I may be drinking, the sandwich or Popsicle I may be eating. And when they come in close, I try to do what my therapist has told me to do and "just notice" what happens in my body. The fear like magma rises up through my core, my arms and legs tense, my heart beats faster, and my breathing changes. There is a memory reel of every time I've been stung (age three, on the cheek; eleven, on the thigh; twenty, on the hand), and I notice that I can *feel* how it felt. Sometimes, this noticing is enough to make me go back inside. Sometimes, I take off down the block, furiously waving and swatting my hands, cursing. But other times, I am able to section off enough space in my body for the fear to see that there are other places containing other things, and I shift my attention to these other places: a place for curiosity, a place for relationality, a place for meeting.

I wonder what it must be like to encounter a giant being. I wonder what they sense on my breath and in my energetic field. I wonder if they like the heat coming off my head. I wonder what drew them in, and I can't help but think, *They are coming close because they want to.* I can assign to them the same decision-making power I have, or I can think about their movements as pure reflex, but neither actually explains why the interaction is happening. All I know is that it *is* happening, an interspecies encounter where risk is present. And in my most solid parts, I sense that there is a structure outside the spectrum between United States–style, individualized, bootstraps "choice" and "our fate is written in stone"—neither free-market free will nor an all-powerful God playing with dolls—a structure that governs what happens, that governs encounters. I sense a structure that is rhizomatic: a locus of power that has no center, that may burst forth anywhere, and that is not solid or still. It is neither inside nor outside any body, not the wasp's or my own. I wonder if (which is to say I sense this too) our shared agency arises in our relationship to each other, in the dance of fear and relation that dwells in interstices and edges, a dance perhaps known by all evolving, adapting creatures, perhaps even older than Earth. There is something not fully wasp, as I know wasps to be, and not fully me, as I know me to be, that governs us. We are entangled and in the midst of a vast network of resonances, a cosmically curated chaos, in which sting or no sting, death or no death, everything is unfolding just as it should.

I practice fear with bugs because I'm often scared, often at night. Sitting on the couch with my partner, my dog, and my cat, I can fall asleep with ease, drifting off halfway through whatever we are watching. But the moment I set the intention *it's time to go to bed*, and I make my way to the bathroom, my physiology changes: my heart starts racing and I begin to see shadows of figures in my mind's eye, standing in corners, breathing behind closed doors, suddenly reflected in mirrors. The moment I close my eyes to attempt sleep, they move in closer, standing over me, peering down. And so there is a nightly flicker of descending into rest, shooting back up and checking behind doors and in corners, and then trying to settle again. Going to bed is a ritual surrender to certain death, or, worse, immobilization in the presence of an unknown other.

As a poet, as a writer and artist, I have always known that nothing is fake about what I imagine. I have always known the mind's eye, the imagination, the psyche as simply another plane of existence, no less real than the material, just alternate, another source of information, a door that can open to any place I need to be. This belief saved me many times as a young person, knowing consciously and unconsciously that I could always be caught and held by my enchantment. I could be whisked away by what interested me. My knowledge of and relationship with the immaterial and the unprovable was as much proclivity as survival skill. To this day, I'm bored by debates over the binary of what's real and what's not real—as if there is one objective reality out there for us to find and prove—a deeply colonial notion— and much more interested in what ensues *as a result of* x y or z reality. I am much more enchanted by a world in which the wasps and I are in a dance neither of us truly understand (but are both alive and conscious as a result of), than I am by a predetermined, measurable, fixed, and predictable existence. If someone tells me wind is what animates the trees to sway and *hushhh*, I know I have learned nothing about *why*. When people explain away cosmic coincidences with rationality ("you keep pulling that tarot card because you haven't properly shuffled the deck and the cards are sticky"), I am left with *but why* that *card though?* There is no reason, to me, not to include bad shuffling and sticky cards as part of the cosmic design through which I was delivered the Ten of Swords every time I pulled for a year before I quit my job.

And yet, seeking the depths and believing in the existence of all I imagine is itself a double-edged sword. A door left open, for some, is an invitation inside, especially for tiny winged creatures looking for warmth.

The central nightmare is this, and it stung me when I was tiny. I am in my bed and my best friend is in the bed next to me. I am just slipping into sleep when I hear foot-steps and see a figure in the corner of the room. I ask my best friend what she is doing up, but the figure says nothing. I hear it breathe. I look to the other bed and it is freshly made, untouched. She was never here. The figure walks closer, reaches out a long spindly finger, touches me between my eyes, and suddenly I can't see or move or breathe. I wake knowing, somehow, that this was no nightmare, and that the creature was not of Earth.

This terrified me enough to give me sleeping issues for, well, the rest of my life. For years I went to sleep in my own bed and woke up in my parents' bed, or on their floor, clueless as to how I got there. My family tells me I used to walk around the whole house in my sleep, having entire conversations with people, once taking a shower without waking up. My sister, with whom I shared the top floor of our house, tells me that the nights I attempted my own bed, she often had to soothe me from night terrors—of which I had no memory.

It terrified me just enough to fear anything alien-related for most of the rest of my life, and just enough to be perfect ammo for older siblings and cousins and parents to poke me with. This fear of aliens, and my ability to withstand it—indeed, my ability to separate the "imagined" from the "real," and to proceed to dismiss the imagined entirely (or at least place it in a neat and tidy box, far away from bedtime)—this ability to not be afraid became a test.

I practice fear with bugs because they are just as real as my nightmare, just as much an encounter, and I am trying to work my way up. I want to see how scared I can be, how much I can tolerate, how big the plume of fear can get while maintaining the entanglement that governs us both, us all—me, the ET, my imagination, the wasps.

I was surprised to find, upon looking up its etymology, that *encounter* has an inherently oppositional connotation. From the old French *encontre*, it is described as a "meeting of adversaries," a "confrontation," a "fight," or an "opportunity." *En* means *in*, "near, at, in, on, within," while *contra* means "against, opposite," or "in comparison with." What strikes me, perhaps unsurprisingly, is the within-ness of the definition: that even in the midst of conflict or fighting, one is *in*, queering the purported opposition. It suggests that any against-ness necessarily exists within a shared body or some other kind of field of entanglement. There is a preceding in-ness to our encounters, even as they categorically bifurcate.

Once, I was scrolling Instagram and I came across what seemed like a hotep-adjacent inspirational page full of archived videos. I couldn't tell you why, but I clicked on one of a woman talking about lessons her elders had taught her. I can't for the life of me remember the page, or the clip, or anything else about it, but I'll never forget the lesson. Her elder had told her, she said, "You meet no one but yourself." My first reaction was instant bodily resonance, like simultaneous expansion and settling. Then I was quickly flung into walking it back, critiquing the message for Western, white, colonial assumptions: *My god, what a self-centered, navel-gazey thing to say. Is that just pure ego? Does it assume individualism and omnipotence?* But then I remembered that I had learned the practice of critique within Western education, so I went back to resonance, and sat with it for a minute. What moved me? Sure, I love the idea that what we think about others has everything to do with ourselves and our history and not much to do with them. I also appreciate the call to self-reflect, and to remember the power of self-knowledge. I can even somewhat get behind the subtle law of attraction written in between the words. However, the thing that grabbed me was what it might mean to expand the singular.

In my graduate studies, which have traversed theories of individual and collective suffering through depth psychological, Indigenous, decolonial, and Black feminist lenses, I have returned time and again to the ancient teaching that we are not individuals, but rather parts in a field of relationality: we are one, wasps, ETs, and all. An expanded *you, yourself, me,* or *I* is wide enough to contain the so-called other, the one being met or confronted, and *not in a way that negates the other.* There is an *I* that does not conflict with the omnipresence of *we,* where both are co-constitutively contained; a cell that is a singular cell at the same time it is my body; a way of being *we* that does not colonize, dominate, or clone; a way of being *we* that folds no one's particulars and experiences into an amorphous abyss.

There is a principle in "classical" philosophy called the law of noncontradiction, which states, essentially, that where A and B are distinct entities, it is impossible for them to be the same thing, at the same time, in the same respect. I completely disagree. Or, rather, I have observed and prefer a reality in which this isn't the case. Perhaps it is my poet-self, or my reverence for metaphor, or my decolonial assignment to question and often reject the Western "rational," but I know that A can be B, C, and D, all at the same time, in the same place, in the same respect.

This is why I love watching murmurations, why I go to check on all my favorite trees on my daily walks, and why I've never been able to stop thinking about the bottom of the ocean. Each is me and not me, at the same time, in the same respect. Each is completely and wholly itself, with its own agential existence, while at the same time, each is us, giving us *us*, in the same way each person knows themselves and what they need best. They are each other's mysteries and mythologies and metaphors, each other's encounterers and visitors in the night, each other's reasons for growing fangs and fins and learning to swim and grasp. There is an unending, whispering web of stories about how we met and how we know each other. Relations have always catalyzed our transformations, and what is encountered was already entangled.

Before I practiced fear, I tried to rationalize it, tried to make that night everything except a true encounter, tried to keep myself separate from the things that scared me most, tried to keep everything out.

The first explanation I went with was that the entity in my room was actually my mom. I don't remember telling my parents about the encounter, but I likely woke up very early and ran straight to their room, jumped on their bed, and spilled the details. And this is when she would have first told me, "Oh, it was just me, coming to check on you, and I kissed you on your forehead." But then, I'd ask, "Why couldn't I move or breathe? If it was you, why was I terrified?" Quickly, she would have followed up with, "Oh, it was just a dream, honey," but even at my young age I had decided dreams were real. And if she had just changed her story, I would know that this was not about helping me, but about appeasing me. I could not trust her. And still I tried to edit her into the memory for years.

When I was ten, *Signs* came out, and my sister, cousin, mom, and grandma were all dying to see it—so I agreed—thinking ten was old enough to stop being scared. It wasn't. I had nightmares and couldn't sleep for weeks, even nestled between my mom and dad. After that period, even saying "signs" in a spooky voice was enough to get a rise out of me and send my brain and body rushing back to the theater, back to my nightmare-encounter that started it all, back to my inability to withstand or disbelieve my imagination.

And still, I tried to theorize my way out of it. I remember going to sleep thinking of ways to justify the violent actions of the ET in *Signs* by imagining the even more violent conditions they were fleeing, or to which they were reacting. Perhaps they were not hostile but in pain: the natural moisture in Earth's air might have made them sick, they might have been escaping a threat on their home planet, there must have been some desperation, some trigger. But while I couldn't attribute their behavior to violence for violence's sake, I also didn't think I was afraid for fear's sake alone. So I took other measures. I moved my clock radio away from my bed so the muffled static wouldn't pick up any extraterrestrial communication; I made sure my broken door was shoved tightly closed, so that if anyone were to open it, the loud scrape it made would wake me; I walked the streets of my neighborhood with my eyes on roofs and trees, always looking for unexpected places the visitors could hide and jump out from.

It's probable that part of the reason I was so scared is because I kept scaring myself. I watched *Alien* and *E.T.* alone in my basement in an attempt to be brave; I binged *Ancient Aliens*, pretending to be uninterested and unbothered; I did a lot of things to try to overcome my fear, and none of them made me less scared, really.

By the time I got to college and was schooled in an array of critical social theories, I was finding new ways to rationalize my memory. Fear of "aliens," as we know them—flying saucers and cow mutilations and abduction and laser beams—emerged during the (second) Red Scare. The storyline of *Invasion of the Body Snatchers* (1956), one of the first "alien" movies that fits neatly into the popular narrative, is well-known to be an allegory for the social hysteria around the spread of communism. Films like *War of the Worlds,* which takes a slightly different narrative arc, had me spotting and questioning the presumption that a completely unknown other would take the shape of colonizer, invading other lands for resources, and destroying or enslaving all those in their path. Movies like these were telling stories about history, stories that were actually psychological repetitions of unhealed and unaddressed collective trauma. Clearly, whatever happened that night in my bedroom had been colored by an endless and profitable production of xenophobic, colonialist propaganda. Capitalism had gotten me once again. Knowing I had been programmed to feel this way quelled my fear for a while.

As I started going to therapy and learning more about intergenerational trauma, I also learned that what we experience in our bodies and psyches is not always exactly linear or literal. It occurred to me that I could have experienced something that wasn't "in" this lifetime, wasn't necessarily "my" experience. I thought of all the invasions my we/I body has undergone: medical trauma, illness, rape. I thought of the echos between my encounter and fear of abduction and all the encounters my Black ancestors had in their hundreds of years of enslavement, how many of us were taken right from our beds by unknown and uncanny humanoid others in the night, frozen by fear or injury, forced upon ships, experimented on, and so on and so on. It occurred to me that I might be feeling all of it, and it occurred to me that even if the experience wasn't "mine," it was showing up through me because it was mine enough to work with, mine enough to heal. I was safe enough in this lifetime to be able to feel what they needed to survive. I was comfortable with this, even as it was a bit daunting. I tried to get good at feeling, and I got really good at reading trauma books.

Still, no matter how much I read and understood, how much I theorized and rationalized, I still had a hard time going to sleep.

And then something changed.

It was the un-nightmare that broke open the nightmare, and it happened on my first day of graduate school. I was enrolled in a low-residency program, so for three very long days each month, our cohort of ten gathered on campus for class, slept in dorms, and ate all our meals in a dining hall. After hours, we often found ourselves in the dorm's living room, deconstructing Jung or archetypal psychology or decolonial philosophy late into the night, no doubt like the depth psychologists who came before us. On our first of these living room nights, Leah, a new classmate with whom I quickly felt kindred, told everyone about a cool thing she knew how to do: she had a client-based healing practice using the Akashic Records—a vibrational record of every soul's journey since its inception, that existed in a specific nonphysical realm of consciousness, accessed by a prayer. On this first night, she offered to open them up for us, and explained that we could ask whatever question we wanted: "Even, like, who really killed JFK." Immediately, I thought of the lifelong thing I had never been able to get out of my head, this question I never thought would be answered. Leah said the prayer and then prompted us. "Okay. They're open. Ask anything you want."

The four or five of us exchanged glances and felt the silence fill up, until I broke it, spewing out through my black hoodie: "Why have I never been able to stop thinking about aliens my whole life?"

"What do you mean?"

"I mean, so, I, like, had this nightmare when I was three—"

"What was the worst part? What was scary about it?" Her voice carried a terse authority, and I trusted it.

"Um, I don't know, loneliness?"

"Deeper."

"Uh—"

"Total isolation. It's total isolation. And that's not something you have to be worried about, because everything in the universe is connected. We can never not be connected. Isolation is a capitalist illusion used to generate profit. You are never alone."

This opened me. Breath swept through a place there had been tightness just moments before. My body shifted and softened, taking the shape of a new belief. I knew Leah, or whoever was speaking through her, was right. I settled and took my first step into a new reality, now able to ask the real question:

"Then what happened that night in my bedroom?"

"You have been visited. But this isn't a bad thing; it's nothing to be worried about. You were visited by your family."

Um, what? Excuse me?

I was enlivened and enchanted and affirmed and still a little tiny bit scared, all at once. A splash of cold fireworks out of my head and down my spine. I think I squealed. Lots of sparking. Some magic. It was a meaning I hadn't yet considered or had room for: that the being truly could have been in my room, that I could have been terrified and that I could have been safe *all at the same time*. I could have been frozen by some alien technology and yet not have been harmed; they might never have meant to harm me, my family. Maybe nothing bad had happened. Which meant that what I understood as danger might not be very dangerous at all, even when it came in the form of what I feared most, this ultimate unknown "other" of my nightmares.

I had tried and tried to make this encounter anything but real, but here it was, real, and presenting an open door, a new place to venture when fear rose up in my body.

Eventually, I practiced becoming them. I practiced becoming them while I was me, at the same time, and in the same respect. I began to imagine it was me creeping around my house, I stood where I thought they might stand and saw what I thought they would see, I began to imagine what I looked like in my bed, and what it might be like to stand over me and startle me awake. I embraced the facts that I contain darkness, that I could be virulently feared, and that I could still be me. I asked myself why I was doing this, how I felt about it, and what it was all for. I imagined all the worlds I had seen, and where I came from. I kindly asked myself to let me sleep. It helped.

When I couldn't stretch that far, I let them be them but I let them come close, trying to feel the safety I knew existed, the one that accompanied the fear, the consistent relational field around the hot point of encounter. This took more work, but it also helped.

There may be a cosmically curated order of things I can't fully perceive but of which I can train myself to be witness and accomplice. I can let things happen if they are happening. Like the wasps, and maybe the extraterrestrial in my room that night, or my nightmare, or intergenerational trauma, or my imagination that refuses to quit, or my capitalist-colonial conditioning, or my need to be brave and worthy, or my fear that plumes up and wants me to run—each is equally *why*. And more importantly, each is also me, also us, also the universe. And when something is present, something is in relation.

I am not a productive poet. Ninety-nine percent of the time, I am a poet who is going to the grocery store, a poet who is walking their dog, a poet who is at the gym; a TV-watching poet, a cooking poet, a taking-a-bath, sitting-in-the-sun, emotionally laboring, drinking, texting, laughing-at-TikToks poet. "Poet" describes not what I spend my time doing, but how I experience the world. More often than not, it is a state of being constantly approached, nagged, encountered, and noticed by things most people don't see or believe in (or perhaps more accurately, the things Western schooling has trained and rewarded us for discounting) and then figuring out what to do next. Usually, I just go about doing what I was doing, and I just feel kind of tormented, buzzy, and—in the early morning, after coffee but before the world wakes up—euphoric. Sometimes I tune out the aliveness, and I feel bored and restless. At my best, at my most rested and watered and fed, I use the nagging as an invitation, an opening into relationality with whatever the thing requesting my attention is. I listen. A dug-up mound of grass and earth is also a dead mammal; the contracting, crisping, shedding, and piling up of leaves each year is how natural death always looks; *sky* is always opening or yearning to open; *fear* sings of the future; *sadness* sings of the past. When I am a good host to what comes to me, each discrete being that I meet is fundamentally multidimensional and referential. It holds the shape of something else, and those two things know one another in some very essential and original way, like how peach flesh knows teeth, and how red knows ripeness, and how lungs know air, even before their first meeting. It is a shimmering language I can never quite grasp and that never leaves me alone. Everything is a metaphor for something else, belonging to and perpetuated by something ancient and archetypal and holy. Everything we have been trained to think is flat has depth.

A poem (and the occasional drawing) is how I host the least believable, least definable, scariest, and most insistent things that knock on my conscious awareness and want to be let in. David Butler, on the other hand, hosted with recycled metal and found objects. Mr. Butler was another who was approached, awoken, and frightened by things that encountered him at bedtime. He never described himself as an artist, nor described his creations as art, but his fantastical creatures, his brightly painted pinwheels and whirligigs, and his light-catching, shadow-casting window screens are now in the Smithsonian. The world saw him differently.

Born in 1898 in Good Hope, Louisiana, as the oldest of eight, he spent much of his time in between household obligations carving small wooden structures and drawing pictures of his environment, "people picking cotton or fishing, shrimp boats, sugar cane fields." As an adult, he worked in sawmills, cut grass, built roads, and labored at a number of other jobs until the early 1960s. Around that time, when he suffered a work-related injury that left him partially disabled, he began making "art"—the cut, hammered, and painted corrugated tin and aluminum sculptures he is most known for—full-time. His creations are spiritual, fantastical, almost storybookish, while at the same time deeply mysterious: nativity scenes, crosses, angels, and immediately recognizable animals, plus "cockatrices" and other creatures officially unknown to science. His pieces, while varying widely, recognize each other by their bright primary colors mixed from neighbors' leftover house paints, their bold spots and stripes, and their cutout stars and hearts, each piece alive and in its own midst, rooted by fence post or dowel.

Mr. Butler seemed to be a man obsessed. In books, the lawn that surrounds his small square brick house is a garden of characters, his "flowers" there to provide color all year long, a library of beings he consistently sold, gave away, replaced, and created anew: "Flying Elephant," "Rooster," "Winged Creature with Gourd," "Two Wise Men on a Camel," "Man with Three Legs," "(Untitled) Angel," "(Untitled) Heart," "(Untitled) Seven Headed Dragon." Each can fill a world with its stories, each both flat and thick with myth. His house is equally adorned. Each of the windows and doors are affixed with "spirit shields," which cast shadows of his beings dancing into and across the house as the light moves and which serve as protection against the negative forces present after his wife's death in 1968. His creations traveled with him, too, as he rode to town each day on his bicycle, itself a city of tin windmills, birds and fanged fish, bows, ribbons, and found objects.

Children called him the "tin man," the "medicine man," and the "voodoo man," and he was described by his great-niece, Algertha Wilson, as a "kind, patient, and loving person," as much as he was the town eccentric. In pictures, Mr. Butler is small and bright under a short-brimmed fedora, his eyes are playful in his deep brown skin, and his smirk is warm yet knowing. "I see them things at night when I lay down, and I get up and cut them out just like I seen them." He died at ninety-nine in 1997 in Patterson, Louisiana.

There is so much I want to know about Mr. Butler, like how his disability affected and enabled his creations, which of his creatures were his favorites and which were his protectors, and what he did when he was scared. From what I do know, I suspect that this man was in intimate contact with what surrounded and approached him, some of which was known to science, some to religion, and some to more ancient myth. I suspect him to have been a person who prioritized relationship with who and what came knocking on his consciousness and, as a part of which, was a person in constant negotiation about proximity, noting which spirits could come in and which should be kept out. His pieces, in his words, were "God given." They did not originate within him. In this I hear God is *heavy*: the spiritual is not immaterial; it has mass. What came to Mr. Butler in dreams and at night literally *moved* him into hammering and painting and drilling and attaching. When I know of this weight, it follows that the work I do to keep the invitations out is *also* physical; it takes physical and energetic effort to keep myself from making poems, from making art, which is to say, I effort with my body when I deny relationality with what surrounds me. Isolation is a psychic *and* physical exertion, because the two aren't separate. And if that's the case, there is always some level of agency present when isolation threatens. I, too, can choose who to let in and who to keep out.

What was the exact shape of Mr. Butler's discerning? Did he dance with the beings that came to him? Were there ones he didn't put to metal and paint, and why? Did they wake him up? Did they wait behind doors and in mirrors? Did they come close when he shut his eyes? Could he hear them breathe? Did they touch him? I want to know if they said anything to him. If they explained why they were there, requested their own colors and patterns or which window to cover. I want to know if he spent any time ignoring their requests and how they responded. What did he call *Untitled (Very Old Mermaid)*? What does it call itself? How did it approach him?

Based on the fate of most of his pieces, it might have been given to a passerby or stolen after his death before it was sold, before it ended up at the Smithsonian, and before I came across gallery photos of it on the museum's website. The figure is unlike how we usually think of mermaids—perhaps earlier in its evolution, more fish than human, with one arm and one brown-red-skinned hand being its only apparent marker of hybridity. The creature struck me as adept in the exploration between worlds—between dim, tight trenches and vast seafloors, between the reality of coral and the reality of a whale shark, between land and sea, sure, but also between what we consider real and what we consider fantasy, between the literal and the metaphorical, the material and the immaterial. This is what came through even before I learned Mr. Butler himself seemed to exist between worlds. The mermaid is certainly in motion, certainly on a journey, almost swimming out of its paint. Blurry as a fixed trait, with no intention of clarity—an image that defies focus, unsteady somehow. You aren't quite sure what you are looking at, but you also know it's a mermaid, the arm nearly turning over in stroke, the logic of its heart matching the logic of its button eye, red bleeding stars, it sees what it feels. I want to know what it's looking at, and what it's looking for.

⌒

Much has been written on the harm Descartes enacted when he proposed *cogito ergo sum*, I think therefore I am. When he and his allies effectively spread the lie of a mind as separate from a body, they also set in motion the template of the fraught, closed, self-iterative binary as an apparatus for measuring and understanding the world. The split of mind from body also split civilized from uncivilized, rational from emotional, man from woman, and so on and so on.

The mind that mainstream science and psychology know sits inside the brain, and it is a brain blueprinted by DNA, built by conditions of nutrition and love and harm as we mature, and is maybe, tangentially, influenced by our ancestors' nutrition and love and harm epigenetically. It is a brain that is computer-like, that if fed the right programming, chemical or otherwise, could be expected to come out a certain, functional, rational way. In this model, we are essentially independent (or, at best, interdependent) beings with unique experiences and symptoms, our pockets full of identities and feelings and beliefs and the things that happened to us. When the emotional or the imaginative outweighs the rational, we are taught that something is wrong. When we don't act like computers, we are erased, reprimanded, pathologized, and imprisoned. (The gag is, even *computers* don't always act like computers—the computers of capitalist fantasy, that is.)

The imagination, in this model, is understood to sit inside the mind, which sits inside the brain. Dominant narratives depict it as an endearing and positive thing for children to possess and wield; we want them to believe the world is wide open and full of possibility. When they become adolescents, the narrative abruptly shifts. The only things teens are said to imagine are what their peers think of them and the things they aren't supposed to do (drugs, sex, etc.). Their world tightens as the imagination becomes something to control. As adults, the scraps of imagination that still exist are understood as out-of-control anxieties and ruminations, seen as pooled only in certain "creative" people, or colonized and corporatized with words like *innovation* and *flow*. Imagination is a part of the brain that, if it's doing what it is supposed to, withers.

Psychologist James Hillman saw it differently. For him, the mind is in the imagination, rather than the imagination being in the mind. I picture a Western, rational mind, which is defined as human because of its ability to order and categorize and predict and analyze and abstract, in the midst of and surrounded by and flooded with fantastical, imaginative, irrational material, flowing freely in and out of it. To give a reductive but clear image: a sponge in the ocean, where the sponge is the mind, and the ocean—all it contains, all its tides, all its storms—is imagination. The sponge has its way of processing the ocean, but it simply cannot contain or understand the whole, and not because the ocean has no rhythm or language, but because the sponge wasn't *designed* to dance or speak.

The lines upon which Enlightenment thinkers defined *human,* with Reason at the forefront, also defined nature in its relief; who was unruly, who resisted control and predictability, who wouldn't or couldn't labor, who felt, who was mysterious, who was the earth, who was winged, who was four legged, who didn't *make sense*—the feminine, the Indigenous, the dark, the erotic, the changing moon—each of these and more was categorized as non- or sub-human, which is to say, at best, conquerable, and at worse, disposable. Interestingly, while entire peoples fall under this category (which, indeed, was a philosophical ignition of colonization and enslavement), no one has gone unscathed—because, as

I understand it now, life in its true authenticity is unruly, is mysterious, and doesn't stay put.

As much as we might deny it, that Cartesian split persists, as does the imprint of the fraught, closed, self-iterative binary, the tug-of-war. When I look out at the Minneapolis skyline, or look down from an airplane, I see a "built" environment versus the "natural" one, not one continually diversifying whole. When I think about the climate emergency, I see a world split into human and nonhuman—as opposed to us as part of the earth, turning over on and rearranging itself because it wants to, it's ready. When I greet my favorite trees, I experience how unlike a tree I am instead of wondering what if "me" is just the vehicle through which I experience the feeling of separateness, and not the truth of it? When I see a video of a UFO on the internet, I see an empty and peaceful sky with an aberration in it, something that belongs and something that doesn't, that couldn't, instead of surrendering to the fact of its presence— whatever *it* is. And when I'm "in" "my own" "mind," in bed at night, flickering up and down struggling to submit to rest, I see something wrong as opposed to just something happening.

I think we are nature. Nothing that has ever happened has happened in a separate story than the meteor that murdered the dinosaurs, or the spiders that cast their webs up and fly on the wind, or every virus or mammal that has ever transformed to become what it is. I think every part of us is nature, and, what's more, I want to know what a world in which I believe I am nature enables and creates. I want to know what happens next. I am built and natural, I am a climate emergency, rearranging myself and letting myself die. I am the sky and the aberration, the breathing moving body and the breathing rooted one, the one approaching and the one being approached.

When I fear, I know I am touching something, I know I am alive. We are what we think we are, we are what we never considered we could be, and we are a mystery, all at once.

———

The same summer I met wasps, I met grasshoppers. Well, one grasshopper in particular. When I took my dog for our first walk in Northeast Minneapolis, I noticed differences. There was more "nature" here. White and red pines towered and dropped their needles right in people's yards, the boulevards were wider, the blocks were longer, everything was more spread out. Just enough that I could feel that this used to be the edge of town. And in all that edge and ecotone, bugs flourished in a diversity different than in Whittier, closer to downtown. I don't remember seeing one grasshopper in the five years we lived there (or even in the two years I spent right off Bde Maka Ska, the lake to the south and west). It was July when we moved, and the hottest day of the year. Even in air you can swim through, I like my morning cup of coffee hot, and I like to sit out on my stoop and greet the day. Our first morning in the new place, I sat on our stoop and was surprised by the explosive athleticism of a grasshopper that burst its way in and out of the tangled daylilies that line our sidewalk. I watched it for a few minutes, until it landed on the concrete in a slice of sunlight, turned its long body, one tiny insect leg at a time, toward the warmth, and exhaled. Well, seemed to exhale. It was directly in front of me. I was a little scared at first, just seeing how big it was, surely longer than my index finger, but I was drawn quiet by our shared affinity for the moment, for the morning stillness. We were in tune enough for me to notice one of its antennae was shorter than the other, and my admiration grew, knowing that even this tiny beast hadn't avoided injury, and still hopped in sunlight.

As we settled into our new home, and I spent many mornings drinking my coffee on our stoop, this grasshopper came back again and again. For the whole rest of the summer. We never made physical contact, but on more than one occasion it sat right next to me, in the same slice of sunlight I was in, and looked out from where I was looking.

I say this to say, I also practice love with bugs. I give them loving, kind eyes, and try to communicate my admiration and wonder. I try to be in my curiosity and fascination around them, in my deepest trust for the universe, and in my reverence for all life, trying to learn from them in the way only relationship can teach, trying to learn that fear might be a lesson of love.

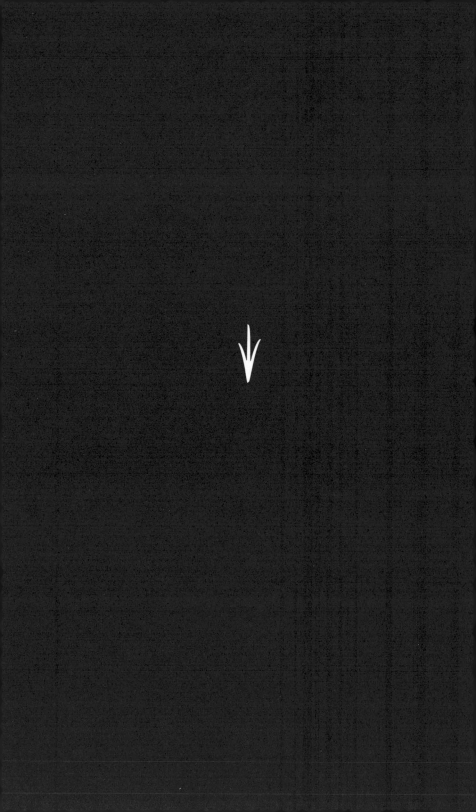

NOTES

"FOREWORD: MEMORY DIVINE"
Carolyn Finney

1   *"Blackness is not"* Reginald Dwayne Betts, "The Lives They
    Lived: Michael K. Williams," *New York Times*, December 22,
    2021, https://www.nytimes.com/interactive/2021/12/22/
    magazine/michael-k-williams.html.

1   *"It is dangerous"* Alexis Pauline Gumbs, *Undrowned: Black
    Feminist Lessons from Marine Mammals* (Chico, CA: AK
    Press, 2020).

1   *"See me, feel me"* "We're Not Gonna Take It," MP3 audio,
    track 24 on The Who, *Tommy*, Decca Records, 1969.

2   *"seesawing between observation"* Seph Rodney,
    "Jennifer Packer Shows Us the Responsibility
    of Seeing," Hyperallergic, February 8,
    2022, https://hyperallergic.com/708648/
    jennifer-packer-shows-us-the-responsibility-of-seeing/.

4   *"the presence of a person"* Dona Nelson, quoted in Rodney,
    "Jennifer Packer Shows Us."

"INTRODUCTION: MORE TO BE SHAPED BY"
Erin Sharkey

Big thanks to Joey and the whole team at Milkweed for their care on this project.

16   *The grave-robbed remains* Canadian Press, "Chicago Museum Gets 'Cultural Repatriation' Award for Returning Inuit Remains to Labrador," Canadian Broadcasting Corporation, September 21, 2017, https://www.cbc.ca/news/canada/newfoundland-labrador/field-museum-cultural-repatriation-award-inuit-remains-1.4299935.

16   *The San Diego Museum of Man* Rachel Hatzipanagos, "The 'Decolonization' of the American Museum," *Washington Post*, October 11, 2018, https://www.washingtonpost.com/nation/2018/10/12/decolonization-american-museum/?noredirect=on.

18   *"someone else's land"* Carolyn Finney, *Black Faces, White Spaces: Reimagining the Relationship of African Americans to the Great Outdoors* (Chapel Hill: University of North Carolina Press, 2014), xiv.

18   *"knew more about the land than the actual owners"* Finney, xiv.

"AN ASPECT OF FREEDOM"
Ama Codjoe

Dedicated to: Diane Peters, Karen Codjoe, Debra Sewell, and Gwendolyn Reese. Grateful acknowledgement to *The Sun* for publishing "An Aspect of Freedom."

29   *"After we died"* Agha Shahid Ali, "Ghazal," in *Rooms Are
      Never Finished: Poems* (New York: W. W. Norton, 2003), 18.

31   *"We shall not"* African-American spiritual, n.d., ca. the 1800s.

38   *"Every day I think about it"* Sarah Collins Rudolph, quoted
      in "Long Forgotten, 16th Street Baptist Church Bombing
      Survivor Speaks Out," *All Things Considered*, NPR, January
      25, 2013, https://www.npr.org/2013/01/25/170279226/
      long-forgotten-16th-street-baptist-church-bombing-
      survivor-speaks-out.

"A FAMILY VACATION"

Glynn Pogue

Big love to Erin Sharkey for curating this powerful collection
of voices and giving us a platform. A gracious thank-you to the
team at Milkweed for their support of this project. And all honor
to my mother, Monique Greenwood, who pours from her own
cup to fill others, tirelessly working to provide a space for her
people to be replenished and find peace in the great outdoors.

49   *"a familiarity with Nature"* William H. H. Murray,
      *Adventures in the Wilderness; or, Camp-Life in the
      Adirondacks* (Boston: De Wolfe, Fiske & Co., 1869), 8.

49   *"were 'born of hunter's breed'"* Murray, 8.

49   *"a breath of mountain air"* Murray, 8.

50   *"the bible of black travel"* J. Freedom du Lac, "Guidebook
      That Aided Black Travelers during Segregation Reveals
      Vastly Different D.C.," *Washington Post*, September 12,
      2010, https://www.washingtonpost.com/wp-dyn/content/
      article/2010/09/11/AR2010091105358.html.

50   *"a vacation without aggravation"* Victor H. Green, *Traveler's
      Green Book: For Vacation without Aggravation, International
      Edition, 1963–64* (New York: Victor H. Green Co., 1963).

54   *"And I'd gladly stand up"* "God Bless the U.S.A.," track 10
      on Lee Greenwood, *You've Got a Good Love Comin'*, MCA
      Records, 1983, compact disc.

"THIS LAND IS MY LAND"
Sean Hill

I want to thank Donald and Mary Hill, my Uncle Butch, Henry
and Diana, my cousins on the lake—the Jarretts, and the rest of
my family. And for their friendship and support, I want to thank
the late Derick Burleson, Camille Dungy, Allen Gee, Renata
Golden, J. Drew Lanham, and Latria Graham. And I'm forever
grateful to Erin Sharkey for inviting me to be a part of this project.

61   ***the violent birth throes of this nation*** The word "nation"
      come to us from the Latin *natus* (that which has been born),
      the past participle of *nasci* (be born) and shares this root with
      words like "natal" and "nature." Black folks were born out
      of the peculiar institution that was chattel slavery in those
      English colonies that became the United States of America.

62   *"an Act"* "An Act Emancipating Austin Dabney," 14 August
      1786, vol. D, Enrolled Acts and Resolutions, House and
      Senate, Legislature, RG 37-1-15, Georgia Archives, accessed
      April 5, 2022, https://vault.georgiaarchives.org/digital/
      collection/adhoc/id/581.

62   *"To emancipate"* The act of emancipating has had a long
      history because slavery has had long history, but the

economic system built on chattel slavery was exceptional in its scale and still today casts a long shadow.

69   *"We were treated"* Unidentified soldier, quoted in John Virtue, *The Black Soldiers Who Built the Alaska Highway: A History of Four U.S. Army Regiments in the North, 1942–1943* (Jefferson, NC: McFarland & Company, 2013), 7.

70   *"Skilled mechanics are needed"* "Alcan Highway under Construction," Schomburg Center for Research in Black Culture, Photographs and Prints Division, New York Public Library, accessed April 5, 2022, https://digitalcollections.nypl.org/items/510d47df-fa5d-a3d9-e040-e00a18064a99.

"CONFRONTING THE NAMES ON THIS LAND"
Lauret Savoy

I am deeply grateful to Erin Sharkey for inviting me to contribute to *A Darker Wilderness*, and for suggesting that I return to a meditation on racist place-names begun several years ago. I also give special thanks to Peter J. Blodgett, H. Russell Smith Foundation Curator of Western American History at the Huntington Library for his research time and kindness. Finally, my loving gratitude will always go to family and dear friends who have helped me understand what it means to inhabit this land and to be a citizen of this nation.

83   *One Hualapai name* Hualapai Tribe Department of Cultural Resources, "Evaluating Hualapai Cultural Resources along the Colorado River," FY 2016 Report to Bureau of Reclamation, HDCR2017-066.

85   *"a masterpiece of American writing"* Matt Weiland,
     introduction to *Names on the Land: A Historical Account
     of Place-Naming in the United States*, by George R.
     Stewart (New York: New York Review Books,
     2008), ix–x.

86   *"Names are magic"* Walt Whitman, "An American Primer,"
     Atlantic Monthly 93, no. 558 (April 1904): 460–70, http://
     www.theatlantic.com/past/docs/issues/04apr/primer.htm.

86   *My parents and I lived at first* On the naming of San Francisco
     and Los Angeles, I consulted Stewart, *Names on the Land*,
     (Boston: Houghton Mifflin Company, 3rd ed. 1967), 156–61.

87   *"bespattered with* **Washingtons, Lafayettes***"* H. L.
     Mencken, *The American Language: An Inquiry into the
     Development of English in the United States* (New York:
     A. A. Knopf, 1921), 345.

88   *"For name, though it seem"* Francis Bacon, "A Brief
     Discourse of the Happy Union of the Kingdoms of England
     and Scotland," in *The Works of Francis Bacon*, vol. III
     (London: F. C. and J. Rivington, 1819), 264.

89   *Columbus couldn't hear "Taíno" speech* There are
     different interpretations of the origin and uses of "Taíno"
     as a term designating certain groups who inhabited what
     are now commonly known as the Bahamas and Greater
     Antilles at the time of Spanish contact. In recent decades
     growing numbers of Caribbean peoples with Indigenous
     ancestry have embraced calling themselves Taíno, and
     their movement challenges still-held notions that Native
     peoples in the islands were wiped out with European
     colonization.

89   *"in order that they might"* Christopher Columbus, translated
     and quoted in David Henige, "To Read Is to Misread,

to Write Is to Miswrite: Las Casas as Transcriber," in
Amerindian Images and the Legacy of Columbus, ed. René
Jara and Nicholas Spadaccini (Minneapolis: University of
Minnesota Press, 1992), 227.

90   **Dakota, Illini, Kansa, Ute** Jack Weatherford, "The Naming
of North America," chap. 15 in *Native Roots: How the
Indians Enriched America* (New York: Ballantine Books,
1992), 218.

90   **Massachusett, *to the Wampanoag*** Wôpanâak Language
Reclamation Project, personal communication, 2015.

90   ***And there is the convoluted origin*** On the origin of the
name Wisconsin: Stewart, *Names on the Land*, 88.

91   ***a shallow, braided river*** On the naming of the Platte River:
Stewart, 136.

91   ***The long range stretching*** On the naming of the
Appalachians, I consulted David Walls, "On the Naming of
Appalachia," in *An Appalachian Symposium: Essays Written
in Honor of Cratis D. Williams*, ed. J. W. Williamson
(Boone, NC: Appalachian State University Press, 1977),
56–76; Stewart, *Names on the Land*, 17–18, 334; Donald
E. Davis, *Where There Are Mountains: An Environmental
History of the Southern Appalachians* (Athens, GA:
University of Georgia Press, 2000), 3–5, 215–216; and
Weatherford, *Native Roots*, 224. Note that the above
authors, including Stewart, mistakenly state that Guyot's
map used "Allegheny." The map used "Alleghany" and can
be seen in Arnold Guyot, "On the Appalachian Mountain
System," *American Journal of Science*, Second Series, XXXI,
no. 92 (1861), 157–87.

92   ***The Oregon story*** On the naming of Oregon: Stewart, *Names
on the Land*, 153–55. Stewart uses the term "River of the West."

92   **Wyoming** *also began* On the naming of Wyoming: Stewart, 310–14.

93   *"Because it is a beautiful name"* James Doolittle, quoted in Stewart, 313.

93   *"roll[ed] with venison richness"* This and the subsequent quotes are from Whitman, "American Primer."

94   *H. L. Mencken acknowledged and matched* See chapter 3, "Geographical Names," in Mencken, *American Language*.

94   *"Such names as* **Tallahassee***"* Mencken, *American Language*, 344–45.

94   *Mencken also drew from the reports* The US Board on Geographic Names was established by executive order in 1890. See https://www.usgs.gov/core-science-systems/ ngp/board-on-geographic-names.

94   *"In its laudable effort"* Mencken, *American Language*, 354.

95   *like the Wampanoag nation* Before the Wampanoag Nation's Wôpanâak Language Reclamation Project, the language of Wampanoag in Massachusetts had not been spoken in more than 150 years, six generations, yet the Wampanoag Nation is reclaiming it because theirs was also among the first Native languages to develop and use an alphabetic writing system, through the efforts of English missionaries trying to convert the Wampanoag to Christianity in the 1600s. The first complete bible printed in New England, and possibly the "new world," was published in the Wampanoag language in 1663. The Wampanoag came to use writing as the means of communicating with the European colonists. See http://wlrp.org/.

95   *the "matrix" of linguistic meaning* Many authors, including David Abram and Leslie Marmon Silko, have written of the land using this language and idea.

95   *"the continuity and accuracy"* Leslie Marmon Silko,
      "Interior and Exterior Landscapes: The Pueblo Migration
      Stories," in *Yellow Woman and a Beauty of the Spirit: Essays
      on Native American Life Today* (New York: Simon &
      Schuster, 1996), 35.

95   *"place-names are arguably"* Keith Basso, *Wisdom Sits
      in Places: Landscape and Language among the Western
      Apache* (Albuquerque: University of New Mexico Press,
      1996), 76.

96   *The Ndee word* **ni'** John Welch and Ramon Riley,
      "Reclaiming Land and Spirit in the Western Apache
      Homeland," *American Indian Quarterly* 25, no. 1 (Winter
      2001): 5.

96   *"most forcefully displayed"* Basso, *Wisdom Sits in Places*, 89.

96   *The land watches over and "stalks"* Basso, 57.

96   *"purposive" behavior* Basso, 75.

96   *"think and act"* Basso, 75.

96   *"sensing of place"* Basso, 143.

96   *"talked names"* Basso, 45.

96   *"I ride that way"* Basso, 46.

96   *"reciprocal appropriation"* N. Scott Momaday, "Native
      American Attitudes to the Environment," in *Seeing with a
      Native Eye: Essays on Native American Religion*, ed. Walter
      Holden Capps (New York: Harper & Row, 1976), 80.

96   *"own most fundamental experience"* Momaday, 80.

96   *"doing human history"* Basso, *Wisdom Sits in Places*, 7.

96   *"a way of constructing"* Basso, 7.

97   *"In contrast to the oppressed Indian"* Stewart, *Names on the
      Land*, 329.

97   *But as diaspora linguists* On African origins of place-
      names, I consulted Annette Kashif, "Africanisms upon the

Land: A Study of African Influenced Place Names in the
USA," in *Places of Cultural Memory: African Reflections on
the American Landscape* (Washington, DC: Department of
the Interior, National Park Service, 2001), 15–34; Winifred
Vass, *The Bantu Speaking Heritage of the United States* (Los
Angeles: Center for Afro-American Studies, University of
California, 1979); and Winifred Vass, "Bantu Place Names
in Nine Southern States," in Joseph Holloway and Winifred
Vass, *African Heritage of American English* (Bloomington:
University of Indiana Press, 1993).

97   *"The name . . . cannot be translated"* William Read, *Florida
Place-Names of Indian Origin and Seminole Personal Names*
(Baton Rouge: Louisiana State University Press, 1934), 53.
On the origins of *Suwannee*, see also Kashif, "Africanisms
upon the Land," 19, 26; and Vass, *African Heritage of
American English*, 116, 134.

98   *The Great Dismal Swamp* At least one Maroon refuge lay
in the Great Dismal Swamp straddling Virginia and North
Carolina's low-country border. Note that the name is
redundant, for *dismal* refers to dreary tracts of swamp.

98   *And hybrid words* Examples of hybrids or "creolizations"
of African, Indigenous, and/or European languages may
include Black Mingo Pocosin, a swamp along the Virginia-
North Carolina border, according to Kashif, "Africanisms
upon the Land," 27. Several place-names once thought to
be solely of Indigenous origin, or of dubious or unknown
origins, may at least in part be rooted in Africa. Wando
River in the Gullah region of South Carolina, for example,
resembles the Kongo word *Kwando*, a large river (and a city
on its banks) in Angola.

99   ***"Black towns" grew in number*** Quintard Taylor, *In Search of the Racial Frontier: African Americans in the American West, 1528–1990* (New York: W. W. Norton, 1998), 69.

99   ***at least two hundred American toponyms*** See US Board of Geographic Names to find the use of racial slurs in place-names at http://geonames.usgs.gov/ or https://www.usgs.gov/core-science-systems/ngp/board-on-geographic-names/domestic-names.

99   ***the "pejorative form"*** On the definitions of "niggerhead," see *Oxford English Dictionary Online*, s.v. "niggerhead," accessed December 9, 2021, https://www.oed.com/viewdictionaryentry/Entry/126937.

103   ***"place names that include"*** Reconciliation in Place Names Act, H.R. 8455, 116th Congress (2020). See https://www.congress.gov/bill/116th-congress/house-bill/8455/text?r=1&s=1. For the 2021 Senate and H.R. bills, see https://www.congress.gov/bill/117th-congress/senate-bill/2400/text?r=4&s=4 and https://www.congress.gov/bill/117th-congress/house-bill/4454?s=8&r=1.

104   ***"Racist terms have no place"*** Deb Haaland, quoted in US Department of the Interior, "Secretary Haaland Takes Action to Remove Derogatory Names from Federal Lands," press release, November 19, 2021, https://www.doi.gov/pressreleases/secretary-haaland-takes-action-remove-derogatory-names-federal-lands.

"AN URBAN FARMER'S ALMANAC"
Erin Sharkey

113 *"And when you look up"* Deut. 4:19.

113 *"And God said"* Gen. 1:14–15.

121 *"being BISSEXTILE"* Benjamin Banneker, *Benjamin Banneker's Pennsylvania, Delaware, Maryland and Virginia Almanack and Ephemeris* (Baltimore: William Goddard and James Angell, 1792), 1, https://www.loc.gov/item/98650590/.

121 *"a sable descendent of Africa"* Banneker, 2.

121 *"a free Negro"* Benjamin Banneker, *Banneker's Almanack and Ephemeris* (Philadelphia: Joseph Crukshank, 1793), 2, https://transcription.si.edu/view/8045/NMAAHC-2014_63_31_002.

121 *"I am annoyed to find"* Benjamin Banneker, quoted in Charles A. Cerami, *Benjamin Banneker: Surveyor, Astronomer, Publisher, Patriot* (New York: John Wiley & Sons, 2002), 150.

"CONCENTRIC MEMORY"
Naima Penniman

149 *"a positive obsession"* With thanks to Octavia Butler:
Kindness eases Change.
Love quiets fear.
And a sweet and powerful
Positive obsession
Blunts pain,
Diverts rage,
And engages each of us

In the greatest,

The most intense

Of our chosen struggles.

Octavia E. Butler, *Parable of the Talents* (New York: Grand Central Publishing, 2019), 41.

153 **"God, grant me the serenity"** This is the Serenity Prayer, written by the American theologian Reinhold Niebuhr.

155 **"Those whose boldness"** C. L. R. James, *The Black Jacobins: Toussaint L'Ouverture and the San Domingo Revolution* (New York: Vintage, 1989), 20.

155 **"he conceived the bold design"** James, *Black Jacobins*, 20.

156 **Makandal's forces killed** James, *Black Jacobins*, 19.

156 **"a basic need"** Alexis Pauline Gumbs, *Undrowned: Black Feminist Lessons from Marine Mammals* (Chico, CA: AK Press, 2020), 88.

157 **"This God who made"** Dutty Boukman, quoted in Laurent Dubois and John D. Garrigus, *Slave Revolution in the Caribbean, 1789–1804: A Brief History with Documents* (New York: Bedford/St. Martin's, 2016).

157 **"For nearly three weeks"** James, *Black Jacobins*, 88.

158 **"And so, right before"** Unidentified storyteller, quoted in "Lands of Freedom: The Oral History and Cultural Heritage of the Matawai Maroons in Suriname," Amazon Conservation Team, accessed March 30, 2022, https://storymaps.arcgis.com/collections/198cd38e98014dbe9b926d3d20011f98?item=1.

161 **the modern equivalent of $21 billion** Jeffrey Sommers, *Race, Reality, and Realpolitik: U.S.–Haiti Relations in the Lead Up to the 1915 Occupation* (Lanham, MD: Lexington Books, 2016), 124.

161 **Millions left the soil behind** For more, read Leah Penniman, *Farming While Black: Soul Fire Farm's Practical Guide to*

Liberation on the Land (White River Junction, VT: Chelsea Green Publishing, 2018).

171   *"I sat in this living room"* Fresh Roberson (@freshertogether), "August 2018 I sat in this living room," Instagram photo, April 25, 2020, https://www.instagram.com/p/B_aEA4ilXT4/.

174   *Like how dolphins evolved* For more, read "Adapt," in Gumbs, *Undrowned*.

174   *Like how plants* Merlin Sheldrake, Entangled Life: How Fungi Make Our Worlds, Change Our Minds, and Shape Our Futures (New York: Random House, 2020), 123.

175   *it sends its surplus sugars* For more, read Suzanne Simard, *Finding the Mother Tree: Discovering the Wisdom of the Forest* (New York: Alfred A. Knopf, 2021).

175   *again and again nature demonstrates* Dan Chodorkoff, *The Anthropology of Utopia: Essays on Social Ecology and Community Development* (Porsgrun, Norway: New Compass Press, 2014), 145–58.

"THERE WAS A TREMENDOUS SOFTNESS"

Michael Kleber-Diggs

I am thankful for my grandparents, Grace and Arthur Glass; my mother, Lequetta Diggs; my father, Dr. James A. Diggs, DDS; my brother, Martin Diggs; my aunt, Joyce Smith; my aunt, Laura Ross; my cousin Karla Smith; my cousin, Bettye Sabree; and all my family members on both sides for their support, encouragement, grace, and space. My family is loving and rich with people who value, cherish, and maintain our memories and artifacts. Together we remember and carry forward the stories of those who came before us.

"WATER AND STONE"
Alexis Pauline Gumbs

Love and gratitude to everyone mentioned and cited who has dedicated their energy to engaging and sharing Audre Lorde's legacy. And special honor and gratitude to recent ancestors Gloria Joseph and Ika Hügel-Marshall.

213 *"Miss Lorde, are you a nature poet?"* Audre Lorde, *Conversations with Audre Lorde*, ed. Joan Wylie Hall (Jackson: University Press of Mississippi, 2004), 41.

213 *"What are you talking about?"* Lorde, 41.

214 *"sensualist"* Audre Lorde, "An Interview with Audre Lorde," interview by Adrienne Rich, *Signs* 6, no. 4 (Summer 1981): 730.

214 *"Audre Lorde is not a nature poet"* Dudley Randall, review of *The First Cities*, by Audre Lorde, *Negro Digest*, September/October 1968, 13.

215 *"feelings and relationships"* Randall, 13.

215 *"inner weather"* Randall, 13.

215 *"We do not have to become"* Audre Lorde, *Dream of Europe*, transcript of a 1990 poetry reading in Stuttgart, Germany, 244.

216 *"not a luxury"* Audre Lorde, "Poetry Is Not a Luxury," in *Sister Outsider* (New York: Penguin Books, 2020), 24.

218 *"means trout fishing"* Audre Lorde, *The Cancer Journals* (New York: Penguin Books, 2020), 10.

218 *"knowing that my work"* Lorde, 10.

219 *"a piece of home"* Audre Lorde, "A Burst of Light: Living with Cancer," in *I Am Your Sister: Collected and Unpublished Writings of Audre Lorde*, ed. Rudolph P. Byrd, Johnetta

Betsch Cole, and Beverly Guy-Sheftall (New York: Oxford University Press, 2009), 119.

221 *"Blackfullness"* Audre Lorde, "Above the Wind: An Interview with Audre Lorde," interview by Charles H. Rowell, *Callaloo* 23, no. 1 (Winter 2000): 56.

224 *"bio/anthology"* "The Wind Is Spirit: A Bio/Anthology of Audre Lorde," Kickstarter, February 11, 2016, https://www.kickstarter.com/projects/1554636407/the-wind-is-spirit-a-bio-anthology-of-audre-lorde.

225 *Turquoise, amber, and malachite* See Audre Lorde, "Digging," in *The Black Unicorn: Poems* (New York: W. W. Norton, 1995).

225 *"those stones in my heart are you"* Audre Lorde, "Scar," in *The Black Unicorn: Poems* (New York: W. W. Norton, 1995).

225 *"language crazure"* Lorde, *Cancer Journals,* 14.

228 *"sterile wordplay"* Lorde, "Poetry Is Not a Luxury," 25.

231 *"Leaving leaving"* Audre Lorde, "On My Way out I Passed over You and the Verrazano Bridge," in *The Collected Poems of Audre Lorde* (New York: W. W. Norton, 2000), 403.

231 *"flights of this journey"* Lorde, 406.

231 *"mapless uncertain"* Lorde, 406.

231 *"but the wind is our teacher"* Audre Lorde, "Hugo I," in *The Collected Poems of Audre Lorde* (New York: W. W. Norton, 2000), 461.

235 *"our teaching means keeping trust"* Audre Lorde, "Dear Toni Instead of a Letter of Congratulation Upon Your Book and Your Daughter Whom You Say You Are Raising to Be a Correct Little Sister," in *The Collected Poems of Audre Lorde* (New York: W. W. Norton, 2000), 94.

235 *"deep aquatic eyes"* Lorde, 94.

236 *"none of us have 300 years"* Lorde, *Cancer Journals,* 19.

"HERE'S HOW I LET THEM COME CLOSE"
katie robinson

Love to my beloved Erin; love to my fiancé, LM; love to my boox, Leah; love to my co-conspirator, Amy; love to Mr. David Butler; love to the wasps and grasshoppers; and love to all my Star Kin.

249   ***Akashic Records*** According to Dr. Linda Howe, "the Akashic Records are a dimension of consciousness that contains a vibrational record of every soul and its journey. This vibrational body of consciousness exists everywhere in its entirety and is completely available at all times and in all places. As such, the Records are an experiential body of knowledge that contains everything every soul has ever thought, said, and done over the course of its existence, as well as all its future possibilities" (Howe, *How to Read the Akashic Records*, 3). For more on the Akashic Records, see Linda Howe, *How to Read The Akashic Records: Accessing the Archive of the Soul and Its Journey* (Boulder, CO: Sounds True, 2010), and Leah Garza (@crystalsofaltamira) on Instagram and www.crystalsofaltamira.com.

253   ***He never described himself as an artist*** For context surrounding David Butler's life and work, I relied in this section on Jane Livingston and John Beardsley, *Black Folk Art in America: 1930–1980* (Jackson: University Press of Mississippi, 1982); and Samella Lewis, *African American Art and Artists* (Berkeley: University of California Press, 1990).

253   ***"people picking cotton"*** William Fagaly, quoted in Livingston and Beardsley, *Black Folk Art*, 66.

254 *"flowers"* David Butler, quoted in Lewis, *African American Art*, 112.

254 *"spirit shields"* David Butler, quoted in Tom Patterson, "David Butler" *Pictured in My Mind: Contemporary American Self-Taught Art*, ed. Gail Andrews Trechsel (Jackson: University Press of Mississippi, 1995), 34.

254 *"tin man"* Algertha Wilson, quoted in Danika Foley, "One Man's Trash, Another Man's Artwork: David Butler Exhibit at Louisiana State Museum," *KWBJ TV 22*, July 27, 2011, YouTube video, 1:22, https://youtu.be/8ct5-QCBqI0.

254 *"kind, patient, and loving person"* Wilson, quoted in Foley, "One Man's Trash," 1:11.

254 *"I see them things"* David Butler, quoted in Foley, "One Man's Trash," 1:36.

255 *"God given"* Butler, quoted in Lewis, *African American Art*, 113.

ILLUSTRATION CREDITS

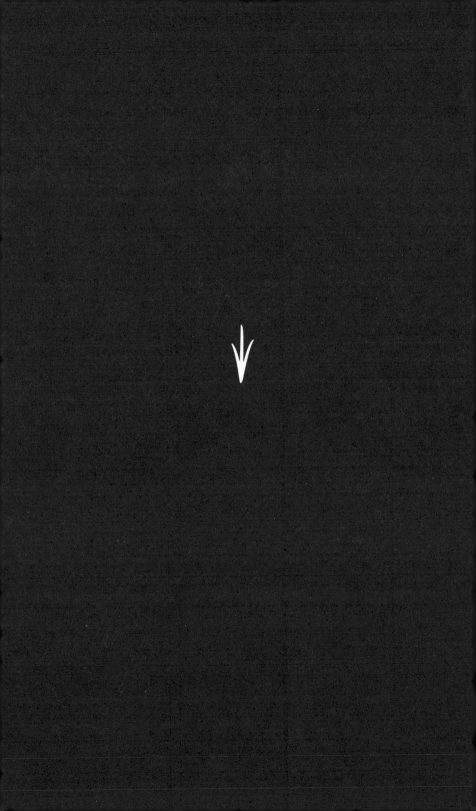

CONTRIBUTORS

AMA CODJOE (she/her) is the author of *Bluest Nude* and *Blood of the Air*, winner of the Drinking Gourd Chapbook Poetry Prize. Her poems and prose have appeared in *The Best American Poetry* series, *Orion*, and elsewhere. Among other honors, she has received a 2017 Rona Jaffe Foundation Writer's Award, a Creative Writing Fellowship from the National Endowment for the Arts, a NYSCA/NYFA Artist Fellowship, and a Jerome Hill Artist Fellowship. She lives in New York City.

CAROLYN FINNEY (she/her) is the author of *Black Faces, White Spaces: Reimagining the Relationship of African Americans to the Great Outdoors*. Her work has appeared in the *New York Times*, *The Guardian*, *Newsweek*, *Outside*, and *Orion*, and she is a columnist at the *Earth Island Journal*. She has served as a Fulbright Scholar, a Canon National Parks Science Scholar, and a Mellon Postdoctoral Fellow in Environmental Studies, and additionally served for eight years on the US National Parks Advisory Board. She was awarded the Alexander and Ilse Melamid Medal from the American Geographical Society and recently received a Mellon grant to work on her performance piece, *The N Word: Nature, Revisited* at the New York Botanical Gardens Humanities Institute. She received her PhD in geography from Clark University and is currently an artist-in-residence and environmental studies professor of practice in the Franklin Environmental Center at Middlebury College.

RONALD L. GREER II (he/him) is a multigenre writer and poet whose poems and stories have appeared in *Doors Adjacent*, *Night Colors*, and *Drop a Kite*, among others. He is the 2019 Pamela J. Caligiuri Broadside Award winner and is coeditor of the forthcoming anthology *America Precariat*. Greer spent his formative years in Detroit, nurturing his grandfather's urban gardens.

ALEXIS PAULINE GUMBS (she/they) is the author of *Undrowned: Black Feminist Lessons of Marine Mammals*, *Dub: Finding Ceremony*, *M Archive: After the End of the World*, and *Spill: Scenes of Black Feminist Fugitivity*. She is also coeditor of *Revolutionary Mothering: Love on the Frontlines*. Her work has been featured in *Best American Experimental Writing*, *The New Inquiry*, *Sierra*, *The Offing*, *Kweli*, *Ebony*, *Southern Cultures*, and more. Gumbs is a 2022 Whiting Award Winner in Nonfiction, a 2022 National Endowment for the Arts Fellow, and was a 2020–2021 National Humanities Center Fellow. She earned her PhD in English, African and African-American studies, and women and gender studies from Duke University. She is creative writing editor of *Feminist Studies*, literary advisor for the Ntozake Shange Trust, and the cocreator of the Mobile Homecoming Trust, a living library amplifying generations of Black LGBTQ brilliance in Durham, North Carolina.

SEAN HILL (he/him) is the author of *Dangerous Goods*, winner of the Minnesota Book Award in poetry, and *Blood Ties & Brown Liquor*, named one of the ten books all Georgians should read by the Georgia Center for the Book. His numerous awards include fellowships from the Cave Canem Foundation, Stanford University, and the National Endowment for the Arts.

Hill's poems and essays have appeared in *Callaloo, Harvard Review, New England Review, Orion, Oxford American, Poetry, Terrain.org, Tin House,* and numerous other journals, and in almost two dozen anthologies, including *Black Nature: Four Centuries of African American Nature Poetry* and *Villanelles.* He lives in Montana with his family and is an Assistant Professor of Creative Writing at the University of Montana.

MICHAEL KLEBER-DIGGS (he/him) is the author of *Worldly Things,* winner of the 2020 Max Ritvo Poetry Prize. His essay "On the Complex Flavors of Black Joy" appears in *There's a Revolution Outside, My Love: Letters from a Crisis,* edited by Tracy K. Smith and John Freeman. Kleber-Diggs's work can be found in Poem-a-Day, Poetry Daily, *Poetry Northwest,* Literary Hub, *Hunger Mountain,* and elsewhere. He is a past winner of the Loft Mentor Series in poetry, and his work has been supported by the Minnesota State Arts Board and the Jerome Foundation. Kleber-Diggs is an instructor with the Minnesota Prison Writing Workshop. He also teaches creative writing in Augsburg University's low-residency MFA program and at the Saint Paul Conservatory for Performing Artists.

NAIMA PENNIMAN (all pronouns) is the director of education at Soul Fire Farm, where she equips a rising generation of Black, Brown, and Indigenous farmers with the skills needed to reclaim dignified futures in relationship to land. She is the cofounder of WILDSEED, a BIPOC-led, land-based community focused on ecological collaboration and transformative justice. She is also an originating member of the Black healers collective, Harriet's Apothecary, and founder of the Haitian resilience project, Ayiti Resurrect.

Penniman is a visionary artist and poet whose performances have inspired thousands of people and movements across the world. Published in *All We Can Save* and *We Are Each Other's Harvest*, Penniman devotes her creativity toward intergenerational healing and planetary interdependence.

GLYNN POGUE (she/her) has written for *Vogue*, *National Geographic Traveler*, *Guernica*, *Eater*, and the *Los Angeles Review of Books*, among others. She holds an MFA in creative writing from The New School and is a former fellow of the Brooklyn Public Library's "Hear Me Out" audio workshop, the *Los Angeles Review of Books* Publishing Workshop, and VONA/ Voices. Pogue is the cofounder and cohost of the *Black Girls Texting* podcast and currently works at Audible Studios.

katie robinson (all pronouns) is a student of love, trauma, and transformation. Their poem "The Biggest Fish I Follow Follows Ghosts" was featured in the anthology *Queer Voices: Poetry, Prose, and Pride*. They attended VONA (Voices of Our Nation) at Minneapolis's Loft Literary Center in 2017 and were a 2015 Givens Foundation for African American Literature Emerging Writer Fellow. They are currently a PhD candidate at Pacifica Graduate Institute, where they are writing a dissertation at the intersections of depth psychology, decoloniality, and police and prison abolition. During the week, robinson is an educator and facilitator in racial justice and abolitionist movements in Minneapolis.

LAURET SAVOY (she/her) is the author of *Trace: Memory, History, Race, and the American Landscape*, winner of the 2016 American Book Award from the Before Columbus

Foundation and the 2017 ASLE Creative Writing Book Award. *Trace* was also a finalist for the 2016 PEN American Open Book Award and Phillis Wheatley Book Award, as well as shortlisted for the William Saroyan International Prize for Writing and Orion Book Award. Savoy is the coeditor of *The Colors of Nature: Culture, Identity, and the Natural World*; *Bedrock: Writers on the Wonders of Geology*; and *Living with the Changing California Coast*. She is the David B. Truman Professor of Environmental Studies and Geology at Mount Holyoke College and a Fellow of the Geological Society of America. Winner of Mount Holyoke's Distinguished Teaching Award and an Andrew Carnegie Fellowship, Savoy has also held fellowships from the Smithsonian Institution and Yale University.

ERIN SHARKEY (she/her) is a writer, arts and abolition organizer, cultural worker, and film producer based in Minneapolis. She is the cofounder, with Junauda Petrus, of an experimental arts collective called Free Black Dirt and is the producer of film projects including *Sweetness of Wild*, an episodic web film project, and *Small Business Revolution* (Hulu), which explored challenges and opportunities for Black-owned businesses in the Twin Cities in the summer of 2021. Sharkey has received fellowships and residencies from the Loft Mentor Series, VONA/Voices, the Givens Foundation, Coffee House Press, the Bell Museum of Natural History, Penumbra Theatre, and the Jerome Foundation. In 2021, Sharkey was awarded the Black Seed Fellowship from Black Visions and the Headwaters Foundation. She has an MFA in creative writing from Hamline University and teaches with the Minnesota Prison Writing Workshop.

milkweed
EDITIONS

Founded as a nonprofit organization in 1980, Milkweed
Editions is an independent publisher. Our mission is to
identify, nurture, and publish transformative literature and
build an engaged community around it.

Milkweed Editions is based in Bdé Óta Othúŋwe
(Minneapolis) within Mní Sota Makhóčhe, the traditional
homeland of the Dakhóta people. Residing here since time
immemorial, Dakhóta people still call Mní Sota Makhóčhe
home, with four federally recognized Dakhóta nations and
many more Dakhóta people residing in what is now the state
of Minnesota. Due to continued legacies of colonization,
genocide, and forced removal, generations of Dakhóta people
remain disenfranchised from their traditional homeland.
Presently, Mní Sota Makhóčhe has become a refuge and
home for many Indigenous nations and peoples, including
seven federally recognized Ojibwe nations. We humbly
encourage our readers to reflect upon the historical legacies
held in the lands they occupy.

milkweed.org

Milkweed Editions, an independent nonprofit publisher, gratefully acknowledges sustaining support from our Board of Directors; the Alan B. Slifka Foundation and its president, Riva Ariella Ritvo-Slifka; the Amazon Literary Partnership; the Ballard Spahr Foundation; *Copper Nickel*; the McKnight Foundation; the National Endowment for the Arts; the National Poetry Series; and other generous contributions from foundations, corporations, and individuals. Also, this activity is made possible by the voters of Minnesota through a Minnesota State Arts Board Operating Support grant, thanks to a legislative appropriation from the arts and cultural heritage fund. For a full listing of Milkweed Editions supporters, please visit milkweed.org.

Interior design by Tijqua Daiker and Mary Austin Speaker
Typeset in Arno

Arno was designed by Robert Slimbach. Slimbach named
this typeface after the river that runs through Florence, Italy.
Arno draws inspiration from a variety of typefaces created
during the Italian Renaissance; its italics were inspired by the
calligraphy and printing of Ludovico degli Arrighi.